OXFORD STUDIES IN AFRICAN AFFAIRS

General Editors
JOHN D. HARGREAVES *and* GEORGE SHEPPERSON

LIBERALISM IN SOUTH AFRICA 1948–1963

LIBERALISM IN
SOUTH AFRICA
1948–1963

BY

JANET ROBERTSON

CLARENDON PRESS · OXFORD

1971

Oxford University Press, Ely House, London W.1

GLASGOW NEW YORK TORONTO MELBOURNE WELLINGTON
CAPE TOWN SALISBURY IBADAN NAIROBI DAR ES SALAAM LUSAKA ADDIS ABABA
BOMBAY CALCUTTA MADRAS KARACHI LAHORE DACCA
KUALA LUMPUR SINGAPORE HONG KONG TOKYO

PRINTED IN GREAT BRITAIN BY
RICHARD CLAY (THE CHAUCER PRESS) LTD
BUNGAY, SUFFOLK

TO MY NIECES
ELIZABETH AND JANE

Preface

THERE have been in South Africa, since the Second World War a number of political groups deserving the 'liberal' *imprimatur*. It is my intention to describe and analyse what happened to these liberals in South Africa between 1948 and 1963. My prime interest is in those whites and blacks who were actively concerned to abolish racial discrimination and to extend equal rights to non-whites within the existing parliamentary system. I have examined black liberals and their changing views as these developed within the African National Congress. On the white side of the colour bar, I have analysed the foundation and growth of the Liberal Party, the first parliamentary party in South Africa created for the express purpose of extending rights to non-whites. I have examined also the fate of white liberals within the United Party, and their emergence into the Progressive Party. In addition, the Torch Commando and the Black Sash are reviewed, since both were extra-parliamentary movements which claimed to uphold liberal values.

This book is not intended to provide an exhaustive study of any of these groups. Nor is its aim merely to record original material, although it will be obvious that much of it is based on fresh sources. Rather, I have sought first and foremost to reconsider old views and well-worn facts by gathering together separate threads which have been all too rarely seen as part of an integrated whole. As such, I hope my work will provide a new synthesis of recent South African history.

This book began as a Ph.D. thesis which I was able to complete only through the material assistance of a Commonwealth Post-graduate Scholarship and the encouragement of my colleagues, first at the University of Adelaide and, since 1967, at the Flinders University of South Australia. I want to thank particularly my supervisors, Philip Lockwood and Peter Phillips.

I also wish to thank: in Australia, the Barr Smith Library, University of Adelaide; the South Australian Parliamentary Library;

the South Australian Public Library; the Library of the Flinders University of South Australia; the Melbourne Public Library; the National Library, Canberra; in the United States, the Program of African Studies, Northwestern University, Evanston, Ill., and especially the Program's Director, Professor Gwendolen Carter and her associates, Professor Jeffrey Butler of Wesleyan, Conn., and Professor Thomas Karis of New York City College; Mr. and Mrs. Edward Williams of Evanston, Ill.; in London, the British Museum; Chatham House Press Library; the Institute of Commonwealth Studies, London University; the School of Oriental and African Studies, London University; in South Africa, the Black Sash office, Johannesburg; the National Union of South African Students' office, Cape Town; the South African Institute of Race Relations, Johannesburg, and Mr. and Mrs. David Lunn of Johannesburg.

I am especially indebted to the people whom I interviewed; nearly all of them were South Africans. Several preferred not to be mentioned by name, but in most cases their names are listed in Section 4 of the Bibliography. In every case, their experiences and their views added to my understanding.

Finally, I want to thank my parents and my brother and sister-in-law for their constant support.

JANET ROBERTSON

Flinders University
1970

Contents

Abbreviations

A.N.C.: African National Congress
A.R.M.: African Resistance Movement
Ass. Debates: South African House of Assembly Debates
C.O.D.: Congress of Democrats
C.O.P.: Congress of the People
G.M.C.: Professor Gwendolen M. Carter, Director of the Program of African Studies, Northwestern University, Evanston, Ill., U.S.A.
L.P.: Liberal Party
N.R.C.: Native Representative Council
N.U.S.A.S.: National Union of South African Students
P.A.C.: Pan Africanist Congress
P.A.S.: Program of African Studies, Northwestern University, Evanston, Ill., U.S.A.
P.D.: Press Digest, issued by the Jewish Board of Deputies, Johannesburg
U.P.: United Party
S.A.C.P.O.: South African Coloured People's Organization
S.A.I.C.: South African Indian Congress
S.A.I.R.R.: South African Institute of Race Relations
S.A.L.A.: South African Liberal Association
S.A.L.G.: South African Liberal Group

TERMINOLOGY

Generally, the term 'whites' has been used to include the Afrikaners and the English-speakers, and the term 'non-whites' to embrace that otherwise unwieldy group comprised of Africans, Coloureds, and Indians. Naturally, the words 'liberal', 'liberals', and 'liberalism' appear frequently. They are capitalized only when reference is being made to the South African Liberal Party or to a member of that party.

Except in quotations etc., 'Lutuli' is spelt in the way his biographer, Mary Benson, prefers it.

Introduction

As plans were made for the unification of the South African colonies in the period of reconstruction after the Boer War, it became apparent that two distinct racial problems were involved: the white race question regarding the future relations between Boer and Briton, and the colour question. Earlier, in 1897, Sir Alfred Milner, High Commissioner for South Africa, had recognized just how closely these two issues were related.[1] In particular, he had expressed to Asquith his uneasy conviction that it was possible for the British Government to unite the white races by adopting a repressive policy towards non-whites:

> . . . *I personally* could win over the Dutch in the [Cape] Colony and indeed in all of the South African dominions in my term of office . . . without offending the English. You have only to sacrifice the 'nigger' absolutely and the game is easy. . . .[2]

In fact, the Liberal Ministry of 1906 chose to reconcile the white races through the granting of self-government and independence.[3] In so doing, they necessarily conceded that the solution of the colour question must be left to the former colonists. Most British parliamentarians finally agreed with the Liberals' priorities.[4] Those who like Ramsay MacDonald warned of the dangers of trusting 'the man on the spot' were in a minority.[5] More generally accepted was the principle expressed in 1906 by Sir Montagu Ommanney, Permanent Under-Secretary of State for the Colonies.

> I am afraid [he said] that it is impossible to devise effectual means of controlling the native policy of a self-governing Colony . . . [for] when

[1] Sir A. Milner to Mr. H. H. Asquith, 18 Nov. 1897, in Cecil Headlam (ed.), *The Milner Papers*, i (London, Cassell, 1931), 177–8.

[2] Quoted in G. H. L. Le May, *British Supremacy in South Africa 1899–1907* (Oxford, Clarendon Press, 1965), p. 11.

[3] G. B. Pyrah, *Imperial Policy and South Africa 1902–10* (Oxford, Clarendon Press, 1955), pp. 81–2.

[4] L. M. Thompson, *The Unification of South Africa, 1902–1910* (Oxford, Clarendon Press, 1960), pp. 422–3.

[5] Quoted in George Bennett (ed.), *The Concept of Empire: Burke to Attlee 1774–1947* (London, Adam and Charles Black, 1953), p. 38.

we decide to give that form of government . . . where there is a large native population, we deliberately accept the risk of having to save the white community from the consequences of its mismanagement of the natives.[1]

It was only in the years following the Act of Union, and the concession of South African autonomy in colour policy, that the British Government developed a harder line; then they sought to guarantee the rights of non-white majorities prior to any transfer of power to a white colonial government.[2]

In South Africa, as the National Convention (1908–9) discussed the form of union, most delegates agreed with Jan Smuts, the Boer general, that the white racial issue was of paramount concern.

> The political status of the Natives [he said] is no doubt a very important matter, but vastly more important . . . is the union of South Africa, which if not carried now will probably remain in abeyance until another deluge has swept over South Africa.[3]

Only a handful of whites held the view that freedom for the white population under the terms embodied in the Draft Act of Union would prejudice the freedom of the non-whites.[4]

This fear was expressed by a group commonly regarded as Cape liberals. Prominent among them were J. H. de Villiers, J. W. Sauer, Walter Stanford, J. X. Merriman, W. P. Schreiner, and James Rose Innes.[5] Such men as these, practising politicians and generally active in other areas of public life, cherished those liberal principles and institutions which had been transplanted from Britain to the Cape Colony during the nineteenth century.[6] Parliamentary government

[1] Quoted in Nicholas Mansergh, *South Africa 1906–1961: The Price of Magnanimity* (New York, Praeger, 1962), p. 68.

[2] Bennett (ed.), *Concept of Empire*, p. 23; also W. K. Hancock (ed.), *Survey of British Commonwealth Affairs*, vol. II, part 2, p. 3.

[3] Letter to J. A. Hobson, 13 July 1908, in W. K. Hancock and Jean van der Poel (eds.), *Selections from the Smuts Papers* ii (C.U.P., 1966), 441.

[4] e.g. W. P. Schreiner to Smuts, 2 Aug. 1908, ibid., ii, 450.

[5] J. H. de Villiers was Chief Justice and President of the Cape Legislative Council, 1873–1910; he was President of the National Convention 1909–10. J. W. Sauer was a solicitor and farmer as well as a parliamentarian. He was Colonial Secretary from 1898–1900. Walter Stanford was a distinguished member of the Cape Civil Service 1863–1907; as well, he was Secretary for Native Affairs for a time and Chief Magistrate of the Transkeian Territories. J. X. Merriman, a business-man, was a parliamentarian from 1869 until 1924; he was Prime Minister of the Cape 1908–10. W. P. Schreiner was a lawyer who became a passionate advocate of non-white rights at the turn of the century. He relinquished his seat at the National Convention in order to defend the Zulu Chief Dinizulu against charges laid by the Natal Government. James Rose Innes was an M.P. and Chief Justice of the Supreme Court of the Transvaal 1902–10.

[6] Hancock (ed.), *Survey of British Commonwealth Affairs*, vol. II, part 2, p. 7.

itself was highly valued as were other guarantees of freedom such as the rule of law, an independent judiciary, a free press, freedom of speech and of conscience.[1] Nor was loyalty to these liberal principles and their practice limited to English-speakers. Some of the most ardent support for such values came from Afrikaners, notably from Jan Hofmeyr, F. D. Malan, and their fellow-members of the Afrikaner Bond.[2] In this way, Cape liberalism served to unify at least an articulate minority of the white races in South Africa. Conversely, it was a set of values antipathetic to uncompromising Afrikaner nationalists, particularly in the Boer Republics.

A major reason for this antipathy was the Cape liberal view on the rights of non-whites. Cape liberals were not initially or primarily concerned with the colour question in South Africa. But they had inherited the principle of racial equality imposed on the Cape by the Imperial authority in the Ordinances of 1828, 1836, and 1842.[3] When the British Government established a parliament in the Cape in 1853 they had acted in accordance with the principle of civil equality, and granted the right to vote to all South Africans regardless of race, providing they could fulfil simple educational and economic qualifications. Those who were eligible to vote were also entitled to seek election in either house.[4] When responsible government was granted in 1872, Gladstone insisted on the retention of the 'colour-blind' franchise.[5] There had been strong, if minority, local support for the British Government's action with regard to the franchise. When, for example, the Legislative Council of the Cape Colony had met in 1852 to consider the draft constitution for the prospective parliament, it was clearly inconceivable to several members that non-whites should not qualify to vote on the same terms as whites. William Field, the Collector of Customs, pointed out: 'We ... are discussing whether the coloured man should have civil rights. *This in a British colony in the year 1852* [author's italic].[6] Yet, by the 1880s, the

[1] Leo Marquard, *Liberalism in South Africa* (Johannesburg, S.A.I.R.R., 1965), p. 22.

[2] ibid.; also Rodney Davenport, *The Afrikaner Bond: The History of a South African Political Party, 1880–1911* (Cape Town, O.U.P., 1966), p. 53.

[3] Eric A. Walker, *A History of Southern Africa*, 3rd edn. (London, Longmans, 1962), p. 243.

[4] ibid.

[5] A point made by Ramsay Muir in 'Liberalism and the Empire', in H. L. Nathan and H. Heathcote Williams (eds.), *Liberal Points of View* (London, Ernest Benn, 1927), p. 266.

[6] J. L. McCracken, *The Cape Parliament 1854–1900* (Oxford, Clarendon Press, 1967), p. 69.

champions of franchise revision were growing in number.[1] There were several reasons for this, for example, the apparent political weight of the non-white vote in the electoral battle between white parties.[2] But one of the most significant reasons was the increasing number of Africans and Coloureds who were qualifying to vote. This was particularly marked when the Transkei with its large African population was annexed to the Cape in 1887.[3] Three laws raising the franchise qualifications were passed by the Cape legislature in 1887, 1892, and 1894.[4] The effect of such measures was to disenfranchise non-whites, although 'down-at-heel Europeans and Coloured folk' were also excluded.[5] Even so, the principle of the vote for every civilized man regardless of race was retained.[6]

When the National Convention (1908–9) came to consider the question of voting rights in the prospective Union, the Cape delegates found themselves in a minority.[7] They advocated the extension of the Cape franchise regulations throughout the Union. This brought them into conflict with almost all politicians in Natal and the two Boer Republics, and with some of their colleagues in the Cape Parliament as well.[8] Furthermore, what evidence there is suggests also that their views on non-white rights found little support among the rank and file of either the Boer or British population in any colony.[9] In fact, the fervent opposition to the Cape liberals on the colour question indicates that, in their own times, they represented a liberal non-white policy qualitatively different from that supported by most whites in the South African colonies. Such support for political rights for non-whites was to remain in a minority after Union.

[1] ibid., p. 88.

[2] Davenport, *The Afrikaner Bond*, pp. 118–23.

[3] McCracken, *The Cape Parliament*, p. 90.

[4] Walker, A. *History of Southern Africa*, p. 432.

[5] ibid.

[6] Thompson, *The Unification of South Africa*, p. 112. The slogan of 'the vote for every civilized man' has become associated with Cecil Rhodes. In fact, in 1887, Rhodes had demanded 'Equal rights for every white man south of the Zambesi'. In 1899, challenged by his potential Coloured supporters he wrote: 'My motto is "Equal rights for every civilized man south of the Zambesi". What is a civilized man? A man, whether white or black, who has sufficient education to write his name, has some property or works, in fact is not a loafer . . .' See Sarah Gertrude Millin, *Rhodes* (London, Chatto Windus, 1933), p. 221.

[7] Thompson, *The Unification of South Africa*, pp. 212–26.

[8] e.g. ibid., pp. 329, 332, 337–9.

[9] ibid., pp. 112–15. Thompson makes particular reference to the evidence taken by the South African Native Affairs Commission of 1903–5.

In the view of Cape liberals, the vote should be reserved for civilized men, but all men, regardless of colour, should have the chance to become civilized. Moreover, it was the whites' duty, they argued, to promote the education and advancement of non-whites.[1] Such an attitude provided the hard core of the Cape liberals' views on colour. And it underpinned their vigorous resistance to any form of union which did not guarantee the existing political rights of non-whites. It was, for example, John X. Merriman's judgement that 'no sympathy for the Boer cause' could 'ever excuse any sort of departure from a liberal native policy'.[2]

There were other important aspects of the Cape liberals' attitude towards colour. Theirs was essentially a gradualist programme: they acknowledged the difficulty and slowness of the 'civilizing process'. There was, said W. P. Schreiner, 'no place for a false denial of the wide social gap' separating white and non-white.[3] Cape liberals also made it clear that they did not advocate social integration. Their views about the political rights of non-whites were modified by a qualified franchise. Yet, in this they did not differ from most of their contemporaries in South Africa, or in England. It was in 1906 that Lord Selborne, as South African High Commissioner, wrote to Smuts concerning the native vote. He accepted the idea of the franchise for those who 'have really reached the average level of civilization of the white man.'[4] But he rejected completely the idea of universal suffrage.

... parliamentary institutions in England [he said] are 550 years old, and yet the bulk of the population, white working men, have not yet had the vote for 50 years ... if the Natives in South Africa are to receive the franchise at all, they must be led up to it in exactly the same gradual way in which the white men were. . . .[5]

[1] cf. J. X. Merriman to Smuts, 13 Oct. 1912, in Hancock and van der Poel, *Selections from the Smuts Papers*, iii, 115: 'I was rather surprised and interested by being asked by a Coloured cab-driver what I thought of the action of the European powers towards Turkey!! . . . it shows you how education and the Press are stirring up the spirit of unrest all over the world. Awkward for the dominant races.'

[2] Letter to F. C. Mackarness, 22 Nov. 1903, in Phyllis Lewsen (ed.) *Selections from the Correspondence of J. X. Merriman*, iii (Cape Town, Van Riebeeck Society, 1966), 409.

[3] Eric A. Walker, *W. P. Schreiner: A South African* (Oxford, Clarendon Press, 1937), p. 311.

[4] Letter dated 9 Jan. 1908, in Hancock and van der Poel, *Selections from the Smuts Papers*, ii, 393.

[5] ibid., p. 394.

B

Nor did the Cape liberals find it easy to accept the prospect of non-white majority rule. John X. Merriman expressed his misgivings in a letter to Smuts in 1906. 'The relative numbers [he said] form the gravest objection as indeed they do constitute, and always will remain, our gravest menace.'[1] He continued:

> To me personally the idea of a Native franchise is repellent but I am convinced that it is a safety-valve and the best safety-valve, and that . . . it will be generations before the European political supremacy will be menaced, while it does undoubtedly not only safeguard the rights of an inferior race but also gives them a content which puts an end to the political unrest that any unrepresented population will always have.[2]

As the debate on the form of South African union drew to a close, Cape liberals were forced to admit defeat. The Draft Act of Union embodied universal adult suffrage for South African males; only in the Cape was the franchise for Africans and Coloureds retained, on the basis of a civilization qualification. Moreover the Cape liberals had been forced to concede the principle of the right of non-whites to be elected to parliament.[3] The stages in the debate at which each of them accepted defeat differed.[4] But, with the notable exception of Schreiner, they finally agreed that the solution of the white race issue warranted a strategic withdrawal;[5] it sufficed to preserve and entrench non-white rights within the Cape. Confronted by resistance on even this score from the other provinces, they may justifiably have regarded what they did achieve as a victory. Meanwhile they were outspoken in their hope of eventually extending Cape rights for non-whites to the rest of the Union. The concessions

---

[1] ibid., p. 447. Letter dated 19 July 1908.

[2] ibid., p. 448; cf. Jan Hofmeyr prior to Union: '. . . whatever my own prejudices of colour and race may be . . . the political and social security of white South Africa would be none the worse for retaining the goodwill of the five million of coloured and aboriginal inhabitants, with whom we live interspersed, and for reconciling them with our political institutions.' Quoted in Eric A. Walker, *The Cape Native Franchise* (a series of articles published in the *Cape Argus*), published by the Continuation Committee of the National Conference on the Native Bills (Cape Town, 1936).

[3] Thompson, *The Unification of South Africa*, pp. 219–20.

[4] ibid., pp. 336–48.

[5] After the Draft Act of Union had been revised, it came before the Cape Parliament for final approval in June 1909. In his opposition, Schreiner was supported only by Sir Gordon Sprigg, an Independent M.P.; his amendment directed at further guarantees of non-white rights was defeated by 94 votes to 2. ibid., pp. 292–3. Schreiner then led a mission of protest in England; it was timed to coincide with the British Parliament's decision on the Draft Act. Ibid., pp. 402–7; also Walker, *W. P. Schreiner*, pp. 312ff.

which they had made were part and parcel of their conviction that *after* Union toleration towards the principle, and practice, of rights for all civilized men would grow. Again with the exception of Schreiner, they were, in the manner of liberals everywhere, optimistic about the future: the white population were bound, they argued, to grow more, not less liberal on the colour question.[1] Their optimism, as well as their gradualism and their faith in the qualified franchise, were to characterize the political outlook of white liberals in South Africa as late as the 1950s.[2] By then, however, it was to be much more evident that the major racial question confronting South Africans was that of colour. This was something which the authoress, Olive Schreiner, had foreseen in 1908:

The problem of the twentieth century will not be a repetition of those of the nineteenth or those which went before it. The walls dividing continents are breaking down; everywhere European, Asiatic and African will interlard. The world on which the twenty-first century will open its eyes will be one widely different from that which the twentieth sees at its awakening. And the problem which this century will have to solve is the accomplishment of this interaction of distinct human varieties on the largest and most beneficent lines, making for the development of humanity as a whole, and carried out in a manner consonant with modern ideals and modern social wants. It will not always be the European who forms the upper layer; but in its essentials the problem will be everywhere the same. We in South Africa [she concluded] are one of the first peoples in the modern world . . . to be brought face to face with the problem in its acutest form. On our power to solve it regally and heroically depends our greatness.[3]

After 1910, however, it was still the white racial question which dominated Union politics. The electoral success of the South African Party in 1910, under the leadership of Botha and Smuts, denoted the victory of moderate Afrikaner opinion. Significantly, Botha recommended the 'placing of the Native question above party politics and the fair and sympathetic treatment of the Coloured races in a broad and liberal spirit'.[4] He may well have foreseen that if this were not agreed upon the colour question would be exploited

[1] Thompson, *The Unification of South Africa*, p. 339.
[2] See below, p. 199.
[3] Olive Schreiner, *Closer Union* (Cape Town, The Constitutional Reform Association, n.d.), pp. 25–6.
[4] See Gen. Louis Botha's Manifesto, 1910, in D. W. Krüger (ed.), *South African Parties and Policies 1910–1960: A Select Source Book* (London, Bowes & Bowes, 1960), p. 49.

in the struggle for power between the white parties. Such a colour policy was no bar to closer political alliance with the predominantly English Unionist Party, and further progress towards the reconciliation of the white races, and absence of serious dispute over the colour question, was indicated by the combination of the South African Party with Jameson's Unionists in 1920.

In 1924 Hertzog's National Party won power. This was a triumph for extremist Afrikaner opinion since Hertzog's Nationalists had seceded from Botha and the moderates late in 1913. Between 1924 and 1929 the Nationalists ruled in a mutually advantageous coalition with the Labour Party. During those years further guarantees of equality of the Afrikaners and English-speakers were secured; the legacy included official recognition of the equality of the two white languages, two flags and two anthems, and the introduction of the 'civilized labour policy'. In 1931 the enactment of the Statute of Westminster acknowledged South Africa's dominion status.

In the 1929 election the Nationalists won a majority of seats in the Assembly after a campaign fought on the colour issue[1]—an omen of their similar success in 1948. Yet the economic crisis of 1933 led to a coalition and then to the Fusion of the National Party and the South African Party. This Fusion, secured in 1934 with the formation of the United Party, signified the high-water mark of Boer–British reconciliation. The only major questions left in abeyance seemed to be the republican issue and the question of neutrality if Britain were to again be involved in war.[2] The process of Fusion had meant the emergence of two extremist groups, the Purified Nationalists, reflecting extremist Afrikaner views particularly in regard to a republic,[3] and the Dominion Party which, by contrast, stood for the paramount importance of the Imperial link.[4] It was the Purified Nationalists who were to win the loyalty of the majority of Afrikaners in the 1940s and assume political power in 1948.

Meanwhile, in the thirties, while the Boer–British conflict appeared resolved, the colour question assumed new prominence. The success of Fusion in 1934 had been dependent on the South African Party's acceptance of the Nationalists' colour policy which was segregationist. To many of the party, this had not been a major concession;

---

[1] Walker, *A History of Southern Africa*, p. 625.
[2] W. K. Hancock, *Smuts*, vol. II: *The Fields of Force 1919–1950* (C.U.P., 1968), pp. 254–5.
[3] ibid., p. 253.   [4] ibid., p. 258.

as Smuts knew, a number of his supporters already sympathized with the Nationalists' views on colour.[1] They had, in fact, threatened the unity of the South African Party on this issue in the twenties; even so, the party had remained, paradoxically, the only political home for liberals. After 1934, the colour question threatened the cohesion of the newly formed United Party. The major crisis occurred over Prime Minister Hertzog's proposed native settlement.[2] He had first drawn up bills to achieve similar aims in 1926, after which a Joint Select Committee had debated the relevant issues for five years.[3]

The central features of the Hertzog legislation which was approved in its final form in 1936 was the removal of the African voters in the Cape from the common roll. Instead, under the terms of the Representation of Natives Act, Africans were entitled to elect three whites as Native Representatives in the House of Assembly. Africans in all provinces were to elect four white Senators. The Act provided, in addition, a degree of communal representation by setting up a Native Representative Council.[4] United Party agreement on this measure—and its counterpart, the Native Land and Trust Act, obligating the Government to extend the areas of the Reserves— was secured on the condition that the Coloured vote in the Cape should be reaffirmed.

Opponents of the Hertzog bills fought under the banner of liberalism.[5] A chief protagonist, J. H. Hofmeyr, declared in November

[1] Hancock, *Smuts*, vol. II, p. 206. See below, p. 15.
[2] ibid., Ch. 14, pp. 259–66.
[3] Walker, *The Cape Native Franchise*, pp. 19, 28, 29.
[4] Muriel Horrell, *Legislation and Race Relations* (Johannesburg, S.A.I.R.R. 1963), pp. 1–2. The Council would include 5 whites and 16 Africans, of whom 4 were to be nominated and 12 elected; the Secretary of Native Affairs was to be chairman.
[5] R. F. Alfred Hoernlé, *South African Native Policy and the Liberal Spirit: Being the Phelps–Stokes Lectures, delivered before the University of Cape Town, May 1939* (Johannesburg, Witwatersrand Univ. Press, 1945), p. 105. As early as 1929 a Non-Racial Franchise Association had been formed to protect the existing rights of non-whites in the Cape, and to promote support for the extension of the 'civilized vote' throughout the Union. At the Association's inaugural meeting, James Rose Innes spoke of the need for a 'reasoned defence of the Cape franchise'. James Rose Innes, *Autobiography* (Cape Town, O.U.P., 1949), p. 312. White liberals were not alone in their opposition to Hertzog's measures; widespread reaction came from non-white political organizations and these combined to form the All-African National Convention in December 1935. Their failure to prevent the passing of Hertzog's bills, and the implications of those measures for the future of non-white rights, stimulated a new militancy among non-whites. See below, pp. 32–4.

1935: 'When I speak of Liberalism I think especially of the Native people of this land.'[1] He had then recommended the Cape liberal view of the franchise. Referring to such men as Schreiner, Sauer, Rose Innes and his relative, Jan Hofmeyr, he said:

Every one of them regarded the retention of the Cape native franchise as the very Ark of the Covenant so far as the Cape is concerned. It would be wrong to deprive any citizen born in this country of the opportunity to aspire to the full rights of citizenship merely because of race or colour.[2]

Hofmeyr's advocacy of shared political rights in an integrated society was not the only liberal method of meeting the South African colour problem. There had been considerable interest among liberals in two alternate solutions: total separation and parallel institutions. The first of these had been a respectable liberal theory since it had been endorsed by Dr. John Philip, the English missionary and champion of racial equality, in the 1820s:[3] but a hundred years later, in the 1930s, the degree of economic integration made such a solution impractical. The policy of parallel development with parallel opportunities *without* territorial segregation was another alternative. The ideal of parallel institutions was, as Hancock points out, generally accepted as 'the liberal orthodoxy of . . . that time'.[4] However, to most liberals in South Africa, it was clear by the thirties that parallelism was not likely to offer a genuinely liberal alternative. As Alfred Hoernlé acknowledged in 1939:

The present Cape Native franchise [of 1936] is a bit of political Parallelism, but so carefully circumscribed that it is . . . impotent to endanger White domination. . . . No general and adequate extension of this principle of having separate registers for voters of different races is conceivable, let alone that the Parliamentary representatives of each race should be members of that race.[5]

Faced with Hertzog's plan to remove the African voters from the Cape common roll, Smuts found himself in a unique dilemma. On the question of political rights for non-whites he had consistently been 'an evolutionist';[6] and had already shown some degree of

---

[1] Quoted in Edward Roux, *Time Longer than Rope*, 2nd edn. (Madison, Univ. of Wisconsin Press, 1964), p. 292.
[2] ibid.
[3] Hoernlé, *South African Native Policy*, p. 63.
[4] Hancock, *Smuts*, ii, 121.
[5] Hoernlé, *South African Native Policy*, p. 165.
[6] Hancock, *Smuts*, ii, 259.

adaptation on the colour question in a liberal direction. In 1913 he had believed parallel development was still possible;[1] but by the 1920s he admitted the intractable difficulties caused by the extent of economic integration.[2] In 1936, however, he saw the price of an uncomprising defence of the existing African franchise as the destruction of the newly won Boer–British unity; he was not prepared to pay such a price. Because of this he found himself regarded with hostility by Hofmeyr's supporters on the issue. In privately pleading his defence he argued: 'Politics is the art of the possible and the practicable',[3] and later stressed: '*I have had to sit tight and save the work in national upbuilding* [author's italic] for which I have been mainly responsible these five years.'[4]

The liberals who regretted the United Party's assent to Hertzog's bills saw clearly how weak their position was. This did not prevent Hofmeyr's defiant stand with the support of ten other M.P.s.[5] Indeed, he made particular reference to their minority attitude:

[The] tide of reaction is still flowing forward. I know that those of us who are opposing that tide cannot hope to check it. The puny breastworks that we put up must be swept away, but I do believe that the mere putting up of the breastworks is going to accelerate the day when the tide will turn, as turn, I believe, it some day will. . . . I know that I am speaking against the feeling of the overwhelming majority of this House. I know I am speaking against the feeling of the great mass of the people of this country. . . . I believe that there is also a rising tide of liberalism in South Africa. It is mostly the younger people who are in the forefront of that tide . . . it is by them that the ultimate connection in this matter will have to be decided.[6]

Other liberals who discussed the implications of the 1936 crisis did not share even this degree of hope. In 1939, Alfred Hoernlé delivered the Phelps–Stokes Lectures at the University of Cape Town. He noted the 'decline and eclipse' of the acceptance of the liberal principle of integration.[7] This was, he said, 'the result of a more race-conscious generation realizing more clearly, and shrinking from, the ultimate consequences of Total Assimilation'.[8] In 1939 also,

---

[1] ibid., pp. 113–14.   [2] ibid., p. 121. See below, p. 24.
[3] ibid., p. 291.   [4] ibid., p. 294.
[5] In the Joint Session required to change the entrenched clauses of the constitution, 168 M.P.s supported Hertzog's bills and 11 opposed them.
[6] Alan Paton, *Hofmeyr* (Cape Town, O.U.P., 1964), p. 228.
[7] Hoernlé, *South African Native Policy*, p. 66.
[8] ibid.

J. S. Marais produced his definitive history of *The Cape Coloured People 1652–1937*. He concluded his analysis with the following:

> What of the future? I believe there is little hope of a reversal of present-day trends. If the last hundred years of South African history have any 'lesson' to teach us it is this: every inch of territory yielded to the supporters of caste is ground irretrievably lost. . . . Today the question is not whether it will be possible to extend the Cape's institutions northward, but how much support the Cape tradition still retains in the Cape itself. *The fact is that European public opinion in the Cape Province during the twenty-eight years since Union has grown used to the idea of colour-bar legislation* [author's italic].[1]

Thus, by the late thirties, the liberal minority had acknowledged themselves impotent within the existing party structure. Their only medium of political expression was the United Party, and that party had been prepared *as a party* to give ground on the colour question, either because they agreed with Hertzog's denial of equal political rights to non-whites or because, like Smuts, they considered the preservation of the unity of the white races, as expressed in Fusion, more important.

Ironically, it was Smuts's decision to enter the European war in 1939 which destroyed Fusion, and destroyed too the reconciliation of Boer and Briton. South Africa's entry into the war, together with other factors, facilitated the resurgence of an Afrikaner nationalist movement. And in the forties Boer–British hostility once again gathered intensity. But by the forties, the colour question had assumed paramount importance. The spread of industrialization and South Africa's involvement in the war both helped to engender a new spirit of African nationalism in the forties. It was in such circumstances—with both racial questions unresolved—that the Nationalists won political power in the election of 1948.

The year 1948 'marks a watershed in South African politics'.[2] The Nationalists immediately began to implement their *apartheid* policy. Here was the beginning, Roux claims, of 'a period of racial legislation more thoroughgoing, more grotesque perhaps, than anything the country or the world had ever seen'.[3] Yet 1948 marked also the opening of the final phase in the resolution of the white

---

[1] J. S. Marais, *The Cape Coloured People 1652–1937* (Johannesburg, Witwatersrand Univ. Press, 1957), p. 284.

[2] Gwendolen M. Carter, *The Politics of Inequality: South Africa Since 1948*, 3rd edn. (London, Thames & Hudson, 1962), p. 37.

[3] Roux, *Time Longer than Rope*, p. 366.

racial issue. At first, the Nationalist victory regenerated hostility between the white races, and white liberals rallied to the United Party's defence. While the formation of a separate liberal party was thus delayed the Nationalist policy of *apartheid* drove the African National Congress to adopt strategies unacceptable to most white liberals. Thus the gulf which had appeared in the forties between the aims and methods of white liberals and those of the African National Congress now widened. These crucial discrepancies were to persist throughout the fifties: the gulf was only bridged by the end of the decade. By then, however, the bulk of the white community had accepted *apartheid* as the only solution to the colour problem. They were at last united: in their support of the Nationalists' non-white policy. And by entering the white laager they had contributed to the gradual dismantling of the liberal state.

CHAPTER I

The background: the two racial issues in the 1940s

i

Prior to the Nationalists' victory in 1948 the principles of political liberalism were already under review in South Africa. This reappraisal had several causes: South Africa's involvement in the Second World War; the increasing pace of industrialization and urbanization; and the ambivalence of the United Party Government's colour policy. These factors did not have the same impact on white liberals as on liberals within the African National Congress (A.N.C.), but they were important in both instances. With white liberals, there was no drastic redefinition of aims. The factors which drove the A.N.C. to adopt a harder, though still moderate, line served also to exacerbate hostility between the white races in the forties. This friction regenerated liberal views about white rights and helped to delay a separate movement among those also concerned with non-white rights. In addition, the United Party did not appear to white liberals as intransigent on the colour question as it did to Congress liberals. Thus, the revival of the white racial question and optimism as to the ultimate direction of U.P. colour policy immobilized white liberals in the forties. In the case of Congress liberals the forties was a period of significant change. Their political aims, while still indisputably liberal, became more radical in the South African context. It was in this period, for example, that Congress leaders adopted the principle of manhood suffrage for the first time and rejected the Native Representative Council and the method of communal representation which it embodied. In ways such as these the principles of liberals within the A.N.C. developed quickly in comparison with those of white liberals before 1948.

ii

The United Party had never given satisfactory expression to liberal principles on colour. Its origins lay in the other race issue—

that between Boer and Briton. The U.P. was, nevertheless, the party for which most English-speakers, who comprised the bulk of the liberal group, were accustomed to vote. True, the Native Representatives preferred to be distinguished as a group and, in fact, consciously thought of themselves—to use Margaret Ballinger's phrase—as 'non-party people'.[1] But when political power was at issue, the Native Representatives had inevitably to support the United Party, not as a liberal party but as the only moderate alternative to the Nationalists. As a result, the U.P. sustained a strong hold on the imaginations—and votes—of liberal whites, even when they might have had reason to suspect the party's liberalism as spurious.

Such a suspicion would have been well founded. Even prior to Fusion, the South African Party had been sharply divided over the colour question. Some members, for example, had openly expressed sympathy with the Nationalist–Labour native policy.[2] As one member expressed it in 1924, General Hertzog did not have 'a monopoly of segregation'.[3] Significantly, when Fusion was completed in 1934, the new United Party's native policy emphasized that 'the essentials of European civilization' were 'paramount'.[4] The principle of 'Christian trusteeship' was stressed, but the key issue of the future political representation of non-whites was left 'to the free exercise of the discretion of individual members'.[5] Basic disagreement on the colour question recurred in U.P. ranks continually in the thirties, most notably over the Hertzog legislation of 1936.[6] Here the liberals' hero was the Cabinet Minister, J. H. Hofmeyr, who led the minority of M.P.s who opposed the 'settlement'.[7] But subject to conflicting pressures, and (according to his biographer, Alan Paton) not the least as a result of his own inertia, Hofmeyr failed to break away from the U.P. to form a separate party based on the extension of civil and political rights to non-whites.[8]

There were, however, a number of principles which the United Party and the liberals shared. The U.P. stood for the preservation of principles and methods historically associated with the Western liberal tradition—minimum Government interference with the rights of the individual, the rule of law, the inviolability of the constitution,

---

[1] Author's interview, Cape Town, 9 Dec. 1965.
[2] W. K. Hancock, *Smuts*, ii, p. 206.   [3] ibid., p. 163.
[4] *Programme of Principles*, as quoted in Hancock, *Smuts*, ii, 257.
[5] ibid.   [6] See above, pp. 9–11.
[7] Roux, *Time Longer than Rope*, pp. 289–93.
[8] Paton, *Hofmeyr*, pp. 311–12.

and the independence of the judiciary. True, both principle and practice represented a liberalism more characteristic of the nineteenth century than the twentieth. But such values were as deeply prized among those who sought a liberal solution to the colour question as they were among U.P. leaders.

Because of this the war years saw a strengthening of the bonds between the U.P. and those with liberal views on colour. In those years United Party principles acquired fresh significance and appeared to need vigorous defence. The colour question became strategically a question of second importance. The late thirties and early forties were marked by a regeneration of English–Afrikaner hostility. This renewed bitterness between the white races had a complex cause. In part it was due to new economic competition between Afrikaners and English-speakers. Also important was the question of South Africa's entry into the Second World War, which led to the breakdown of Fusion.

The traditional hostility of Boer and Briton was exacerbated by the Afrikaner movement to the towns in the thirties and forties. Between the censuses of 1936 and 1951 the net urban migration of whites, almost all Afrikaners, was just short of a quarter of a million. In 1936 Afrikaans-speakers constituted 48 per cent of South Africa's white urban population; by 1951 69 per cent.[1] Among the whites the English-speakers had previously enjoyed a monopoly of the profits of the industrial wealth of South Africa. The late thirties and early forties saw the beginnings of a concerted effort on the part of a small group of Afrikaners literally to 'buy into' this monopoly.[2] But the wall of English economic privilege was slow to yield. And while it remained the old jealousies aggravated day-to-day dealings between the white races in the big cities, not least because the Afrikaners were at the bottom of the economic—and social—scale. In 1948 it was these Afrikaners newly arrived in the cities who swung the balance for the Nationalists in crucial urban constituencies.[3]

Not all Afrikaners opposed the South African war commitment. Smuts's most bitter opponents, however, were Afrikaners. The war years were marked—marred, in the U.P. view—by outbreaks of

[1] Hancock, *Smuts*, ii, 289.

[2] Sheila Patterson, *The Last Trek: A Study of the Boer People and the Afrikaner Nation* (London, Routledge & Kegan Paul, 1957), pp. 167–70.

[3] Carter, *The Politics of Inequality*, p. 159; also N. M. Stultz, 'The Electoral Revival of the National Party in South Africa, 1934 to 1948', unpublished Ph.D. thesis, Boston Grad. School, 1965, pp. 327–8.

violence against men in arms, and the uncompromising opposition of Nationalist newspapers such as *Die Transvaler*.[1] In addition, during the war the resurgence of Afrikaner nationalism which had begun in the mid thirties continued. This aggravated the fears of United Party supporters about the future of white unity and white rights in South Africa. The struggle against dictatorship—whether personified by Hitler and Mussolini in Europe or threatened by the Afrikaner nationalists at home—became the first priority with most white liberals in the war years.

Hertzog's refusal to follow Smuts into the war meant that Hertzog and his supporters were thrust out of the Boer–British camp into the political wilderness. The Afrikaner Party which they formed in 1941 was based on a respect for equal rights for the white groups, but at the same time a struggle for the political leadership of Afrikaners took place with frightening implications for United Party principles of reconciliation between Boer and Briton—and for the U.P.'s political future. By 1942 there were four Afrikaner political organizations— Hertzog's party, Malan's Reunited National Party (H.N.P.),[2] the Ossewa Brandwag and Pirow's New Order.[3] These organizations reflected important ideological differences, but they shared, with different degrees of vehemence, in the opposition to South Africa's

[1] A memorable instance of *Die Transvaler* support for the Nazis was embodied in the judgement passed on Dr. H. F. Verwoerd by Judge Philip Millin in May 1943. One of the newspaper's directors, Verwoerd had taken action against the Johannesburg *Star* over their charge that he had falsified names in support of the Nazis. He lost the case, and in delivering the judgement, Millin claimed Verwoerd 'did support Nazi propaganda, he did make his paper a tool of the Nazis in South Africa, and he knew it' (Paton, *Hofmeyr*, p. 370). In post-war years, this incident became one of the customary means by which anti-Nationalists demonstrated the fascist sympathies of Verwoerd in particular, and the Nationalists in general.

[2] In December 1933, a group of Nationalists reacted to the prospect of Fusion by forming a separate Purified National Party under Dr. D. F. Malan. Those moderate Afrikaners who, under Hertzog, left the U.P. in 1939, subsequently reached sufficient agreement with the Malanites to form Die Herenigdne Nasionale of Volksparty, or Reunited National Party (H.N.P.) in 1940. The moderates were only temporarily reconciled; in 1941 they seceded to form a separate Afrikaner Party based on equal rights for the white groups. See Hancock, *Smuts*; ii, 253; Carter, *The Politics of Inequality*, pp. 33–4.

[3] M. Roberts and A. E. G. Trollip, *The South African Opposition 1939–1945* (London, Longmans, 1947), p. 126. The Ossewa Brandwag or 'oxwagon guard' was a cultural organization set up in 1938, at the time of the centenary of the Great Trek, to stimulate an exclusive Afrikaner nationalism (ibid., pp. 73–4). cf. Eric A. Walker, *A History of Southern Africa*, p. 678. The New Order was formed by Oswald Pirow in 1941 within the ranks of H.N.P. Pirow and seven other M.P.s soon seceded to form the New Order Party, based on National-Socialist doctrines. Roberts and Trollip, *South African Opposition*, p. 97.

involvement in the war. Such opposition was bound to provoke suspicion among those who supported Smuts's stand, particularly the English-speakers.

This suspicion of Afrikaner nationalism, whatever its particular medium, was increased immeasurably by a significant totalitarian element which developed in Afrikaner political theory in this period.[1] A number of vocal Afrikaners revealed a lack of sympathy for the values of Western parliamentary democracy, if not overt support for fascist principles. The Ossewa Brandwag, for example, were prepared to condemn 'unnational elements' to inferior civic status, oppose bilingualism, support ideals of race purity, and approve the overthrow of democracy in Germany and Italy.[2]

Whatever the distinctions which marked off one set of Afrikaner nationalist values from another in the war years, the English-speakers were always ready both then and later to associate all hostile Afrikaner nationalism with its most illiberal elements. This was, of course, to ignore the important differences between men such as Malan and Eric Louw.[3] But it was a basic reason for the intensity of the clash which followed the Nationalists' election victory in 1948. A recurring theme in the United Party's attacks on the Government after that date was that they were forced by circumstance to assume their role of the war years as defenders of freedom. After the loss of Hertzog's support in 1939, the United Party could no longer represent the principles of Fusion in the same sense as they had before the war. But they found in the history of white politics in South Africa during the war an additional *raison d'être*—that of the defence of basic liberal principles.

In fact, the extremism of an organization such as the New Order was rejected by Malan, whose party rapidly came to represent the mainstream of Afrikaner nationalist opinion.[4] He was prepared to guarantee the English-speakers in South Africa full equality of political, cultural, and language rights.[5] But even though this more moderate view prevailed the more extremist groups had been re-

---

[1] Roberts and Trollip, *South African Opposition*, p. 4; Patterson, *Last Trek*, p. 93.

[2] Roberts and Trollip, *South African Opposition*, p. 152.

[3] ibid., p. 174.

[4] By the 1943 election Malan was able to establish the H.N.P. as the strongest party competing for Afrikaner votes in elections. Roberts and Trollip, *South African Opposition*, pp. 158–9.

[5] ibid., p. 149; Patterson, *Last Trek*, p. 105.

sponsible for increasing the political awareness of rank-and-file Afrikaners. It had been, for example, the Ossewa Brandwag which had brought the Nationalist cause home to the people, 'from the bywoner [farmer] to the banker, from the university student to the railway ganger'.[1] In the wartime election of 1943 the Afrikaans-speaking vote for the United Party dropped and the H.N.P. increased the ratio of their support.[2] Thus the war years augured well for the future of a strong Nationalist Party. In peacetime conditions electora support for the H.N.P. was likely to grow—the rate of population increase was higher among Afrikaners than English-speakers[3] and those Afrikaners who had backed Smuts over the war would be freshly susceptible to the appeal of Afrikaner nationalism. In addition, the Afrikaner migration to the towns held the possibility of increased support for the Nationalist Party in vital urban constituencies.[4] For these reasons alone it was evident long before 1948 that the post-war election would be closely fought. In the face of this threat liberals were encouraged to postpone any secessionist move; they believed it more immediately important to prevent the Nationalists from gaining power.

As the 1948 election approached the Nationalists represented not only threats to white rights; clearly, also, their policy of *apartheid* constituted a challenge to the liberals' hopes for the extension of rights to non-whites. It thus proved important for the future of liberals that United Party racial policy in the forties appeared, for a number of reasons, qualitatively different from that of the Nationalists. The U.P. disagreed—fundamentally, they thought—over the nature of the colour problem and its solution. In the forties their area of disagreement appeared extensive because they differed radically on what were later to be proved tangential questions.

The fact that the United Party did not share Nationalist fears or approve Nationalist non-white policy derived largely from the nature of traditional relationships between English-speakers and non-whites, relationships crucially unlike those of most Afrikaners.[5] Over the

---

[1] Roberts and Trollip, *South African Opposition*, p. 122.
[2] ibid., p. 159.   [3] ibid.   [4] See above, p. 16.
[5] It was Smuts's contention that when the native question was discussed the Nationalists were 'back at Dingaan' (*Cape Times*, 12 Jan. 1949). This was a reference to the importance which the Afrikaners attached to the Voortrekkers' encounter with the Zulus in the 1830s, and in particular, to their clashes with Dingaan, the Zulu King. The Zulus' killing of Piet Retief, the Boer leader, and his negotiating party, as well as the subsequent Battle of Blood River in 1838,

years the different historical experiences of the two white groups had become mythologized, and the myths were transmitted and perpetuated by a number of effective agencies. Notable among these were national-language newpapers.[1] Perhaps the most glaring instance was the difference in the attitudes encouraged by the English-speaking churches on the one hand, and the Dutch Reformed churches on the other—the second exerting what Patterson calls 'a major social influence in Afrikaner life'.[2]

The English had not struggled for survival as had the Afrikaners. The Boers had trekked into a hostile interior in the mid-nineteenth century, and were forced to protect their families and their hard-earned gains from the frighteningly unfamiliar Bantu. Nor had the English shared the Afrikaner experience of 'poor-whiteism'.[3] This was a crisis which had engendered fresh hostility between Afrikaners and Africans competing for the more poorly paid jobs on the frontier of the racial economic dividing line after the turn of the century, particularly in the twenties.[4] And it was a form of competition which threatened to recur in a newer and perhaps more explosive form in the South African cities of the forties and early fifties as both Afrikaners and non-whites trekked there from the platteland. These Afrikaners were, at least temporarily, marginal men, thrust into an alien society. And as their African counterparts had done, they too brought their tribal backgrounds—in particular, a series of preconceptions about non-whites which were as much an integral part of their baggage as was their family Bible.[5] But the new relationships in the cities were not ordered in the same way as the traditional ones on the Afrikaner farms. There were here, in the life of the cities, manifold opportunities for abrasive contact between Afrikaners and

---

when the Trekkers inflicted a heavy defeat on the Zulus, became, in the view of Afrikaners generally, events of prime significance in the history of their relations with the Africans.

[1] Carter, *The Politics of Inequality*, pp. 37 ff.

[2] Patterson, *Last Trek*, p. 215.

[3] According to the findings of the Carnegie Commission, in 1929 those classified as Poor Whites had constituted one-tenth of the white population—and one-fifth of the Afrikaans-speaking population. Quoted in Sheila T. van der Horst, 'The Effects of Industrialisation on Race Relations in South Africa', in Guy Hunter (ed.). *Industrialization and Race Relations: A Symposium* (London, O.U.P., 1965), p. 116.

[4] *Last Trek*, p. 140.

[5] I. D. MacCrone, 'Race Attitudes', in Ellen Hellmann (ed.), *Handbook on Race Relations in South Africa* (Cape Town, O.U.P., 1949), p. 704.

non-whites.[1] The unaccustomed 'cheekiness' of the city 'kaffir' would have alone sufficed seriously to alarm the rapidly increasing Afrikaner population, for instance, in the Johannesburg industrial complex. In addition, theirs was a situation which was economically precarious. They were, in Malan's words, 'meeting the non-European at the new Blood River' and they were 'defenceless in the open plains of economic competition'.[2] Although the influx of Afrikaners did not reproduce the 'poor-white' problem it did introduce into the labour market a group not sufficiently skilled to take jobs normally the prerogative of the whites, and, because of their whiteness, not prepared to take the unskilled jobs reserved for non-whites at lower rates of pay. Job opportunities for Afrikaners were limited, for example, to low-grade civil service positions, the ranks of the police force or to manning the public transport system.[3] Such jobs brought them into daily contact with large numbers of non-whites. With the memory of 'poor-whiteism' less than a generation old, they could scarcely avoid reacting with fear; it was, after all, the presence of a pool of readily available black labour which most directly threatened their economic security.

The English in the cities did not feel their economic security threatened to any comparable extent by the increasing number of Africans seeking employment in urban areas. The non-white population shift guaranteed an abundant supply of cheap labour and ensured steady profits for English investors whose stakes in industry in the forties were considerably higher than those of the Afrikaners. In addition, the English-speakers' monopoly of the skilled labour force was not threatened by the non-white migration to the cities. There was less day-to-day contact between English-speakers and Africans than there was between Afrikaners and Africans. Generally it was Afrikaners who staffed public services like post offices and pass offices, where they would regularly come into contact with non-whites in the normal course of their duties.

Distinctions were noticeable too, in what were, to whites at least, striking regional differences. One of the most marked contrasts was

---

[1] e.g. the incident recounted by Ezekiel Mphahlele in his autobiography, *Down Second Avenue* (Berlin, Seven Seas, 1962), pp. 100–1.

[2] Quoted in W. K. Hancock (ed.), *Survey of British Commonwealth Affairs*, i, 20.

[3] Jan Goudriaan and D. G. Franzen, 'Economic Factors', in G. H. Calpin (ed.), *The South African Way of Life: Values and Ideals of a Multi-racial Society* (London), Heinemann, 1953), p. 180.

that between the outlook of the whites in the Western Cape where the non-white population was Coloured rather than African, and those in the Orange Free State, where the whites, almost entirely Afrikaners, were heavily outnumbered by an uneducated African majority. No doubt the descendants of the Trekkers remembered that the Cape had given little or no assistance to the Northern Republics in the Boer War. The Western Cape, in particular, seemed to them 'un-South African and "jingoistic" '.[1] As Patterson noted of their reaction to Cape Town as late as the mid fifties:

> They feel ill at ease in a city where liberalism lingers to the extent that coloured people sit on the municipal council and on the same park bench or bus seat, where a motorist may be directed or even corrected by a coloured traffic policeman, and where a tourist may find coloured people using the same piece of beach or sea.[2]

This was a reaction to the traditional relationship between whites and Coloureds. Historically, the English-speakers in the Cape, like the Afrikaners living there too, had been associated with the Coloureds, rather than with the Africans whose numbers in that area were proportionately very small. This long association meant that Coloureds had been exposed consistently to European cultural traditions and had been integrated into the way of life in the Cape in a way in which Africans never were. Consequently, Hertzog had held from the mid twenties that while Africans should be segregated, the Coloureds belonged with the European group. In addition, not only were the political rights of the Coloureds entrenched in the South Africa Act, but they had been guaranteed afresh in 1936, as the *sine qua non* of United Party connivance at the diminution of African voting rights.[3]

In the rural areas also Afrikaners were associated with Africans to a far greater degree than were the English. In 1946, 85·54 per cent of white farmers were Afrikaans-speaking.[4] Except in Natal, there were comparatively few English-speaking farmers. On all European farms, whites generally had what van den Berghe describes as only 'highly segmental and utilitarian relations with Africans'. These were,

---

[1] Patterson, *Last Trek*, p. 83.

[2] ibid. These observations remained valid until the early sixties when the Nationalists applied *apartheid* much more rigidly in the Western Cape.

[3] See above, p. 9.

[4] Pierre L. van den Berghe, *South Africa: A Study in Conflict* (Middletown, Wesleyan Univ. Press, 1965), p. 109.

he adds, relations 'defined by a vigorous strait-jacket of master-servant etiquette'.[1] Consequently, the whites in the countryside usually held the most obviously stereotyped views about non-whites —and held them most steadfastly.

This bred among many Afrikaners an attitude of 'platteland superiority' which was frequently displayed by Government members. 'We Nationalists come from the Platteland and know the natives', Mr. P. W. Botha declared in the House of Assembly in September 1948.[2] He went on to challenge the judgement of a U.P. member, Mr. A. E. Robinson, who had not lived and worked with the natives in the same way:

> If he has not done that what right has he to come here and scold people whose forefathers and whose church have contributed greatly to . . . their education and development and what right has he to scold them for wanting them to oppress the Natives and deprive them of their rights?[3]

Ironically, this line of argument served less to convince the United Party of the validity of the Government's viewpoint, than to accentuate the urban–rural dichotomy between English and Afrikaners and to encourage the English further in their despising of platteland opinion.[4] In part such conflicts were evidence of city–country rivalry, a universal enough phenomenon. It was, however, a particularly bitter rivalry in South Africa, since it was underscored by other differences—such as those of national origin and language—and these combined to sustain and intensify the old hostility between Boer and Briton.

During and after the war such differences were underlined by the development of a United Party colour policy which was distinguishable from that of the Nationalists and which, at least to the optimistic, augured well for further liberalization. Little ground was gained, from the liberal point of view, on the question of political

---

[1] ibid., p. 224.

[2] *Ass. Debates*, vol. 64, 6 Sept. 1948, col. 1684.

[3] ibid. Mr. Botha was supported by Mr. J. S. Labuschagne who stated 'I'm a platteland farmer', and explained why this gave him a special insight: '. . . on my farm there are many natives whose parents trekked from Natal to the Transvaal with my father more than 60 years ago. The children of these natives are on my farm and I repose great confidence in them. I give them responsibilities which I would not entrust to every European, unless I knew him. Those labourers are happy and prosperous . . .' ibid., 1685.

[4] Commented on by Basil Davidson, *Report on Southern Africa* (London, Jonathan Cape, 1952), p. 151.

rights for non-whites. But none was lost either. There persisted in Smuts's mind a conflict between the social and economic advances he was prepared to initiate and the issue of political equality.[1] But the U.P. stood firmly on two aspects of political rights. First, party spokesmen stressed repeatedly that they would oppose the abolition of those political rights for non-whites which already existed. Not only was this a liberal principle, but the pursuit of it always held (for the optimists) the possibility of extending such rights. Second, the policy of the U.P. towards the Native Representative Council was, at least in the white world, different from that of the Nationalist Government.[2] Then, too, in the forties, the views of almost all white liberals were marked by their belief in gradualism and the qualified franchise. For such reasons they did not yet feel alienated from the main body of the United Party on the question of political rights.

The greatest hope for liberals lay in the dramatic change in the official U.P. attitude towards economic segregation. Such a change appeared to the liberals associated with the party to promise the eventual extension of political rights to non-whites.[3] Earlier, in 1923, Smuts had shown basic agreement with Hertzog by the terms in which he had promoted the Native (Urban Areas) Bill.[4] While making provision for non-whites to live in cities, Smuts had expressed the hope that they would eventually choose life in the villages. By the mid-war years his view had radically altered. Addressing the Institute of Race Relations in Cape Town in February 1942, Smuts acknowledged that segregation had failed:

A revolutionary change [he said] is taking place among the Native peoples of Africa [sic] through the movement from the country to the towns—the movement from the old Reserves in the Native areas to the big European centres of population. Segregation tried to stop it. . . . The process has been accelerated. You might as well try to sweep the ocean back with a broom.[5]

Smuts was chiefly concerned with the social effects of this migration. The Government must be prepared, he argued, to provide wages,

---

[1] Hancock, *Smuts*, ii, 481.

[2] In particular, the concessions which Smuts made to the N.R.C. in October 1947 were in contrast to the Nationalists' early announcement—after their victory in 1948—that they intended to abolish the Council (Benson, *The African Patriots* (London, Faber & Faber, 1963), pp. 145, 152).

[3] Ellen Hellmann, 'Urban Areas', in Ellen Hellmann (ed.), *Handbook on Race Relations*, p. 268.

[4] Hancock, *Smuts*, ii, 123–5.   [5] ibid., pp. 475–6. See below, pp. 43–4.

housing, education, and other social services for the non-white urban population. For the investigation of such problems related to non-white migration, the U.P. Government set up the Native Laws Commission in August 1946, under the chairmanship of Justice H. A. Fagan. The Commissioners presented their report in March 1948. They argued, as Smuts had done, that the 'townward movement of Natives . . . can be guided and regulated but it is impossible to prevent it or to turn it into the opposite direction.'[1] They concluded that territorial segregation was a dream and migratory labour an obsolete system.[2] Henceforth, non-whites must be accepted as a permanent part of the urban population and the Government must stream-line the relevant laws accordingly.

The Nationalist Party's emphasis was fundamentally different. In the face of the recent migration, they considered old-fashioned segregation to be no longer adequate. Their determination to arrest and, if possible, abolish economic integration was expressed in the 1948 election cry of *apartheid*—and, following their victory, in the laws introduced to effect economic and social apartness.[3] Thus the increased rate of industrialization and urbanization of non-whites had provided new ground in which old grievances between Afrikaner and English-speaker could be nurtured. In ordering their priorities, the Nationalists were responding to their 'tribal past'. The U.P. were equally affected by their traditions, not least as the party of English-speaking big business, in their capacity to see the issue of economic integration as a separate question, distinct from other aspects of non-white policy.

Meanwhile, during and after the war, there were other important reasons why those with liberal views on colour did not dissociate themselves from the U.P. in the forties. Most liberals interested in 'the native question' were involved in specialized ways. Their common concern was a strong and lasting bond between them, but their field of activity varied. Within the general framework of race relations they tended to be absorbed in their immediate areas of interest. This may

[1] *Report of the Native Laws Commission* (The Fagan Report) U.G. No. 28 (1948), par. 65.
[2] Hancock, *Smuts*, ii, 490.
[3] Van der Horst, 'The Effects of Industrialisation on Race Relations in South Africa', p. 102: 'The policy of apartheid which conditions the lives of all South Africans is a direct reaction to the new conditions arising from industrialisation. It was industrialisation, the growth of towns associated with it, and the movement of Africans to meet the labour needs of the expanding towns and industries which led to the enunciation of this policy as a political doctrine and to the attempt to impose separation between white and black in all spheres.'

help to explain why they did not divert their energy to form a new party sooner. John Cope and René de Villiers, for example, associated with the journal, *Forum*, which first appeared in 1938, were interested in English–Afrikaner reconciliation as a necessary prerequisite to an equitable solution to the colour problem.[1] The Hoernlés and the Rheinallt Jones devoted much of their energy to the Institute of Race Relations.[2] Alfred Hoernlé, together with two other Institute members, Leo Marquard and E. G. Malherbe, established the Army Educational Services, which encouraged interracial understanding.[3] From 1938 to 1943 J. D. Rheinallt Jones was a Senator representing the Africans of the Transvaal and Orange Free State, a job in which, according to Roux, he was tireless and thorough.[4] Both Margaret and William Ballinger were engaged in multiple enterprises. Margaret Ballinger was the only Native Representative to hold a seat for the entire period the scheme of native representation was in operation— from 1938 until 1960. In addition she was a member of the Joint Council of Africans and Europeans in Johannesburg, her home city. Edgar Brookes was a foundation member of the Institute of Race Relations and continued to support the Institute. As well, he was Native Senator for Natal from 1938 to 1943, and maintained throughout this period his interest and active work in and for African education.[5] Julius Lewin, Donald Molteno, and Douglas Buchanan were all lawyers who applied their ability to the colour question in different ways. Lewin, for example, became a teacher in Native Law at the University of the Witwatersrand. The other two were each for a time in Parliament as Native Representatives, Molteno for Cape Western from 1938 to 1949, and Buchanan for the Transkei from 1947 to 1954. There was in these self-chosen tasks a degree of absorption—and a satisfaction—which could, as well as provide the foundations for a separate Liberal Party, militate *against* the liberals taking steps to create one. Such liberals were so busy working on immediate problems that it would have been difficult to find time to plan a party to promote broader, more lasting, prescriptions.

It was important, too, that these people saw themselves as the inheritors of the Cape liberal tradition.[6] Their forerunners in the nineteenth century and at the time of Union had been men content to

[1] Paton, *Hofmeyr*, pp. 293–4.   [2] ibid., p. 296.
[3] ibid., p. 341.   [4] Roux, *Time Longer than Rope*, p. 300.
[5] Roux, *Time Longer than Rope*, p. 296.
[6] See above, pp. 2 ff.; also below, p. 111.

work through non-parliamentary agencies, or through existing political parties. These means had to show themselves clearly inadequate before the liberals would construct alternate methods. Disillusionment was not sufficiently widespread among them until the Nationalists' second electoral victory in 1953. By then a number of these liberals—but not all of them—were convinced that the United Party would not serve their purposes, or at best would do so only if pressed by the emergence of a Liberal Party.[1]

In any case, the practical difficulties involved in establishing a new political party were innumerable, and not to be dismissed lightly.[2] The extensive planning, the prospect of competing for votes, and the need for financial backing were all the kind of considerations which would tend to prevent the liberals from making such a move, providing there seemed any likelihood of affecting change through the existing parties. It is possible, too, that another factor which discouraged them from establishing a Liberal Party earlier was a reluctance to move away from what had been traditionally a two-party system.

Throughout the forties liberals active in the U.P. as well as those without close party ties continued to build their hopes around Hofmeyr until his death in 1948. The presence within the U.P. of a man of Hofmeyr's reputation seemed powerful evidence that the party might become liberal on the colour question.[3] Hofmeyr was prominent in the United Party administration from the outbreak of war; he was Vice-President of the Institute of Race Relations from 1944 until his death; and he was an inspiring and seemingly progressive speaker on public occasions.[4] There was no question that Hofmeyr wished the U.P. would liberalize its racial policies. Yet the

---

[1] See below, pp. 108 ff.

[2] See Sir Ivor Jennings, *The Queen's Government* (London, Penguin Books, 1954), p. 65. 'If . . . the reader wants to form a party to forward the policy of which he approves, he knows what to do. He must form an organization in each of 600 constituencies. He must establish a headquarters in London and issue posters, pamphlets, notes for speakers, and other forms of propaganda. He must secure the support of at least one of the national newspapers. At the next election he must put up 600 candidates and persuade the electors that 350 of them are likely to be elected. Frankly, it is easier and cheaper, to join the Conservative or the Labour Party.'   [3] See above, pp. 9–11, 15.

[4] One of Hofmeyr's most memorable addresses was that which he delivered in March 1946 at the University of the Witwatersrand where he was Chancellor. 'Surely it is a mockery [Hofmeyr said] for us to talk of ourselves as a free people, to acclaim ourselves as the inheritors of a tradition of freedom, while we are as a nation to so large an extent the slaves of prejudice, while we allow our dislike of some of our fellow South Africans to stand in the way of dealing fairly

articulate idealist—as in his stand on the Asiatic Land Tenure Bill in 1946[1]—was forced time and again by the inflexibilities of the situation, including his position in the Cabinet, to be the spokesman for compromise.[2] He was sufficiently the product of his own white world to delay as long as possible any open break with the United Party—a break which he acknowledged privately would have to come.[3] On almost every crucial occasion he took the line of least resistance. In this he was influenced by Smuts, to whom he almost always deferred. Those liberals who realized this cherished the hope that once Smuts had retired, or died, the younger Hofmeyr and his policies would dominate the party.[4] As it happened Hofmeyr, the liberal, predeceased Smuts, the paternalist.[5] Meanwhile, the result of the post-war election had raised English–Afrikaner hostility to a new pitch and further postponed a liberal breakaway.

iii

The forerunner of the A.N.C., the South African Native National Congress, had been (like the A.N.C.) conceived as a nationalist organization. Its leaders aimed to unite Africans regardless of tribe and background in the pursuit of common objectives. These objectives—set down in the Constitution of 1912—were liberal ones.[6] In reaction to the settlement of the colour question incorporated in the Act of Union, the Congressmen sought the extension of political rights to non-whites, as well as the removal of other forms of racial discrimination. When Congress was recast in 1919 and the A.N.C. was founded these objectives remained substantially the same. In the Constitution of 1919 Congress leaders emphasized their intention to completely remove the colour bar by the use of 'constitutional

with them.' Quoted in Julius Lewin (ed.) *The Struggle for Racial Equality* (London, Longmans, 1967), pp. 46–7. cf. Paton, *Hofmeyr*, p. 422.

[1] *Ass. Debates*, vol. 56, 28 Mar. 1946, cols. 4430–9.

[2] Paton, *Hofmeyr*, p. 449. It was Hofmeyr, as Acting Prime Minister in Smuts's absence, who was responsible for the crushing of the African Mineworkers' Strike in 1946 (ibid., p. 431). See below, p. 33–4.

[3] Paton, *Hofmeyr*, p. 311.

[4] Smuts appears to have thought of Hofmeyr as his successor (Hancock, *Smuts*, ii, 511). One liberal, the Native Representative, Margaret Ballinger, later contended that she never considered Hofmeyr had the necessary qualities of leadership (author's interview, Cape Town, 10 Dec. 1965); but her misgivings, however valid, do not seem to have been widely shared by other liberals.

[5] In Eric Walker's view, Hofmeyr's death was 'an irreparable blow to the dwindling forces of liberalism . . .' *A History of Southern Africa*, p. 780.

[6] Hellmann (ed.), *Handbook on Race Relations*, p. 519.

means'.[1] They denied they had any 'legislative pretensions'; their role was to be that of spokesmen for the African people and their function was to be a consultative one.[2] This outlook, marked by a tolerance of white paternalism and a qualified franchise, dominated Congress until the crisis over the Hertzog legislation in the 1930s. Even then the moderate view prevailed. After division the A.N.C. accepted the principle of communal representation and agreed to use the two channels provided by the 1936 Act—the white Members of Parliament who were to be the Native Representatives and the consultative body, the Native Representative Council.

This spirit of conciliation and compromise in Congress circles did not survive the forties. Before 1948 liberal views among Congressmen had been transmuted into a philosophy clearly different from that which had characterized Congress leadership as recently as the late thirties. This change was evident in three phases of A.N.C. activity in the period: Congress reactions to South Africa's involvement in the Second World War; Congress support for the adjournment of the N.R.C. in 1946; and the emergence of the A.N.C. Youth League, established in 1944. Each of these signified the transformation of liberal thinking which took place in the A.N.C. before the United Party lost power in 1948.

Congress reactions to the war illustrate clearly the degree of support for liberal principles in the A.N.C. The loyalties of the older Congressmen were torn in a way that those of the younger generation were not.[3] The A.N.C. leadership deliberately rejected a policy of non-co-operation, despite deeply-felt grievances. Yet those Africans who enlisted were not allowed to bear arms. Africans were urged to fight abroad as they had lived at home—as men of inferior status. They were wanted, as Lutuli later said, 'as drivers and potato peelers'.[4]

But, in the A.N.C. view, Congress demands for 'democratic rights and trade unions' could not be divorced from 'the world-wide struggle for freedom and social justice'.[5] Moreover, the overt Nazi sympathizers in South Africa were those who advocated a blatantly repressive non-white policy.[6] A more radical resolution was amended by Dr. A. B. Xuma, President of the A.N.C. and typifying the older, conservative opinion. The official statement, issued by the Executive

[1] Carter, *The Politics of Inequality*, Appendix IV, pp. 482–4.
[2] ibid.   [3] See below, p. 37.
[4] Albert Luthuli, *Let My People Go* (London, Fontana Books, 1963), p. 98.
[5] Minutes of the Executive Committee of the A.N.C., 7 July 1940, mim., P.A.S.
[6] Roux, *Time Longer than Rope*, p. 305.

Committee in July 1940, made a plea for the abolition of racial discrimination in the armed services and asked that, after the war, Parliament consider full citizenship rights for Africans.[1]

There is no doubt that A.N.C. leaders realized how dependent the Government was on African labour, not only in active service but in industries vital to the military effort, like iron and steel works, and munition factories.[2] Yet, when Congress could have easily provoked a crisis—though not without cost to themselves—they were still willing to state their principles, and postpone the satisfaction of their demands. They preferred not to embarrass the white Government with whom they could obviously still identify. Rather, they acted in a manner intended to promote interracial goodwill, and—with a trust typical of liberals—hoped as a result eventually to win recognition of their rights.

The publication of the Atlantic Charter in August 1941 fostered African hopes of a better deal after the war.[3] Such faith appeared justified in 1942 when Smuts made public his conviction that economic segregation was no longer possible in South Africa.[4] In so doing he introduced a new and central theme to United Party colour policy. The timing of the speech was apparently dictated by the possibility of Japanese attack.[5] Smuts's admission that segregation had 'fallen on evil days'[6] was clearly useful in reinforcing non-white loyalty. The A.N.C. shared in a deputation which took this opportunity to protest against the pass laws. Dramatically, the laws were partially suspended. But after the United States fleet engaged the Japanese in the Battles of the Coral Sea and Midway fear of invasion diminished and the pass laws were reintroduced.[7] The A.N.C. reacted to this reversal in a manner consistent with their earlier moderation. No full-scale protests were planned; Xuma stressed that the A.N.C. had only postponed their claims until the end of the war.[8]

When peace came, the A.N.C. shared the general optimism about the future.[9] To mark the occasion and embody their wartime hopes,

[1] Minutes of the Executive Committee of the A.N.C., 7 July 1940.
[2] Roux, *Time Longer than Rope*, p. 305.
[3] Benson, *The African Patriots*, p. 98.   [4] See above, p. 24.
[5] Roux, *Time Longer than Rope*, p. 71.   [6] Hancock, *Smuts*, ii, 475.
[7] Benson, *The African Patriots*, p. 100.   [8] ibid., p. 98.
[9] Anthony Sampson, *The Treason Cage* (London, Heinemann, 1958), p.73 'The victory of the Allies, and the breath of new liberal ideas that had blown into the South African hothouse as a result of the Atlantic Charter, the establishment of the United Nations, and the defeat of the Nazi doctrine of racial supremacy, all seemed to indicate a new deal for South Africa.'

the A.N.C. published a Bill of Rights in 1945.[1] Its debt to the Atlantic Charter was obvious. For the first time, the A.N.C. voiced a claim for one man, one vote. In addition, they sought equal justice before the courts, freedom of residence and movement, and the right to own land. They sought, too, the abolition of the industrial colour bar and the recognition of the Africans' rights to collective bargaining. And they protested against the theory that there was 'a need of a special type of education for Africans as such'. They demanded, in short: '. . . the repeal of any and all laws as well as the abandonment of any policy and all practices that discriminate against the African in any way whatsoever on the basis of race, creed or colour in the Union of South Africa.'[2]

Congress here sought freedoms which democrats outside South Africa regarded as inalienable rights. Their claims were indisputably moderate in tone; this is borne out by the way in which they were drawn up, ratified, and proposed as a 'Bill of Rights', which, it seemed, would automatically recommend itself to all reasonable people. As yet no ultimatums or threats were included, nor was there any prescription as to new methods to be adopted in the face of white intransigence. In these ways, although the Bill of Rights constituted a profound change of demands, it did not embody a breakaway from traditional methods honoured by the A.N.C.—those of formal protest, petition, and deputation.

Yet, it should be noted that in the context of South African society the Bill of Rights had revolutionary implications. If, for example, political rights were extended to 'all adults, regardless of race'[3] South Africa was bound to be governed by the will of a non-white majority. Whether or not such a government ruled in a liberal manner—for example, with regard for the rights of minorities and the rule of law— the prospect was, in the forties, totally unacceptable to almost all South African whites, including those who regarded themselves as liberals.[4]

In the immediate post-war years there was a further indication

[1] Carter, *The Politics of Inequality*, Appendix IV, pp. 484–5.
[2] ibid., p. 485.
[3] ibid., p. 484.
[4] An exception was Mrs. Rheinallt Jones who challenged Roux in 1943 when he claimed that liberals were satisfied with a 'token' native vote. Africans, she said, 'would under any progressive system receive the right to vote gradually as the numbers of those capable of exercising it increase. *Africans would finally be in the majority and there would be nothing to fear in that* [author's italic].' Roux, *Time Longer than Rope*, pp. 290–1.

that the character of liberalism within the A.N.C. was changing. Those Congress members who belonged also to the Native Representative Council shared with other Councillors a newly critical attitude towards the inadequacies of the N.R.C. The method of communal representation embodied in the Council was no longer acceptable to Congress. They were not prepared to postpone any longer their demand for full parliamentary representation. The A.N.C. members of the Council supported the motion moved by their fellow Congressman, Professor Z. K. Matthews, to adjourn the N.R.C.[1] The A.N.C.s' severest critics at the time, including the militant Youth Leaguers, considered this a hopelessly belated gesture of defiance. To such people the whole idea of collaboration had been repugnant from the instigation of the Council. But Congress leaders of the thirties and early forties had been constrained by their own individual backgrounds, as well as that of the A.N.C. as a whole, to plump for the use of communal representation. Sampson speaks of the 1936 Act, which set up the Council, as creating the 'vital component of political agitation, a frustrated intelligentsia'.[2] But theirs was a frustration not fully evident for some years. It was ten years before A.N.C. leaders dismissed the N.R.C. as unlikely to be an effective mouthpiece for African opinion.[3] This fact alone suggests the moderateness of their position.

With the Johannesburg Mine Workers' Strike of August 1946, the harsh realities of the modern industrialized society impinged directly on the remote, ordered—and it seemed, irrelevant—proceedings of the N.R.C.[4] When the Council assembled in Pretoria forty miles away, 4,000 Africans were marching from the mines into Johannesburg. Yet the Under-Secretary of Native Affairs made a speech without reference to the crisis. The Council's requests for an adjournment or permission to go to Johannesburg from Pretoria to assess the situation were refused. It was at this point that the burden of their impotence lay heaviest. And Paul Mosaka, who was chiefly concerned with his people being caught in the 'maelstrom of industralism'[5] spoke of the Council as 'a toy telephone'.[6]

[1] Benson, *The African Patriots*, p. 136.
[2] Sampson, *Treason Cage*, p. 89.   [3] See below, p. 34.
[4] Sampson, *Treason Cage*, pp. 77–8. 'For thousands of politically-minded Africans 1946 was the year in which they ceased to have serious hopes of a change of heart among Whites, the year in which the Youth League won its point over the Old Guard of Congress.'
[5] Benson, *The African Patriots*, p. 114.   [6] Paton, *Hofmeyr*, p. 433.

When the Council reassembled the next day, Dr. James Moroka condemned 'the reactionary character of the Union Native Policy of segregation in all its ramifications'.[1] He made reference to the guarantee of freedom embodied in the Atlantic Charter and the United Nations Charter and, echoing the clarion call of the Bill of Rights, he called on the Government 'forthwith to abolish all discriminatory legislation affecting Non-Europeans in this country'.[2] His motion to adjourn the session of the N.R.C. was carried unanimously.[3] Yet it was clear that the Councillors were reluctant to make this move. It is significant in assessing how liberal they were, that as late as 1946 a forced adjournment of a legally constituted, albeit ineffective, body should seem such a drastic step.

Following the adjournment the A.N.C. held a 'crisis conference' in Bloemfontein in October 1946.[4] The outcome indicates how far Congress had changed since 1936. The idea of the N.R.C. petitioning Parliament was rejected outright. But this rejection of a method earlier acceptable to Congress did not mean the A.N.C. was as yet prepared to sponsor the total boycott of the N.R.C. which Anton Lembede proposed. The final decision on strategy combined conciliation and a new toughness. The Councillors should, as requested, meet the Government but the A.N.C. would in future boycott the elections both to the N.R.C. and of Native Representatives to Parliament.[5] The principle of communal representation was no longer acceptable to Congress.

Meanwhile, Hofmeyr, acting as Prime Minister in Smuts's absence, saw that some kind of turning-point had been reached. In particular, he saw the danger of African leaders, who were once moderate, now being forced by the rigidity of the United Party Government into a more radical position. Writing to Smuts in September 1946 he said:

It seems that (hitherto) moderate intellectuals of the Professor Matthews type are now committed to an extreme line against colour discrimination, and have carried the Chiefs with them. We can't afford to allow them to be swept into the extremist camp, but I don't see what we can do to satisfy them, which would be tolerated by European public opinion.[6]

Hofmeyr here expressed what was to remain the dilemma of white

[1] Quoted by Oliver Walker, the English journalist, in *Kaffirs are Lively* (London, Gollancz, 1948), p. 121.
[2] Paton, *Hofmeyr*, p. 433.   [3] Benson, *The African Patriots*, p. 131.
[4] ibid., p. 134.   [5] ibid., p. 135.
[6] Paton, *Hofmeyr*, p. 435.

liberals in South Africa: how to find a compromise agreeable to both non-white leaders as well as to the white electorate. Confronted by the N.R.C. ultimatum Hofmeyr continued to hope for a climb-down, and he overlooked signs of relatively wide support for the N.R.C. move.[1]

The palliatives which Hofmeyr offered in his role of Government spokesman when the new session of the N.R.C. reopened in November 1946 were rejected. As Matthews pointed out, Hofmeyr appeared to be 'oblivious of the progressive force not only in the world in general but in South Africa itself.'[2] He made no attempt to deal with pass laws, colour bar in industry, or the political rights of non-whites. His statement seemed 'merely an apologia for the *status quo*'.[3]

Selope Thema, supporting Matthews's motion to again adjourn the N.R.C., was noticeably disillusioned. He asked: 'Do you want us to join those forces that are outside, those forces which are out to destroy? If you drive us to that we shall know what to do; but we don't want to do that.'[4] Moroka was puzzled too. He wondered how Smuts, who had helped draw up the Atlantic Charter, could allow the colour bar to continue. It seemed Smuts—and white South Africa—were, as Lutuli later suggested, 'impenetrably deaf'.[5] And the N.R.C. supported Matthews's motion to suspend the Council's activities.[6]

The response of the younger generation of the A.N.C. to the impact of the war and urbanization was the foundation of the A.N.C. Youth League in Johannesburg in 1944. It was not until 1949 that the Leaguers' influence within the A.N.C. reached its peak,[7] but in the mid forties they already provided the most graphic evidence of radical change in the outlook of the A.N.C. It was no coincidence that the Youth League was first formed in Orlando, one of the biggest African locations in South Africa. Increasing urbanization played a large part in the growth of support for the A.N.C. in the forties.

The rate of South Africa's industrial growth was already increasing

[1] ibid., p. 436.   [2] ibid., pp. 438–9.
[3] ibid.   [4] Paton, *Hofmeyr*, p. 440.
[5] Luthuli, *Let My People Go*, p. 93.
[6] In October 1947 Smuts offered the N.R.C. some concessions, including an increase in the number of African Councillors. The N.R.C. was sceptical about the Government's good faith, but Congress agreed to support the new elections. They did not officially boycott the Council again until after the Nationalists came to power. Moroka and Matthews did not comply with this boycott until late in 1950 (Benson, *The African Patriots*, pp. 145, 151, 170).
[7] See below, p. 65.

prior to the Second World War.[1] This rate of growth was, however, overshadowed by that of the war years. The necessity to use non-white labour to provide unskilled manpower and, in some instances, in semi-skilled positions meant a sharp increase in the number of non-white workers employed in manufacturing. The number increased from 143,000 in 1938–9 to 249,000 in 1944–5. This represented an increase of 74 per cent in non-whites as compared with only a 20 per cent increase in the number of white employees in the same period.[2] One striking feature of this pattern of industrial growth in South Africa was the increase in the number of non-whites living in urban areas. Between 1921 and 1936 the total number rose from 587,000 to 1,141,634, and by 1946 it had climbed to 1,794,212.[3] How far this increase represented permanent urbanization is difficult to estimate. The persistence of migratory labour, as well as the varying degrees of adaptation to Western standards of living, make an accurate calculation impossible.[4] But the increase in the number of African women who migrated to the cities indicates a trend towards permanence. Particularly the post-war situations in the cities—the expansion of industry, the size of the urban African population, and the urgent need for African housing—underlined the fact, as Sheila van der Horst claims, 'that the urban movement was no temporary phenomenon and that many Africans had come to town permanently.'.[5]

Since the A.N.C. was an urban-based organization, its ambitions and prospects grew as the non-white population in the cities increased. Earlier, the political initiative had passed to groups like the Industrial and Commercial Workers Union of Africa (I.C.U.) and the African Democratic Party (A.D.P.) which had championed the grievances of urban non-whites.[6] If the A.N.C. wished to be the foremost nationalist organization among Africans it needed to build on its newly enlarged urban base. Africans living permanently in the cities made for readily captive audiences and for stable Congress

[1] Van der Horst, 'The Effects of Industrialisation on Race Relations in South Africa', pp. 109–10.

[2] D. Hobart Houghton, *The South African Economy* (Cape Town, O.U.P., 1964), pp. 119–20.

[3] Ellen Hellmann, 'Urban Areas', in Ellen Hellmann (ed.), *Handbook on Race Relations*, p. 239.

[4] G. V. Doxey, *The Industrial Colour Bar in South Africa* (Cape Town, O.U.P., 1961), p. 106.

[5] Van der Horst, ibid., p. 135.

[6] Roux, *Time Longer than Rope*, pp. 153, 319.

membership. In addition, they were subjected to an increasing degree of governmental control. Furthermore, the facts of residential segregation of the races planted A.N.C. leaders in the context of the location. Life in industrialized Johannesburg was a potent influence in the lives of the League's founders. The political education of some of them was restricted to the environment of mine, factory, and location.[1] Living here was hard and hazardous. The realities of what Anthony Sampson calls 'the industrial jungle' must have impinged sharply on the minds of the young men who formed the League.[2]

The League marked the beginning of a new nationalism among Africans.[3] But the Leaguers were not necessarily anti-white. They no doubt sounded exclusivist to a suspicious white community. But in challenging the practice of white supremacy the Leaguers did not automatically deny to the whites (or to any other racial group) the rights which they sought for Africans.[4] By the early fifties, they had modified their outlook considerably; the antipathy which some of them had earlier felt towards Indians and communists, for example, was noticeably lessened. Meanwhile, their specific rejection of Cape liberal principles did not spell the end of liberal ideals and strategies within the A.N.C. In its initial stages there was an evident plasticity about the League despite its tough line on issues such as the need for African unity, a mass party, and independent action. True, there was much that was latently anti-liberal, but the League was not intentionally, and certainly not irrevocably, anti-liberal at this point.

The Youth League Manifesto was not concerned with the expression of liberal values. It was a document preoccupied with the

[1] Benson, *The African Patriots*, p. 101.

[2] This was strikingly true of Walter Sisulu. As a young man he had worked in a Johannesburg mine, and later held a succession of factory jobs. By the time the League was founded he was a real estate agent. Benson comments: 'He, more than any other individual in the League, and probably more than any other Congress leader, knew just what it meant to be "a native". . . .' (*The African Patriots*, pp. 104–5.)

[3] The League's Manifesto expressed their determination to be 'the brains-trust and power-station of the spirit of African nationalism'. (Congress Youth League Manifesto issued by the Provincial Committee of the Congress Youth League, March 1944, mim., P.A.S., p. 5.)

[4] Jordan K. Ngubane, *An African Explains Apartheid* (New York, Praeger, 1963), p. 79: '. . . [the Youth League] was not anti-white, anti-Indian, or anti-coloured. It was intensely pro-African.' See also Statement taken from Chief Albert J. Luthuli in the case *R.* v. *Adams and Others* (i.e. during the Treason Trial) n.d., mim., P.A.S.: 'I would not say that they [the Youth Leaguers] were anti-white but they looked forward to an essentially African State with minorities enjoying democratic rights.'

necessity to develop the spirit of self-determination among Africans, to encourage an African nationalism. However, to this end the Leaguers vehemently rejected the idea of trusteeship. The deeds of the Trustees, they claimed, had '... shown clearly that talk of Trusteeship is an eyewash for the Civilised world and an empty platitude to soothe Africans into believing that after all oppression is a pleasant experience under Christian democratic rule.'[1] This much was a rejection of what many whites regarded as a liberal attitude, but it was a rejection rooted in proper liberal misgivings. The Manifesto continued: '... [the African] demands the right to be a free citizen in the South African democracy; the right to an unhampered pursuit of his national destiny and the freedom to make his legitimate contribution to human advancement.'[2] In addition, the Leaguers were angered by the anomalous position of non-whites serving in the South African armed forces. 'South African blood ... of Whites and Africans alike ... [the Manifesto said] has been shed to free the White peoples of Europe while Africans within the Union remain in bondage.'[3]

The impression of flexibility is borne out by other evidence. There was, for example, considerable difference of opinion among the League's founders over the degree to which African nationalists should alienate potential allies across the colour line. There was also disagreement over the type of society to be established in the event of political victory. One of the group's founders, the prominent journalist, Jordan Ngubane recalls his differences with his fellow theorists, Anton Lembede and Peter Mda.[4] Lembede was attached to a philosophy called Africanism, an ideology developed to shape and direct African opinion. Ngubane thought Lembede's thinking 'too racially angular'.[5]

It laid too much stress on the African [he argued] and ran the danger of producing a racially exclusive attitude among the Africans which would be similar to that of the Afrikaner nationalists. ... I wanted an ideology which, while unifying the Africans, would at the same time leave room for the European and the Indian to take their places by our side when we were ready to receive them.[6]

[1] Youth League Manifesto, p. 2.   [2] ibid., p. 3.   [3] ibid.
[4] See 'Lembede and Africanism', ch. 10 of a typewritten MS. by Jordan Ngubane, n.d., P.A.S.
[5] 'Lembede and Africanism', pp. 2–3.
[6] ibid., p. 3.

D

Ngubane claims that some, including himself, wanted a liberal democratic republic.

I felt that the element of liberalism on the race question had always been an important ingredient in the make-up of African nationalism. When the A.N.C. was established our fathers did not set themselves the goal of driving the white man into the sea. On the contrary they worked to extend the area of liberty in South African national life.[1]

This 'element of liberalism on the race question' which Ngubane emphasized was (like the urbanization of non-whites) part of the background of the Leaguers. Although they had been subject to formative influences often very different from those of an earlier generation, the thinking of some of them had been shaped in institutions where Western liberal values were highly respected. This is true, for example, of Oliver Tambo and Congress Mbata who were both teaching at St. Peter's School in Rossetenville, Johannesburg, in the early forties.[2] Commonly known as the 'black Eton' of South Africa, St. Peter's was run by the Anglican Community of the Resurrection in a liberal Christian tradition similar to an English public school; St. Peter's was soon to provide an effective medium for the spread of Youth League views.[3] Oliver Tambo and Nelson Mandela had both been students at Fort Hare, the chief centre of African higher education.[4] Situated in the Eastern Cape, an area where Africans had been longest associated with whites, and relatively better-treated, Fort Hare, like St. Peter's, proved a breeding ground for young African nationalists. A number of the original Youth Leaguers were students at the University of the Witwatersrand in the early forties—William Nkomo, M. Majombozi, Zame Conco, and J. L. Z. Njongwe were medical students, and Lembede and Mandela were studying law.[5] By this time both 'Wits' and the University of Cape Town had produced what Roux calls 'a new generation of radical or liberal minded students.'[6] This is not to suggest that such educative influences automatically produced men with liberal views. On the contrary, part of the political importance of Fort Hare seems to have been that life there sparked in some of the students a radical reaction to

[1] ibid., p. 8.
[2] Author's interview with Congress Mbata, Johannesburg, 29 Nov. 1965.
[3] Sampson, *Treason Cage*, p. 131.
[4] Benson, *The African Patriots*, p. 108.
[5] See pamphlet issued by the Bureau of Political Information of the Youth League, n.d., P.A.S.
[6] Roux, *Time Longer than Rope*, p. 345.

the Cape liberal tradition. But such a reaction did not necessarily mean the immediate abandonment of all liberal values.

Neither the Youth League nor the other signs of militancy which appeared in the A.N.C. while the U.P. was still in power meant that that Congress had veered away from liberal principles and methods. But before 1948 Congress had already diverged sharply from values which continued to distinguish white liberals in South Africa. Such discrepancies between liberalism in Congress and in the white world were to become more marked under the impact of the Nationalist victory in 1948.

CHAPTER II

The Nationalist victory and the white community

i

In the period 1948–52 the gap between white liberals and Congress widened. The new Government's prospectus of *apartheid* might have been expected to encourage an alliance between liberals across the colour line. But the Nationalists' victory affected whites and non-whites very differently. In the white world the election result re-generated hostility between English-speakers and Afrikaners. Confronted by Afrikaner nationalism in power, non-Nationalist whites displayed fresh fear of Afrikaner domination. The new Prime Minister, Dr. D. F. Malan, nourished this fear immediately his party won power in 1948: 'Today South Africa belongs to us once more. For the first time since Union, South Africa is our own, and may God grant that it will always remain our own.'[1] Thus after 1948 the white race issue assumed an importance unequalled since the days prior to Union.[2] The main substance of political debate in the years 1948–52 was *apartheid*, but for non-Nationalist whites the Government's colour policy was only one of the ways in which Malan's party would infringe liberty. Recalling the different roles which the political parties had played during the war, non-Nationalists saw the United Party, rather than the Government, as the defenders of freedom. And they closed ranks to defend existing rights and restore the United Party to power.

Particularly important in maintaining non-Nationalist unity after 1948 was the widely held belief that the U.P. would regain power in the next election. The result of the 1948 election had been unexpected and close.[3] It appeared to non-Nationalists as an aberration from the

[1] Patterson, *Last Trek*, p. 104.

[2] The irony of this struck the writer, Basil Davidson, who visited South Africa in the early fifties: 'Strangely enough . . . at the very time when relations between whites and non-whites approach exploding point, the whites remain almost exclusively occupied in a private feud of their own.' *Report on Southern Africa*, p. 151.

[3] Stultz, 'Electoral Revival of the National Party', p. 315.

norm. Their prime objective became that of ousting the Government. The emergence of the Torch Commando in 1951 illustrates both the nature and intensity of anti-Nationalist feeling and the general acceptance among non-Nationalists of the crucial importance of the 1953 election.[1]

These considerations weighed heavily with white liberals.[2] They judged it imperative that they temporarily divert their energies to whole-hearted support of the United Party. It was politically expedient to postpone their advocacy of non-white rights; it was more urgent to defend existing rights, white as well as non-white. In any case, basic principles for which the U.P. stood in this period were generally shared by that minority of whites who sought the adoption of a liberal colour policy. It seemed eminently reasonable to hope that the U.P. would eventually modify its colour policy in a liberal direction. This would be a step consistent with the attitude towards colour embodied in post-war Imperial policy. It would be consistent, too, with well-established U.P. values such as individual rights and the rule of law. Such reasoning led to the liberals' decision to postpone the question of forming a separate party until after the 1953 election.

ii

A major factor dividing the U.P. from the Nationalists after 1948 was the Opposition's claim to identification with prevailing opinion outside South Africa. Consistent with the United Party's role in the war years, U.P. members stressed the importance of South Africa's maintaining good relations with England and the Commonwealth. This view was typically represented by the M.P. Colin Steyn. Emphasizing that South Africa was 'no longer an isolated spot in the world', he claimed that '. . . the cornerstone of . . . [U.P.] policy should be co-operation and mutual goodwill between our country and Great Britain in the first place, and the Commonwealth in the second place.[3] This relationship involved acknowledging Britain's post-war policy towards former colonial territories, in particular, the development within the Commonwealth of independent non-white nations such as India, Pakistan, and Ceylon. The implications of this were profound. By advocating the maintenance of the Imperial link, the U.P. conveyed the impression that they too were willing to extend

[1] See below, pp. 51 ff.
[2] See below, p. 62.
[3] Address to Natal U.P. Congress, reported in *Cape Times*, 12 Sept. 1951.

political rights to non-whites. In fact, this was not true. They were liberal only as far as they were involved in the defence of existing rights, and in this they were far more concerned with those of whites than those of non-whites.

Meanwhile, the Nationalists refused to make themselves in the Commonwealth image.[1] Rather, they spoke with an exclusivist voice. One such voice was that of the Government M.P. S. M. Loubser: 'It will not help us if we allow ourselves to be dictated to by other countries. They do not know of this black peril . . . South Africa cannot afford to look at other countries for guidance.'[2] Such disregard for overseas opinion incensed non-Nationalists in general, and the United Party in particular. In the early fifties they wanted, as one U.P. member put it, to be identified with 'all civilised and democratic countries of the world'.[3] Thus the editor of the *Cape Times* claimed that, if the Government's attempt to manipulate the constitution were successful, South Africa would 'be left without a shred of self-respect before the world'.[4] It was only in the 1960s, when the U.P. could no longer pretend to be a party concerned with liberal principles, that they were prepared to defend their white laager against hostile criticism from abroad.

During the period 1948–52 the sense that the U.P. stood for a significantly different—and potentially, more liberal—non-white policy was sustained by the nature of the political controversies between the parties. This was so despite the fact that on the fundamental principles of political and social segregation the United Party was in total agreement with the Nationalists. Smuts underlined this agreement shortly after his party had been defeated in 1948:

> Our policy has been European paramountcy in this country. Our policy has not been equal rights. It is an abstraction forced upon us by our opponents. We stand and have always stood for European supremacy in this country. We have said that we have a position of guardianship, of trusteeship, over the non-European peoples in the country, and we must carry out that trust in the true spirit of guardianship. . . . We have never

---

[1] A visiting journalist, John Hatch, gained a 'definite impression from T. E. Dönges, the Minister of the Interior and of Mines, that the emergence of non-white dominions within the Commonwealth had done much to increase the Nationalists' wish that South Africa become an independent Republic. *The Dilemma of South Africa* (London, Dennis Dobson, 1952), p. 95.

[2] During the debate on the Immorality Amendment Bill, *Ass. Debates*, vol. 70, 2 Mar. 1950, col. 2260.

[3] Dr. A. Jonker, *Ass. Debates*, vol. 64, 19 Aug. 1948, col. 526.

[4] *Cape Times*, 17 Apr. 1952.

been in favour of equal rights. We have always stood and we stand for social and residential separation in this country, and for the avoidance of all racial mixture.[1]

Even more explicitly, he conceded, 'There is a great deal about apartheid which is common to all parties in this country'.[2] For Smuts—or the U.P.—to dispute this was political suicide. Political integration on a basis of equal rights held the certainty of non-white majority rule, and social integration at least the threat of miscegenation and the loss of identity of the white races. Both these were eventualities unacceptable to the vast majority of whites.

Liberals, however, were able temporarily to reconcile their principles with the United Party's refusal to countenance the extension of rights to non-whites. It was of strategic importance to their cause that the United Party regain power in a white electorate; they could only do this with a conservative colour policy. Conversion of the electorate to liberal principles could be delayed until the Nationalists were removed from power. Meanwhile, liberals' hopes of eventually liberalizing U.P. colour policy were grounded in the disagreements between the U.P. and the Nationalists on several aspects of the Government's *apartheid* plan. These disagreements were major themes of political debate between 1948 and 1952 and obscured the fact that the U.P. would never extend full equality to non-whites.

On the question of economic segregation, the United Party were fundamentally opposed to the Government.[3] Smuts had the widest support from his party when he challenged the Government's plan for the development of the Reserves as the national homeland of Africans:[4] 'The native has been integrated into our economic system . . . he is part and parcel of the whole which constitutes South African economic society. . . .'[5] In expressing this view Smuts was making use of the Fagan Commission Report, which, because of his party's defeat, he had never had the chance to implement. A number of other

[1] *Ass. Debates*, vol. 65, 21 Sept. 1948, col. 2905.
[2] ibid.
[3] See above, pp. 24–5.
[4] This plan was discussed by the Minister of Native Affairs, Dr. E. G. Jansen, in terms characteristic of the Nationalists: 'The reserves must be regarded as the national home of the natives. They must have rights and privileges concentrated in the reserves, and as far as possible they must be settled there according to their tribal associations. The presence of tribal natives in urban areas must be regarded as temporary. They must be periodically returned to their homes to renew their tribal connections.' *Ass. Debates*, vol. 64, 6 Sept. 1948, col. 1660.
[5] *Ass. Debates*, vol. 64, 16 Aug. 1948, col. 203.

U.P. members who spoke in his support also referred to the Fagan findings as irrefutable evidence of permanent economic integration. There was 'only one conclusion' argued the Hon. C. M. van Coller: '. . . no matter how desirable apartheid might be and how much it be desired by us in this country, conditions have been created in this country which have made it absolutely impractical.'[1] Such a view led U.P. supporters to consider long-term plans to accommodate permanent non-white population in urban areas. This problem rather than the needs of migratory labour, they believed, should have prior claim. The Native Representatives were in agreement. Mr. Douglas Buchanan, for example, argued: 'We must provide compulsory education which must be followed up immediately by vocational or industrial or professional training so that the younger generation can contribute to the full measure to the upliftment of their own people.'[2]

The Nationalists agreed with van Coller and the Opposition that there was 'only one conclusion', but theirs differed radically from that of the U.P.: what concerned *them* most deeply was the eventual outcome of economic integration. It was not that the Nationalists wished necessarily to repress the non-whites, but non-white development should, in their view, be made only in a context which would not threaten either directly or indirectly the identity of the whites, and in particular, that of the Afrikaners. The Nationalist M.P. Mr. J. H. Conradie, expressed this when he explained:

If we yield in every sphere, in the political sphere and in the economic sphere, we shall be forced later on to yield in the social sphere. We would like to see the native develop in his own sphere and there attain a high standard of civilisation. We are not opposed to that but he must be separated from us.[3]

Except for the question of economic segregation it was not theory but method which aroused the United Party against the Government over the laws to implement *apartheid*. The Opposition rarely challenged the purpose of such laws; for example, like the Govern-

---

[1] ibid., 6 Sept. 1948, col. 1643; also Mr. I. G. Fleming, President of the South African Federated Chamber of Industries, in an address reported in the *Cape Times*, 3 Feb. 1949: 'The urban Native had been integrated into every level in the economic system, and whether in the producing stage, in the distributing link, or at the consumer end his function is unquestionably permanent.'

[2] *Ass. Debates*, vol. 64, 6 Sept. 1948, col. 1602.

[3] *Ass. Debates*, vol. 64, 7 Sept. 1948, col. 1724. See also Dr. D. Diederichs, ibid., 21 Sept. 1948, col. 2990.

ment, they too, objected to interracial marriages and integrated housing. But they constantly expressed misgivings because the methods which the Government proposed to use entailed the infringement of liberty. The nature of these scruples earned the U.P. the scorn of the Nationalists. The Government's Minister for Economic Affairs, Dr. D. Diederichs, displayed this contempt during the debate on the Suppression of Communism Bill in 1950:

... [The United Party] always and in everything agrees with us. They agreed with us on social segregation. They agreed with us on mixed marriages. They agreed with us regarding immorality between Europeans and non-Europeans; they agreed with us on apartheid. They always agree —but! ... I think we could almost call them the 'but' party. ....[1]

From the Nationalists' point of view the United Party was, in fact, a 'but' party in this period. To the Nationalists the central political issue was the maintenance of white supremacy in the face of the 'swart gevaar' or 'black peril'. Since the United Party also wanted to maintain white political control, their objections to the *apartheid* laws seemed to the Nationalists to be specious. However, the ways by which the Government proposed to enforce *apartheid* aroused non-Nationalist fears for the freedoms of whites in South Africa. And consequently the defence of liberal methods seemed as important to non-Nationalists as the pursuit of liberal aims. Thus, in the lengthy debates on *apartheid* legislation in the first term of Nationalist rule, non-Nationalists were encouraged to see the U.P., in contrast with the Nationalists, as the defenders of liberty.

The U.P. were much more *laissez-faire* than the Nationalists in their approach to the business of legislation, and found distasteful the kind of precise, far-reaching regulations which the Nationalists considered necessary to implement *apartheid*. 'Their broad humanitarianism and dislike of precise rules contrasted sharply with the Nationalist belief in systems and final solutions. ....'[2] This difference was clearly reflected in the debate on the Prohibition of Mixed Marriages Bill introduced into the House of Assembly on 28 April 1949.[3] The Government had little patience with those who were concerned that if such a law were implemented there were bound to be many instances of individuals suffering because of the arbitrary

---

[1] *Ass. Debates*, vol. 73, 14 June 1950, col. 9558.
[2] Carter, *The Politics of Inequality*, p. 98.
[3] *Ass. Debates*, vol. 67, 28 Apr. 1949, col. 4695.

categories provided in the terms of the Bill.[1] Mr. A Steyn was typical in his support of the Bill:

If a person has to be affected, affect him and be done with it: fix the future of your people's composition. Determine that. Affect him tonight and be done with it. Personally he may stand in the way of maintaining a white nation in South Africa. You dare not allow that.[2]

The U.P. perspective was quite different. Sir de Villiers Graaff—to be elected United Party leader in November 1956—voiced the general feeling of the party:

In the 300 years Europeans have been in this country they have done pretty well and this race has remained reasonably white. . . . It seems to me . . . there is no need for us at this stage to put up the white flag of surrender and condemn our nation for a failure, a moral failure of race pride, before it has been established clearly that all other methods that can be applied are ineffective.[3]

No doubt this argument appeared a spurious one to the politically conscious non-whites. The Nationalists and the U.P. seemed merely to be hair-splitting over the most efficient means of maintaining white supremacy. But to the U.P. much was at stake. Misgivings such as that voiced by de Villiers Graaff sprang from a deep-rooted suspicion that the Nationalists would disregard the rights of individuals, that they would enforce regulation in areas where individuals should be free, that they would gather too much power to the Central Government. Fearing these things, they sprang to defend the basic liberal principle of minimum Government interference. United Party objections to the Population Registration Bill (1950) were of the same order.[4] They arose not from any conviction that it was wrong to entrench racial division by rigid classification, but rather from the fear that the terms of the bill provided the Government with too much Ministerial power, and eliminated recourse to the courts.[5]

---

[1] e.g. the onus of deciding the race of persons wishing to marry lay with the marriage officer concerned. If it was subsequently discovered—after population registration was complete—that the marriage officer had mistakenly married a couple of different races, their marriage could be declared invalid. See Horrell, *Legislation and Race Relations*, p. 11.

[2] *Ass. Debates*, vol. 68, 19 May 1949, col. 6191; also Mr. D. J. Mostert, ibid., col. 6196.

[3] ibid., 24 May 1959, col. 6407; also Mr. Myr van der Byl, ibid., col. 6436.

[4] The terms of the bill are detailed in Horrell, *Legislation and Race Relations*, p. 10.

[5] e.g. Mr. G. N. Hayward, *Assn. Debates*, vol. 72, 16 May 1950, col. 6620.

United Party reactions to the Suppression of Communism Bill were similar. The terms of the Bill provided the Government with extensive powers enabling them to ban any person or organization they deemed 'communist'.[1] Smuts's successor, J. G. N. Strauss, made it clear that the U.P. stood 'four-square in favour of the eradication of Communism'.[2] Yet they opposed it at every stage. Aspects of the Bill which particularly concerned them were the breadth of the definition of communism, the wide powers to be given to the executive, and the elimination of a right of appeal to the courts.[3] Such misgivings were shared by all non-Nationalists. Despite differences of emphasis in their criticism,[4] they were united in their opposition to the Bill because it embodied threats to liberty. Labour Party M.P.s and Native Representatives, as well as Strauss's own supporters, endorsed the U.P. leader's rejection of the Bill on the grounds that 'in seeking to combat Communist totalitarianism' it created 'a Fascist despotism'.[5]

Also typical of the U.P. reaction was their attempt to avoid the use of the guillotine in the debate on the Suppression of Communism Bill.[6] With the Nationalists, time was of the essence—not so with the United Party. They objected to the Government 'rushing difficult, contentious and far-reaching legislation through Parliament. . . .'[7] Such an attitude was part and parcel of what Carter calls the United Party's 'Royal Commission approach'.[8] They regularly pressed for a 'careful study of complicated situations by an impartial examining body'.[9] An instance of this was the party's reaction to the Group Areas Bill (1950), which provided for increasingly rigid residential segregation of the races.[10] Strauss acknowledged 'the general acceptance in South Africa of the principle of residential and social

---

[1] The bill—and the subsequent Act—defined 'communism' broadly. Communism included, for example, any doctrine aimed 'at bringing about any political, industrial, social or economic change within the Union by the promotion of disturbances or disorder, by unlawful acts or omissions or by the threat of such acts or omissions. . . .' Quoted in Carter, *The Politics of Inequality*, p. 65.

[2] *Ass. Debates*, vol. 73, 14 June 1950, col. 8933.

[3] Carter, *The Politics of Inequality*, p. 68.

[4] ibid., p. 67. See below, p. 61.

[5] *Ass. Debates*, vol. 73, 14 June 1950, col. 8933.

[6] cf. the comment which Smuts made in a letter to a friend in 1940: 'How good it is for Democracy to have some of the weapons captured from the armoury of Autocracy! Democracy plus the guillotine is good for erring politicians.' Hancock, *Smuts*, ii, 338.

[7] Hon. J. G. N. Strauss, *Ass. Debates*, vol. 73, 13 June 1950, col. 8840.

[8] Carter, *The Politics of Inequality*, p. 89.   [9] ibid.

[10] Horrell, *Legislation and Race Relations*, p. 19.

separation'.[1] But he—and the United Party—wanted the Government
to set up a commission to report on the 'necessity and practicability'
of the measure, as well as on the Bill's financial implications, particularly the 'extent to which it may be necessary to interfere with vested
rights. . . .'[2]

The major clash between the Nationalists and the U.P. in the
period was that over the primacy of the Constitution.[3] Here was a
fundamental liberal principle which all non-Nationalists were bound
to defend. Those who wanted a liberal redirection of U.P. colour
policy were necessarily involved, for the particular aspect of the
Constitution under attack was that relating to the rights of Coloureds.
A feeling more widely shared was the suspicion that the removal of
one entrenched clause—that relating to the political rights of the
Coloureds—was merely a precedent for the removal of the other
entrenched clause—that which guaranteed the equality of the languages of the two white races.[4] Thus both racial issues were at least
implicit in the Nationalists' move against Coloured rights. In this
way the constitutional issue aroused non-Nationalists in particular
solidarity.

Smuts did not wait for the Government's concrete proposals of
February 1951.[5] As early as September 1948 he criticized the Govern-
ment for not airing the 'constitutional aspect' during the elections. It
presented, he claimed, a situation 'very different, far more serious . . .
than that of apartheid itself.'[6] Raising the issue again in a speech at
Witbank in January 1949, he claimed that: 'To break away from the
Constitution is to break away from the very foundation of Union.
That is a form of revolution the results of which no one can foresee.
I am certain the people of South Africa will never allow it.'[7] For non-

---

[1] *Ass. Debates*, vol. 73, 13 June 1950, col. 8873.

[2] ibid.

[3] 'The issue on which the Nationalist Government and the Opposition most
clearly divided was the attempt to ensure full political apartheid by removing
the Coloured voters in the Cape Province from the common roll.' Carter
The Politics of Inequality, p. 119.

[4] The relevant clauses of the South African Act were Sections 35 and 152,
by which the political rights and status of the Coloureds were defended, and
Section 36, which guaranteed the equality of the two official languages. See
Sheila Patterson, *Colour and Culture in South Africa*, p. 38; Carter, *The Politics
of Inequality*, p. 123.

[5] The terms of the Separate Representation of Voters Bill were published in
February 1951.

[6] *Ass. Debates*, vol. 65, 21 Sept. 1948, col. 2901.

[7] *Cape Times*, 10 Jan. 1949.

whites there must have been ironic overtones in the U.P. defence of the entrenched clauses. Smuts was prepared to say that the Constitution was more important than *apartheid*—an ominously legalistic approach from a non-white point of view. Moreover, he used the word 'revolution' in a context meaningful only to whites, and almost totally irrelevant to the situation in which non-whites found themselves. But he rallied the widest support among non-Nationalist whites, including those with liberal views on colour.

The Government's priorities were of a fundamentally different kind. To the Nationalists no question was more critical than how to preserve the white race in South Africa. This was made unmistakably clear by the Hon. J. G. Strijdom, leader of the Transvaal Nationalists and Minister of Lands:

> What difference will it make to the Native whether Native representation is abolished by a 2/3rds majority or whether it is done by a majority of one? There is no moral obligation, except the moral obligation on you to safeguard the future of White South Africa. The future of White South Africa is at stake. Unless there is separation of the races we have no more hope of remaining White than we have of reaching out with our hands and touching the moon.[1]

The strength of purpose suggested here was characteristic of the manner in which the Nationalists discussed the issue. The fact that they sometimes spoke in the more particular terms of the survival of the Afrikaner race was hardly guaranteed to convert the U.P. to their general principle.[2] Instead it served to reinforce non-Nationalist fears for white freedom.

The United Party did not share the Nationalists' sense of threat from the non-white races. References to the 'black peril' are absent from Opposition arguments and assumptions in this period. Furthermore, the Coloureds constituted a special cause; here U.P. members shared certain attitudes which clearly distinguished their policy from that of the Nationalists. There was a general feeling among U.P. followers that the Coloureds ought to be regarded 'as part, an appendage,

---

[1] *Cape Times*, 31 Jan. 1949; also Eric Louw, Nationalist Minister of Economic Affairs, ibid., 10 Jan. 1949.
[2] e.g. Professor I. A. Malan, M.P., in August 1949: 'The whole question of the driving power of Nationalism reduces to that of survival. This point is cardinal. He who fails to recognize the fundamental fact that the Afrikaner is fanatically determined to survive as a European race, has failed to grasp the most elementary fact of South African politics.' Quoted in René de Villiers, 'Political Parties and Trends', in G. H. Calpin (ed.). *The South African Way of Life*, p. 136.

of the European community'.[1] It was certainly valid to make distinctions between Coloureds as a group, and Africans and Indians.[2] There were, of course, limits to the United Party's tolerance of Coloureds; they were never likely to actively promote social integration, or press for an extension of political rights. But they were determined to defend the Coloureds' existing privileges.[3] Thus, on the Coloured issue, the U.P. offered a more liberal alternative than the Nationalists. This bolstered the image of the U.P. as a party genuinely representing political liberalism, and discouraged those who wished to extend that liberalism to non-whites from abandoning the Opposition.

In fact, United Party M.P.s took up cudgels on the constitutional question for a number of different reasons, and, more often than not, for a combination of reasons, some less ambiguous than others. For example, the former U.P. Secretary for Native Affairs, Dr. D. L. Smit, argued that the Coloureds were a unique responsibility of the whites.[4] Consistent with this, a number shared Dr. Colin Steyn's view that the Government ought at least to consult the Coloureds.[5] Frequently, however, the objections which the United Party raised to the Government's proposals were more equivocal. Correctly or otherwise, it was widely assumed among the ranks of the United Party—and by the Nationalists too[6]—that the Coloured vote was a crucial factor in a number of Cape constituencies, and that United Party electoral strength in these areas depended on the political goodwill of the Coloureds.[7] It seems likely that the Coloured vote had

[1] Smuts's phrases, *Ass. Debates*, vol. 65, 21 Sept. 1948, col. 2904.

[2] e.g. the U.P. member, Mr. A. Bloomberg, ibid., cols. 1970–1.

[3] e.g. the U.P. member, Mr. J. Hamilton Russell, in *Cape Times*, 5 Jan. 1949.

[4] Carter, *The Politics of Inequality*, pp. 125–6; also Dr. A. H. Jonker, *Ass. Debates*, vol. 68, 19 May 1949, col. 6188.

[5] Carter, *The Politics of Inquality*, p. 125.

[6] e.g. The Prime Minister, Dr. D. F. Malan, claimed that the Coloureds would be losing 'only the power to turn the scales between the Europeans in their constituencies.' *Ass. Debates*, vol. 75, 17 Apr. 1951, col. 4590.

[7] In 1929 Coloured voters in the Cape numbered nearly 24,000; they held the balance in at least ten of the fifty-eight Cape constituencies. But the value of the Coloured vote declined with the enfranchisement of European women in 1930, and further in 1931, with the extension of manhood suffrage to European males in Cape Province and Natal. By then too, the names on the Provincial Voters' lists could be challenged, an indignity which discouraged voters from registering. Nevertheless, in the 1948 national election and the 1949 provincial election the Coloured votes appeared decisive in four constituencies where the United Party narrowly won, and in two where they narrowly lost. See J. S. Marais, *The Cape Coloured People 1652–1937*, pp. 279–80; also Sheila Patterson, *Colour and Culture*, p. 207. Gwendolen Carter points out that this 'balance of power' factor was never proved conclusively (*The Politics of Inequality*, p. 126).

declined in importance by the early fifties. What remained important was the whites' belief that it was influential, for it was a belief which helped to increase antagonism between the two major parties in the struggle for political power. In addition, like a large number of his followers, Smuts saw the dangers of alienating the sympathies of the Coloureds, and building a hostile, non-white bloc: 'We are going to drive the Coloured people away from us. We are going to help make a united front of all the colour in this country. We talk about a united front—we are making it. It is not the Communists that are making it, it is we that are driving them to it. . . .'[1]

But at the heart of the United Party misgivings was the way in which the Nationalist Government were prepared to act on the matter. Again, it was the means, rather than the end in view, which fired the Opposition to resist. 'It was not the rights of the Coloured which aroused such deep feeling, . . . but the means which the Government used . . ., means which most non-Nationalists considered unconstitutional.'[2] Here was the fulcrum in the relationship of the two parties. The United Party persisted, as one Government member expressed it, in whining 'the Constitution';[3] the Nationalists continued to be incredulous that anyone could consider 'the Constitution was of greater importance . . . than the maintenance of white civilization. . . .'[4]

iii

In May 1951, a small group of ex-servicemen, incensed at the Government's proposed violation of the Constitution, organized public protests against the Separate Representation of Voters Bill.[5]

[1] *Ass. Debates*, vol. 65, 21 Sept. 1948, col. 2904. A similar claim was made by Mr. J. G. N. Strauss, then the Leader of the Opposition, during the debate on the Separate Representation of Voters Bill. In his opinion, the implementing of the Bill could 'only lead to the formation of a solid non-European bloc' (*Ass. Debates*, vol. 75, 25 Apr. 1951, col. 5409).

[2] Carter, *The Politics of Inequality*, p. 119.

[3] Mr. S. M. Loubser during the High Court of Parliament Bill debate. See *Ass. Debates*, vol. 78, 5 May 1952, col. 5003.

[4] ibid.

[5] These details of the founding of the Torch Commando are taken from Gwendolen Carter's account (*The Politics of Inequality*, pp. 302ff.). This section of the book relies heavily on Gwendolen Carter's work on the Commando. However, the main purpose of my inquiry is not to trace the history of the movement, but to discover in what ways, if any, the Torch Commando was a liberal movement. This is a question which Gwendolen Carter raises, but it is only one of her questions, and not her overriding concern.

These demonstrations were so successful in terms of public support that the organizers established a War Veterans' Action Committee to capitalize on the widespread interest in their objective of ousting the Nationalists from power. The Committee's future was discussed at a first National Congress late in June 1951. The delegates agreed that it was time to put down deeper roots, and widen the base of support for the movement, which they renamed the War Veterans' Torch Commando. The emergence of the Torch Commando illustrates the way in which the constitutional issue and the prospective election of 1953 preoccupied non-Nationalist whites in the early fifties. In addition, the nature of the Commando's relations with the United Party underlines the fact that in the same period the U.P. was widely regarded among non-Nationalist whites as a party representing political liberalism.

Influenced by their memories of the war years, the Torchers detected in National Party policy elements which had characterized fascism in Europe and extremist Afrikaner nationalism at home, notably the importance of the *volk* or race, an intense nationalism and the desire for powerful, even dictatorial government. Such an interpretation of the Government's motives was made explicit by 'Sailor' Malan, the newly appointed National President when he said at the Commando's formal launching, 'Our aim is to defeat the Government, which is fascist in spirit.'[1] After considerable debate, the ranks of the movement were opened to others besides ex-servicemen, but the leaders were always men who had fought the Nazis.[2] Echoes of their wartime experiences sounded again and again in their public statements and political activities. For example, when Malan—during the war, an ace fighter pilot—spoke at the group's first rally on 4 May 1951, he said: 'In Abyssinia, at Alamein and a score of bloody campaigns we won the right to a voice in our country's affairs. And we are determined that our voice shall not only be heard but that it shall also be heeded.'[3]

But the Torchers' concern to defend democratic rights, expressed as it was in terms of vocal antifascism, conflicted with another liberal principle, namely, the reconciliation of the white races. The Com-

[1] *Cape Times*, 2 July 1951.

[2] Carter, *The Politics of Inequality*, p. 307; also *Cape Times*, 1 Oct. 1951.

[3] Carter, *The Politics of Inequality*, p. 304. During the 1953 election campaign members of the Commando, in their support of the United Party against the Nationalist Government, plastered stickers which read 'Remember Alamein' (Hatch, *The Dilemma of South Africa*, p. 122).

mando's persistent attempt to equate Afrikaner nationalism with fascism led to the further deterioration of relations between English-speaker and Afrikaner. In this way memories of the war exacerbated old hostilities between the white groups. Ironically, as the Torchers sought to find a firmer base for a lasting unity between the white races they continually struck a note guaranteed to alienate support from the many Afrikaner nationalists who without becoming Hitler's sympathizers or admirers had opposed South Africa's entry into the war.[1] Eventually, too, the Commando lost the support of many of the more moderate Afrikaners who had initially identified themselves with Smuts's war policy.[2] For these men the memory of the war would have faded more rapidly than with the English-speakers; in peace-time they were plunged back into an Afrikaner community where traditional Afrikaner values, for example on the colour question, took priority.

Yet, from their beginning, the Torchers were concerned with the preservation of principles generally recognized in South Africa and elsewhere as liberal. The themes recur: the sacredness of the constitution, the value of democracy, the priority of individual liberties, the importance of the rule of law, anti-totalitarianism in general, anti-fascism in particular.[3] The history of the movement demonstrates conclusively that these were principles widely shared by Commando supporters. It also reveals the limitations which marked the thinking of those South African whites who subscribed to political liberalism in this period. Generally, these people begged the colour question, which they failed to acknowledge—in fact, failed to see—was newly urgent.

In ways such as these, the Torch Commando proved to be a reflection of the United Party. Indeed United Party M.P.s were frequently drawn to defend the Commando from Government attack, and, in so doing, obviously shared the Commando's basic tenets. Dr. Bernard Friedman, for example, explained to the House of Assembly: 'Torchmen did not divest themselves of their concern for democracy when

[1] See D. W. Kruger's comment that 'public sentiment in a large part of the country was resolutely set against any active participation in a war in which South Africa was not militarily threatened.' *The Age of the Generals* (Johannesburg, Dagbreek, 1961), p. 193.
[2] In an interview with the author (Johannesburg, 22 November 1965) Louis Kane-Berman, who had been National Chairman of Torch, estimated that 20 per cent of the early membership of the movement was Afrikaner.
[3] *Cape Times*, 2 July 1951. cf. the version in Carter, *The Politics of Inequality*, p. 308.

E

they took off their uniforms. They are determined to safeguard on their home front the fruits of victory which they gained on the battlefield.'[1] There were, however, important distinctions between the Torch Commando and the U.P. The enthusiasm which the Commando aroused among non-Nationalists was without precedent.[2] Within a year the paid-up membership exceeded 125,000.[3] A large number of the rank and file were U.P. sympathizers, if not U.P. members. But, in addition, the movement succeeded in capturing the imagination and support of that section of the population which had traditionally been phlegmatic about politics.[4] In particular, few leading Torchers had previously been committed to the U.P.[5]

A basic feature of the Torchers' liberalism was their belief in the rights of the individual. The Nationalists, 'Sailor' Malan claimed, had made 'steady inroads . . . on the liberty and freedom of the individual.'[6] Such an outlook—again underpinned by memories of the war—apparently prompted the letter to the *Cape Times* from a Torchman, Captain Roy Strange. He wrote:

. . . we do not want our children to tell the state police the things their parents say; we do not want our country turned into a cattle kraal with no gate opened to the outer world; we do not want to live in the shadow of fear. . . . As South Africans we want to look the whole world in the face and say: 'Where our flags wave all men are free.'[7]

There was unquestioned agreement between Torchmen and the United Party over the importance of individual rights. Evidence of this agreement was indicated by the course of a debate in the Assembly in May 1951. On the evening of 19 May the Torch Commando staged a highly successful torchlight procession in the streets of Cape Town. Later that night, a large crowd, many of whom had presum-

---

[1] *Ass. Debates*, vol. 78, 28 Apr. 1952, col. 4521; see also Mr. H. G. Lawrence, ibid., vol. 76, 20 June 1951, col. 10135; Mr. A. Barlow, ibid., vol. 78, 25 Apr. 1952, col. 4425.

[2] Carter, *The Politics of Inequality*, p. 203.

[3] ibid., p. 330. The author interviewed several people who had been leading Torchmen (Louis Kane-Berman, John Lang, Gerald Gordon) and their evidence, albeit sympathetic, supports such an estimate. Basil Davidson sets the figure as high as 150,000 by mid 1952 in his *Report on Southern Africa*, p. 166.

[4] See the reference made by the United Party M.P., J. Hamilton Russell, to the 'usually non-political, non-party men' who gave their support to the Torch Commando. (*Ass. Debates*, vol. 78, 28 Apr. 1952, col. 4531.)

[5] Carter, *The Politics of Inequality*, p. 330.

[6] *Cape Times*, 26 July 1951.

[7] *Cape Times*, 10 Sept. 1951.

ably either watched or participated in the demonstration, gathered outside the Houses of Parliament. Reports of what followed naturally differ. But there was police intervention, rioting, damage to property, and a number of people were injured.[1] On the following day the Government and the Opposition crossed swords on the proper role of the police in the keeping of law and order. It was clear that there was fundamental disagreements on the limits to police power and on the related question of the rights of the individual in such circumstances. In the ensuing debate the Torch Commando was frequently the centre of attention, since the gravamen of the Government's charge was that the Torchmen were to blame for the rioting. As a result, the United Party was drawn to defend the Torchmen's innocence, and the movement's concern with individual rights, a concern which they clearly shared.[2]

Mr. A. E. Robinson, a United Party M.P., made this mutual understanding quite explicit. He referred to the Torch Commando's demonstration as 'magnificent'.

It was intended to ensure in this country for the future equality of language rights; . . . freedom of movement according to the laws of the land; . . . the future freedom of religion and the freedom of the Press; . . . the future free access to the courts of the land, and a guarantee of their independence. It was intended to ensure for the future freedom of speech with proper safeguards to preserve democracy in this country; and we are proud, as ex-servicemen and members of the United Party, to see that magnificent body of men last night fighting for these freedoms in South Africa.[3]

For their part, the Nationalists were enraged. Mr. H. G. Lawrence, the United Party M.P. who initially questioned the action of the police, had conceded that the police were entitled to protection against injury, but he had added, 'we also want to be assured . . . that every step is taken to protect the safety and the integrity of the individual.'[4] To the Government such a priority was, in the circumstances, beyond

[1] Walker, *A History of Southern Africa*, p. 823.

[2] Here was an issue on which the non-Nationalists showed an unusual degree of unanimity. The Labour Party M.P.s as well as the Native Representatives vigorously supported the United Party view. For example, the Labour Party M.P., Mr. Lovell, said: '. . . I will not have it as long as I have breath in my body, that any person in this country is above suspicion, no matter what office he holds, neither the police, nor civilians, nor Ministers, nor members of Parliament.' *Ass. Debates*, vol. 76, 20 May 1951, col. 7963.

[3] ibid., col. 7991.   [4] ibid., col. 7916.

comprehension, and the Nationalist M.P.s poured invective on the United Party and the Torchmen.[1] Here is further evidence that the Nationalists' assessment of where the immediate danger to the security of South African society lay was crucially different from that of the U.P. By contrast, the United Party's sense of urgency on the colour question was mild. Like the Nationalists, they too wanted 'to make the country safe for white civilization'.[2] But for U.P. supporters and Torchmen there was a more urgent issue: the white race question and the defence of white rights.[3] Their experiences during the war as well as the political triumph of Afrikaner nationalism in 1948 had made this seem the crucial question in South African politics during the first term of Nationalist rule.

This is strikingly evident in the Commando's attitude towards the Constitution. Two of the six principles of the movement emphasized the sacredness of constitutional rights. The veterans planned to uphold 'the letter and spirit of the solemn contracts entered on at the time of Union and the pledges given in this regard since Union'.[4] They also expressed their determination to 'secure the repeal of measures enacted in violation of these obligations'.[5] The constitutional rights most immediately threatened were, of course, those of the Coloureds to vote on the common roll.[6] In this instance, as in others, the war had accentuated differences already existing between Nationalists and non-Nationalists. The latter had, before the war, already been predisposed to consider that the Coloureds deserved different treatment than the Africans.[7] During the war, Coloured units had been separated from white ones. Even so their participation in the struggle against fascism gave the Coloureds added status in the

[1] e.g. The Minister of Justice, Mr. C. R. Swart, whom Lawrence had challenged to set up an inquiry, refused 'to defame the police' by doing so. The Minister of Economic Affairs, Mr. E. H. Louw, characterized the crowd as a 'mob' and implied that Torch Commando leaders were directly responsible for what had happened. Dr. K. Bremer, Minister of Health, denounced the United Party for defending 'rioting and attempted murder'. *Ass. Debates*, vol. 76, 20 May 1951, cols. 7929, 7937, 7991.

[2] Mr. H. G. Lawrence, ibid., 7917.

[3] e.g. the statement made by Gerald Gordon, a Cape Town solicitor and Vice-Chairman of the Commando's National Executive: 'The issues are plain. Never before in South African history has there been such a threat to fundamental liberties. ... We intend exerting ... pressure on anyone or any party that refuses to uphold the letter and the spirit of the Constitution.' *Cape Times*, 11 Aug. 1951.

[4] *Cape Times*, 2 July 1951.   [5] ibid.
[6] See above, p. 9.   [7] See above, p. 22.

eyes of many white servicemen.[1] Thus the Torchers, in as far as they were ex-servicemen, may well have had especially strong reasons for objecting to the Government's plan to diminish Coloured rights. The Nationalists, by contrast, valued the Coloureds' contribution to the war effort differently; the Nationalist Minister for Defence, Mr. F. C. Erasmus, disbanded the Coloured units at his earliest opportunity.[2] To accept Coloured servicemen in South Africa's defence force was to concede non-whites a status unacceptable to the Nationalists; such a status was bound to encourage non-white demands for further extensions of equality, not least for equal political rights.

Basically though, the fundamental objection which the Torchers raised regarding the Government's 'constitutional strip-tease'[3] was not that Coloured rights were threatened, but rather that they were threatened by unconstitutional means. As with the majority of the United Party M.P.s, most Torchers were incensed chiefly over the method rather than the purpose of the Nationalist move.[4] This did not necessarily make their defence of the Constitution any less liberal, but it did underline that, in this regard, theirs was a principle about liberal methods, rather than a principle about a liberal colour policy. Moreover, in as far as the Torchers were concerned about the particular rights which were threatened there was scope for quite different priorities. The threat to Coloured rights had peculiar implications for the English-speakers from whom the Torch Commando consistently received wide support.[5] The second of the two entrenched clauses in the Constitution related to the equality of the language rights of English and Afrikaners.[6] To concede one of the entrenched clauses was the thin end of the wedge. Thus the constitutional issue, ostensibly a struggle over non-white rights, regenerated the old white racial issue.

As this ambiguity on the question of Coloured rights illustrates, the Torch Commando had not been intended as a movement concerned with the colour question. It was, however, an issue which could not be completely side-stepped in South Africa in the early

[1] Such an attitude had been encouraged by the Army Educational Services. See above, p. 26.
[2] Walker, *A History of Southern Africa*, p. 788.
[3] The phrase was used in an editorial in the *Cape Times*, 17 April 1952.
[4] Carter, *The Politics of Inequality*, p. 310. See above, p. 51.
[5] This is indicated by the wide support for the movement in predominantly English-speaking Natal. Here the Torch Commando had a membership over twice that of the U.P. (Carter, *The Politics of Inequality*, p. 322.)
[6] See above, p. 48.

fifties—although many non-Nationalists, including many Torchers, obviously still considered the white racial issue of paramount importance. The Commando's original principles had included the Torchmen's intention to promote 'racial harmony' but, as Gwendolen Carter points out, the term was left undefined.[1] The decisions which the Torchers reached suggest that the majority held a conservative position. Initially, the questions raised in the Torch Commando about non-whites were questions about Coloured rights, and especially the rights of Coloured ex-servicemen.[2] The division which existed on this last question was indicated by the heat of the debate over the place of Coloured ex-servicemen in the Commando. The final decision of the National Executive—six months after the movement had begun—was an equivocal one. There were to be separate branches for Coloured members, and only those who had the right to vote could join.[3] The issue was eventually resolved by the Coloureds themselves. In November 1951, representatives of Coloured ex-servicemen announced that Coloureds would withdraw from the Commando on the grounds that they had no part in what was essentially 'the white man's fight'.[4] But before this gesture was made it was clear that the majority of the Commando were not interested in the extension of rights to non-whites and that the colour question was a potential source of deep dissension among the Torchers.

Thus, the official policy of the Commando on the colour question offered little immediate satisfaction to those members interested in the extension of rights to non-whites. But the Commando had been planned primarily to defend existing rights rather than to extend them. Moreover the question of rights was one traditionally associated with the white community. When such rights were endangered most whites considered it was their own responsibility to safeguard them. The Torchman who wrote to the *Cape Times* in October 1951 may have been misguided; he was not necessarily hypocritical:

> Basically, surely, Torch was conceived because the present Government has broken the white man's word to the non-European. Therefore it seems quite wrong to suggest that the non-European peoples should become embroiled in what is, singularly, a white man's affair.[5]

[1] Carter, *The Politics of Inequality*, p. 308. After the Government had been returned to power in 1953 the Commando's executive determined to elaborate on this principle of 'racial harmony'. The terms in which they did so suggest they originally had in mind the black–white racial issue. ibid., p. 328.

[2] ibid., pp. 308–10.   [3] ibid., p. 309.
[4] ibid.   [5] *Cape Times*, 12 Oct. 1951.

Such an attitude suggests the strong feeling of paternalism which was so integral a part of liberalism on the colour question among South African whites—a paternalism which continued to distinguish even the Liberal Party after its formation in May 1953.[1]

In addition, there were important practical reasons underlying the Commando's colour policy—or lack of one. The Torchmen planned to whip up a degree of enthusiasm sufficient to remove the Nationalists from power in 1953.[2] To build a large pressure group— the only kind they thought would be effective—they had to focus attention on issues guaranteed to unite rather than divide.[3] Such issues were those which concentrated opposition against the Government, rather than proposals for the extension of rights to non-whites. That minority which hoped for the development of a liberal colour policy were, at least temporarily, impressed by such arguments of expediency.

It was the overriding importance of defeating the Nationalists which drove the Torch Commando into close co-operation with the U.P. Initially, the Torchmen sought to avoid any close or formal relationship with the party.[4] Some of them were disillusioned with what they regarded as the vague policy and weak leadership of the Opposition.[5] Many Natal Torchmen wished to retain Natal's right to secede from the Union if the Nationalists acted arbitrarily over the constitutional question.[6] But the origin and expressed aims of the Commando committed the movement to constitutional means.[7] This entailed a further commitment to parliamentary methods. And the United Party was the only party with any chance of wresting political power from the Nationalists. Malan expressed the Torchmen's dilemma when the Commando was launched in the Cape late in July 1951: 'We have no intention of affiliating with the United Party but since the National Party was elected to power in a constitutional way, we must fight them constitutionally, and we can only do that by helping the United Party.'[8] There was as yet no public questioning from the Torchers with liberal views on colour about the efficacy of such methods. Those working outside the Commando were

---

[1] See below, p. 118.
[2] cf. the claim made by the U.P. member, Mr. H. G. Lawrence, that the 'sole objective' of the Torch Commando was to ensure 'that the present Government is displaced by the electorate. . . .' *Ass. Debates*, vol. 78, 25 Apr. 1952, col. 4408.
[3] Carter, *The Politics of Inequality*, p. 308.   [4] *Cape Times*, 26 July 1951.
[5] Carter, *The Politics of Inequality*, p. 314.   [6] ibid., pp. 318–23.
[7] ibid., p. 332.   [8] *Cape Times*, 26 July 1951.

equally reluctant to abandon the U.P. prior to the election.[1] Since Hofmeyr had chosen to remain within the U.P. in the thirties, such liberals had continued to debate about the most effective way of advancing their principles.[2] Constitutional methods and parliamentary means were not at issue.[3] Rather, it was a question of forming the best kind of pressure group to influence the existing Opposition or, as a much more desperate measure, of creating a new party. Significantly, the Torch Commando opted for the more conservative of these alternatives. They hoped to become a 'new democratic spark in the political life of South Africa' but a new spark, they acknowledged, would be useless unless it was 'harnessed to the proper machinery' of the existing opposition parties in the House of Assembly.[4]

The formation of the United Democratic Front was announced in Cape Town on 16 April 1952.[5] The alliance created was one between the United Party, the Labour Party, and the Torch Commando.[6] Their common, overriding interest was to oust the Government at the election scheduled for a year's time.[7] The joint declaration which they

[1] See below, p. 62.

[2] See above, p. 15. The impact of Hofmeyr's decision was suggested by the National Chairman of Torch, Kane-Berman, who subsequently spoke in glowing terms of the way in which Hofmeyr had inspired liberals. He himself would have been willing 'to follow Hofmeyr to the end of the earth'. (Author's interview Johannesburg, 22 Nov. 1965.)

[3] Just how deep-rooted this commitment to constitutional action was is indicated by a story recounted by John Lang, a member of the Torch Commando's National Executive and later active in the Liberal Party. According to Lang, Jock Isacowitz, a leading figure in the left-wing Springbok Legion, another smaller, ex-servicemen's organization, approached the National Executive of the Torch Commando with a plan for the Torchmen to capitalize on their popular support by marching on the Houses of Parliament and assuming control from the Nationalists, through a show of force. One of the older members objected to the scheme on the grounds that such an 'invasion' would involve marching against the traffic in a one-way street, and that would mean the Torchmen would be breaking the law. (Author's interview, London, 14 Sept. 1965.)

[4] Star, 26 Feb. 1952. Quoted in Carter, The Politics of Inequality, p. 315.

[5] Cape Times, 17 Apr. 1952. The protracted negotiations which preceded this move and the crises which marked the United Front's brief life are detailed in Carter, The Politics of Inequality, pp. 315–27.

[6] The Labour Party made a natural third partner; long-since stripped of its artisan colour-bar character, it now stood to the left of the U.P., especially in its views on apartheid. It was a move likely to pay both parties political dividends, since both the United Party and the Labour Party were anxious to avoid splitting the anti-Nationalist vote.

[7] It is also true that the United Party was much in need of the finances which Harry Oppenheimer and others had chosen to put at the disposal of the Torch Commando rather than the U.P. as they had done in the past. Hatch, The Dilemma of South Africa, p. 120.

issued made clear the highest common factor of their liberalism. Stress was laid on free institutions, the equality of the white races, the rule of law, the 'sacred heritage' of the Constitution and the importance of restoring South Africa 'to her rightful place as an honoured member of Western society'.[1] The one reference to the colour question was basically conservative. It said: 'We shall see to it that . . . rights as they extended to the less fortunate shall be defended and that the word of the white man . . . shall be honoured.'[2]

iv

It is significant that it was a group such as the Torch Commando, rather than a separate Liberal Party which emerged in this period. The political issue of immediate importance to all non-Nationalist whites was not the colour question, but that of defeating the Government. This short-term aim took precedence with white liberals and prevented them from forming a Liberal Party prior to the 1953 election.

Meanwhile, liberals played a prominent part in attempting to combat Nationalist moves which involved infringement of liberal principles. For example, part of Edgar Brookes's objection to the Group Areas Bill when it reached the Senate (where he was a Native Representative) was that its administration depended on excessive Ministerial power,[3] a point made frequently by U.P. parliamentarians.[4] In the debate on the Suppression of Communism Bill, the Native Representatives and the Labour Party adopted a stronger line than the U.P.[5] Margaret Ballinger, for example, shared the Opposition's misgivings. But her line of attack diverged significantly from that of the U.P. She stressed that the whites had left the field of race relations open to the communists, and she forecast that the new law would be used against the leaders of non-white political organizations.[6] On the major issue of the future of Coloured voting rights, those with liberal views on the non-white question had no choice but to back firmly the U.P. protests against the Government's proposals. The Institute of Race Relations, for instance, made clear

---

[1] Carter, *The Politics of Inequality*, pp. 316–17.
[2] *Cape Times*, 17 Apr. 1952.
[3] *Senate Debates*, IV, 19 June 1950, col. 5560.
[4] See above, p. 47.
[5] e.g. the Native Representatives supported the amendments which the Labour Party moved unsuccessfully. (Carter, *The Politics of Inequality*, p. 68.)
[6] *Ass. Debates*, vol. 73, 14 June, 1950, col. 8999.

that they shared the U.P. horror that such a move would mean violating the Constitution. It was, in their view—and the most right-wing U.P. member would concur—'a retrograde step, totally at variance with the principles of Western civilization and procedures now being adopted by the rest of the Western world'.[1] Such important points of agreement acted as anchorages mooring liberals loosely, but at least for the time being, securely, to the United Party position.

Confronted by the Nationalists' strength and determination, there could be no capital for the liberal cause in splitting the anti-Nationalist vote. This seemed at the time to be an overwhelming strategical argument for at least postponing the creation of a new party. But in any case those who agreed on the necessity of an extension of rights to non-whites were not in agreement that a new political party was the best or only means of effecting change. Friction over this question marked the life of the South African Liberal Group (S.A.L.G.) formed in Cape Town in January 1952. Composed chiefly of intellectuals and professional people, the S.A.L.G. committed themselves to a ten-point programme advocating the extension of political rights to non-whites, and the alleviation of hardships arising from the colour bar.[2] At their inaugural meeting, Dr. Oscar Wollheim (who initiated the move and was later to be first National Chairman of the Liberal Party) expressed the dilemma in which white liberals found themselves. Although, he said, 'it would be impracticable to form a new political party at this stage', they ought to make some move, for 'unless some organisation were formed immediately the matter would be postponed indefinitely.'[3]

This dilemma persisted. Opinions within the group about their prospective role ranged from those who were reluctant to jeopardize the chances of the United Party in the election by splitting the anti-Nationalist vote, to a minority, sufficiently disillusioned with the U.P. as an alternative, to find any delay until after the elections only irritating.[4] A prolonged discussion at a meeting in June 1952 ended in a compromise to encourage people to join the group, and consolidate their membership.[5] Hesitancy to act more drastically was partly due

---

[1] *Race Relations News*, xiii, 4 (Apr. 1951), 48.
[2] Minutes of the Inaugural Meeting of the South African Liberal Group, Retreat, 8 Jan. 1952, mim., P.A.S.
[3] ibid.
[4] Minutes of the Meeting of the S.A.L.G., Cape Town, 24 June 1952, mim., P.A.S.
[5] ibid.

to a reluctance to cut the ground from under the feet of other groups with comparable aims, and the Torch Commando was cited in this connection. Nevertheless, the liberals agreed that if, as a result of 'increasing restlessness' in the country, there was any kind of coalition between the Nationalists and the U.P., the Group should be prepared 'to spring into action'.[1] It was in this situation of extreme tension that the liberals' dilemma was to be heightened by the non-white Defiance Campaign and its aftermath. Even then—with additional pressures for the formation of a Liberal Party—the unity of the non-Nationalist front was to remain the prime consideration.[2]

[1] ibid.
[2] See below, pp. 90, 95.

CHAPTER III

The Nationalist victory and the African National Congress

i

In the white world the 1948 election result diverted the attention of liberals to the white racial issue and the question of white rights; among Congressmen, however, the Nationalist victory accelerated the process of re-evaluating liberalism as it applied to the colour question. To Congress leaders, the distinctions between the Nationalists and the United Party were distinctions without practical difference. Before the 1948 election the hopes which Congress leaders had held of the U.P. initiating liberal change in the post-war years had dwindled rapidly.[1] What the new Government did, in the A.N.C. view, was to intensify the 'experience of serfdom'.[2] Thus, the Nationalist rule provided fresh impetus to the process of radical change which had already begun before 1948.

Yet the A.N.C. did not abandon political liberalism in the period 1948–52. Their aims remained the same as those set out in the Bill of Rights in 1945. But they adopted new means which had serious implications for the future of liberalism within the A.N.C. and in South Africa as a whole. It was in respect of these methods that the disparity with the views of contemporary white liberals was most evident. The gulf which, prior to 1948, separated Congress from white liberals widened even further in the first years of Nationalist rule. In the late forties, Youth League influence reached its height, signifying the militancy of Congress. In the Programme of Action, endorsed in December 1949, the A.N.C. rejected the use of petition and deputation, as well as the paternalism of the whites, which such an approach denoted. At the same time, they officially approved strategies not generally acceptable to white liberals in South Africa: boycott, strike action and civil disobedience. In the early fifties, again for strategic reasons, the A.N.C. deliberately entered a phase of close co-operation

[1] See above, p. 34.
[2] Luthuli, *Let My People Go*, p. 98.

with communists. In June 1952 the non-white Defiance Campaign was launched and Congress played a major role in this protest against discriminatory legislation. The use of such a spectacular extra-parliamentary strategy as non-violent passive resistance marked clearly the extent of the change in Congress methods in this period. It marked also the widening of the gulf which divided them from white liberals by mid 1952.

ii

Prior to 1948 the clearest sign of radical change within the A.N.C. had been the emergence of the Youth League, characterized by a newly militant nationalism.[1] Youth League influence within Congress reached its height at the National Conference of the A.N.C. held in Johannesburg, in December 1949. It was the Youth League's nominee for President, Dr. James Moroka, who was elected to office in what Benson calls an 'unconstitutional coup'.[2] Among the seventeen elected to the new National Executive were five of the founding members of the League—Dan Tloome, A. P. Mda, Oliver Tambo, and Godfrey Pitje were appointed to the Committee, and Walter Sisulu was made Secretary-General.[3] The Conference delegates endorsed the Pro-gramme of Action, which proposed new strategies at the insistence of the Leaguers.[4] It appeared, as Sampson contends, that the Youth Leaguers had 'virtually won control of Congress'.[5]

Yet the Leaguers' victory was not total; their influence had been significant but they had been forced to make major concessions to other elements within Congress, not least to the liberals and moder-ates. Support for an African nationalism as intense as the League's was slow to develop not only among the older Congressmen but also among those of the Leaguers' own generation. Congress could

[1] See above, pp. 35 ff.

[2] Benson, The African Patriots, pp. 158–9.

[3] See the list of members of the A.N.C. National Executive 1949–60 in Duma Nokwe, 'The Great Smear: Communism and Congress in South Africa', Africa South, v, 4 (1961). In addition to the five mentioned, it seems likely that Dr. J. Z. L. Njongwe, also on the new Committee in 1949, was already a Youth Leaguer. Describing his work as President of the A.N.C. in Port Elizabeth, Benson mentions that he had been 'an early member' of the League (The African Patriots, p. 167). Tloome's position is not clear. He had been one of the original members of the League, but the League preferred to support Sisulu's nomination for Secretary-General at the 1949 election, while the 'left-wing' countered with Tloome (ibid., p. 161).

[4] Benson, The African Patriots, pp. 161–2.

[5] Sampson, Treason Cage, p. 79.

not instantly outgrow its earlier character, despite Youth League pressure. Late in 1948 Peter Mda had conceded in a letter to the Rev. James Calata, then Secretary-General of Congress, that the Youth League anticipated general difficulty in persuading the older members of the A.N.C.—as well as the communist members—to endorse the League's programme of militant African nationalism.[1] Even with Youth Leaguers in some positions of prominence it would take time to convert the older professional men into ardent African nationalists—and with some they would never succeed. The difficulties of the task were implicit in a letter which Mda wrote to Godfrey Pitje in the month before the 1949 Conference. 'The outlook [of African Nationalism] has made advances [he said] but it has not yet taken root among the African Intelligentsia and the bulk of the Youth.'[2]

Thus the Youth Leaguers curbed their ambitions. But for a last-minute change of plan, they even intended to support Xuma's re-election as President in 1949 for want of a more suitable candidate—despite the fact that he had earlier refused to support the Programme of Action.[3] Dr. James Moroka, whom they nominated instead, represented opinion clearly distinguishable from Xuma and the earlier Congress leaders.[4] He had, for example, used his membership of the N.R.C. to voice hard-hitting criticism of United Party equivocation.[5] Yet, as Sampson suggests, he was 'in several ways an odd choice for the uncompromising Youth League to have made for their leader'.[6] Moroka was an unusually prosperous African, with large farms in Thaba 'Nchu, an African reserve in the Orange Free State, where he also ran a thriving medical practice. There he had a number of white patients, as well as several Afrikaner friends.[7] As late as August 1952—before he fell from grace with the A.N.C. executive[8]—a Youth Leaguer described him as one of 'the most moderate of the moderates'.[9]

[1] Letter from Mda to Calata, 17 Nov. 1948, mim., P.A.S.
[2] Letter from Mda to Pitje, 10 Nov. 1949, mim., P.A.S.
[3] Benson, *The African Patriots*, pp. 157–9.
[4] e.g. the article entitled 'Real Troubles of Natal Congress', in *Inkundla ya Bantu* (19 Aug. 1950), p. 4. Here the writer sees Xuma's policy as one of 'drift', and identifies Moroka as one of the advocates of 'planned movement towards clearly defined objectives'.
[5] See above, p. 33.   [6] Sampson, *Treason Cage*, pp. 82–3.
[7] ibid., p. 83.   [8] See below, p. 101.
[9] Joe Matthews's letter to his father, Prof. Z. K. Matthews, 22 Aug. 1952, mim., P.A.S.

Yet, it seems unlikely that Moroka was 'a fake figurehead', as some have suggested.[1] There were on the National Executive a number of other men of similar stamp[2]—for instance, Dr. S. M. Molema, the A.N.C. Treasurer, who like Moroka had trained in Edinburgh,[3] and the Rev. James Calata, who had been Secretary-General from 1935 to 1949 and refused re-election partly because the Programme of Action seemed too drastic.[4] There was also Professor Z. K. Matthews from Fort Hare, who had refused Youth League nomination for the Presidency in 1949, on the grounds that the organization was to be run by a clique.[5] In particular, some of the Youth Leaguers reacted with dislike to Matthews's consistent respectability. Godfrey Pitje thought of him as a 'Black Liberal'[6]—in his own terms, not a flattering label. And Peter Mda was furious when Matthews banned the Youth League at Fort Hare after members had been involved in a boycott. In a letter to Pitje he spoke of 'the inexplicable attitude which an eminent "intellectual" like Professor Matthews has taken', and condemned him for his 'downright and monstrous treachery'.[7] Nevertheless, Matthews was widely admired as one of the most distinguished figures in Congress.[8] In March 1950, Moses Kotane, Secretary of the Communist Party in Johannesburg and a member of the A.N.C. National Executive, wrote to Matthews, seeking a statement on the Government's proposal to introduce passes for women: 'I regard you as our leader: the leading African intellectually and legally, the President of the leading African organisation

[1] This is one of the possible interpretations offered by Sampson, *Treason Cage*, p. 83.
[2] See the list of the A.N.C. National Executive 1949–60 in Nokwe, 'The Great Smear', p. 6.
[3] Benson, *The African Patriots*, p. 161. At the meeting of African leaders held in Bloemfontein in October 1948, Molema had been among those who had voiced caution and stressed the necessity of adequate organization (ibid., p. 151).
[4] ibid., p. 161.
[5] G.M.C. interview with Z. K. Matthews, 19 Mar. 1964, p. 16.
[6] Pitje to Jordan Ngubane, 9 Nov. 1949, mim., P.A.S.
[7] Mda to Pitje, 10 Nov. 1949, mim., P.A.S.
[8] In 1923 Z. K. Matthews had been the first African to graduate in South Africa from Fort Hare, and was soon afterwards appointed as the first African Headmaster at Adams College in Natal. In 1930 he became the first Bachelor of Laws in South Africa. After several years abroad, spent mostly at Yale University and London School of Economics, Matthews was appointed a member of a Commission on Higher Education for Africans in East Africa and the Sudan. He was a member also of the Committee of the Institute of Race Relations and the Union Advisory Board on Native Education. (Benson, *The African Patriots*, pp. 166–7; Sampson, *Treason Cage*, p. 124.)

(provincially, I grant you) and the Chairman of the N.R.C. Caucus. Yes, *the* leader.'[1] There is nothing to suggest this was spurious flattery. Kotane had been an A.N.C. member since 1927, and had more recently helped reorganize the Congress in the Cape.[2] He and Matthews had sat together on the sub-committee appointed to finally frame the Programme of Action.[3] It seems likely that his admiration for the moderate Matthews was much more widely shared than the view expressed by Mda.

The Youth League had been unable to monopolize the elections to the National Executive, but they were able to win the Conference's acceptance of the Programme of Action.[4] The ideals expressed in the Programme were not new; they had already been firmly established in the mid forties. Their debt to the Youth League Manifesto and the Bill of Rights was obvious.[5] The Programme rejected equally the concepts of segregation, *apartheid*, trusteeship, and white leadership, and stressed the desire to achieve 'freedom from white domination and the attainment of political independence'.[6] The A.N.C. would work for 'the abolition of all differential institutions' and seek the right of 'direct representation in all the governing bodies of the country. . . .'[7]

What was new was the strategy which the Programme recommended for achieving Congress aims.[8] These methods were clearly a response

---

[1] Kotane to Z. K. Matthews, 23 Mar. 1950, mim., P.A.S.
[2] Benson, *The African Patriots*, pp. 75, 91.   [3] ibid., p. 151.
[4] This was despite the diversity of the delegates which Sampson notes: '. . . there were still many of the "Old Guard". . . . Most of them were Christians, brought up by missionaries. . . . There was a sprinkling of hard-core Communists. . . . There was a group of distinguished professional men. . . . And there was the younger generation. . . . Mixed with the better-educated Congressmen were all kinds of factory workers, housewives, farm labourers or messengers. . . . (*Treason Cage*, pp. 80–1.)
[5] See above, pp. 31, 36–7.
[6] See '1949 Programme of Action of the African National Congress', in Helen Joseph, *If This Be Treason* (London, André Deutsch, 1963), Appendix A, p. 185.
[7] ibid.
[8] This is borne out by Lutuli's statement made during the Treason Trial. It should be noted that it was then to his advantage to stress that A.N.C. aims continued to be moderate after 1949. But since the case against the accused was eventually dismissed, his evidence seems to retain its validity. He said:
'Since the adoption of the 1949 programme, the A.N.C. has been a militant organisation. I use the word "militant" in contrast to the previous methods used by the A.N.C., such as interviews with or deputations to persons in authority. . . .
'The object of the militant methods was to bring pressure to bear on the Govern-

to a changed situation, the results of a reluctant comprehension that discussion and deputation had been fruitless. By accepting them, the delegates acknowledged that Congress must make use of new weapons, particularly those made available by the still increasing degree of industrialization, so patently dependent on non-white labour. The Programme committed the A.N.C. to the use of 'immediate and active boycott, strike, civil disobedience, non-cooperation . . .' and endorsed in particular 'a national stoppage of work for one day as a mark of protest against the reactionary policy of the Government.'[1]

The adoption of the Programme of Action marked a turning-point in the history of the A.N.C. What the A.N.C. sought to gain through the Programme of Action was perfectly consistent with the tenets of Western liberal democracy. But in South African circumstances the implications were revolutionary: they meant the establishment of non-white majority rule.[2] The novel methods to which Congressmen now pledged themselves were even less acceptable to white liberals in South Africa, and even to many liberals elsewhere. It was the application of these new methods, as well as the implications of A.N.C. aims, that in the fifties were to help cast into a crucible both the values held by Congress and those of the white community. And from that crucible there emerged by the early sixties two mutually hostile nationalisms, both intolerant of liberal principles and liberal methods.

iii

The growth of co-operation with communists was another major development in A.N.C. policy in the period 1948–52. This new tolerance and close collaboration was to be a main factor preventing more effective co-operation between the A.N.C. and white liberals in the middle and late fifties.[3] By 1953 when the Liberal Party was formed[4]—and declared itself opposed to 'all forms of totalitarianism,

---

ment in contrast to the previous method of asking favours from the Government. It was envisaged that militant action would compel the Government to change its attitude towards the Africans and would compel them for the first time to give serious consideration to African political demands.'
(Statement taken from Chief Albert J. Luthuli in the case *R.* v. *Adams and Others*, n.d., mim., P.A.S.)
[1] 'Programme of Action', in Joseph, *If This Be Treason*, p. 186.
[2] See above, p. 31.
[3] See below, pp. 115–6, 165–8.
[4] See below, p. 113.
F

including fascism and communism'—the debate over communism in the A.N.C. had largely subsided. The anti-collaborationist view was still represented within Congress by the Africanists but it was not until 1959 that this element seceded from the A.N.C. to form the Pan-Africanist Congress (P.A.C.).[1] Even then the majority of the A.N.C. leaders were only confirmed in their forbearance. Meanwhile, the issue of communism was one over which Congress leaders and white liberals were deeply divided.

The question of how far the A.N.C. should co-operate with communists arose in two different connections. It was automatically related to the question of co-operation with other racial groups; the leadership of the South African Indian Congress (S.A.I.C.) was communist and that of the more radical Coloured organizations, Trotskyite.[2] But it was not only a question of accepting or refusing help from communist outsiders. There were Africans who were simultaneously members of the Communist Party and the A.N.C. They were never many,[3] but three were members of the A.N.C. National Executive in the period 1949–52—Dan Tloome, J. B. Marks, and Moses Kotane.[4]

Stiff opposition to communists, whether they were outsiders or members of the A.N.C., came from the Youth League. To the Leaguers, communists represented a 'foreign' influence;[5] they feared that co-operation with communists would lead 'to a watering down of the concept of African Nationalism'.[6] But circumstances eventually forced most Leaguers to accept the practical necessity of co-operation with communists. Moreover, some came to accept that communism was not incompatible with African nationalism. This gradual growth in toleration in the early fifties reflected some diminution of the Youth League's influence; freemasonry across racial and ideological barriers was a move away from the exclusivist nationalism of the League.

The marked increase in interracial co-operation after 1948—and consequently in co-operation with communists—owed much to the

[1] See below, p. 200.

[2] Sampson, *Treason Cage*, p. 180; Roux, *Time Longer than Rope*, pp. 357–9.

[3] Benson, *The African Patriots*, p. 62.

[4] Nokwe, 'The Great Smear', p. 6.

[5] G.M.C. interview with Joe Matthews, Maseru, Basutoland, July 1963, p. 9, P.A.S.

[6] Nelson Mandela, *No Easy Walk to Freedom* (London, Heinemann, 1965), p. 180.

thoroughgoing nature of the new Government's *apartheid* policy.[1] The Nationalists soon made it clear that this was to be more all-embracing than the segregation policy of the United Party. They ceased, for example, to observe the kind of distinctions that the United Party had traditionally respected with regard to the Coloureds. And they showed even less tolerance than the United Party had done, when the Indian Government reacted to their treatment of Indians in South Africa. This Nationalist blindness to shade of colour imposed an artificial unity on the non-whites which was soon reinforced by common suffering under new racial laws, and by participation in joint protests.

Paradoxically, it was the Durban riots—and the Government's reaction—which accelerated the move to co-operation between A.N.C. leaders and those of the Indian Congress. In January 1949, African–Indian relations exploded into violence which resulted in death, injury, and widespread damage to property.[2] One of the root causes of the riots was the deep antipathy between the Zulus and the Indians in Natal,[3] but this was an antipathy fostered by social and economic inequities between these two races.[4] And the riots generally served to exacerbate existing hostility.[5]

Indian and Congress leaders no doubt felt that the Government, by their constant emphasizing of racial differences, and in particular by their anti-Indian propaganda had helped provide an atmosphere ripe for racial rioting.[6] To allow existing animosity to increase was

[1] The affinity which was to grow between A.N.C. leaders in the Transvaal and Natal and their opposite numbers in the S.A.I.C. had weak roots in the pre-Nationalist period. e.g. the Germiston branch of the A.N.C. from the Witwatersrand had joined the Indian passive resistance campaign in Durban in 1946; in 1947 the leaders hoped to encourage harmony with the signing of the Xuma–Naicker–Dadoo Pact. (Roux, *Time Longer than Rope*, pp. 365–6; Benson, *The African Patriots*, pp. 140, 162). According to Dadoo himself, the leaders attached great significance to this formal declaration of common interests (author's interview with Dr. Yusuf Dadoo, London, 15 Oct. 1965).
[2] According to the official figures, 142 people were killed and 1,087 injured, 58 of whom died as a result of their injuries. See Maurice Webb and Kenneth Kirkwood, *The Durban Riots and After* (Johannesburg, S.A.I.R.R., 1949), part I, p. 4.
[3] A point made by the Commission of Inquiry. See Webb and Kirkwood, *The Durban Riots*, part II, p. 16.
[4] ibid., part I, p. 11.
[5] There were instances of Africans and Indians helping each other during and after the upheaval (Benson, *The African Patriots*, p. 154). But during the Defiance Campaign in 1952 the organizers hesitated to encourage a wide response in Natal for fear of reactivating African–Indian animosity. Leo Kuper, *Passive Resistance in South Africa* (New Haven, Yale Univ. Press, 1957), p. 111.
[6] Webb and Kirkwood, *The Durban Riots*, part I, p. 7.

to add grist to the Government's mill. The persuasiveness of individuals apparently played a crucial part in relieving tensions. Dr. A. B. Xuma, President-General of the A.N.C., argued with those Congress leaders in Natal who felt strongly against co-operation with the Indians.[1] The idea of co-operation gained support, too, from the Natal Youth League, where one influential figure was the moderate M. B. Yengwa.[2] Yengwa joined with Xuma, George Champion, J. B. Marks, and the Rev. Z. R. Mahabane, the mild early President-General of Congress, and together with the two leaders of the S.A.I.C., Dr. Yusuf Dadoo and Dr. Monty Naicker, issued statements condemning violence.[3]

The white reaction to the riots—in particular, the findings of the Commission of Inquiry—provided a powerful additional incentive to co-operate. The Commission consisted only of whites, and from the outset it refused to allow the cross-examination of any of the witnesses.[4] Here was a paternalism which smacked of dictatorship, and the Joint Committee of the S.A.I.C. and A.N.C. was only one of a number of organizations which withdrew their observers.[5] In the face of the intransigence of white officialdom, a policy of self-help on a joint basis seemed one of the few alternatives.[6]

Meanwhile, Nationalist legislation emphasized the common plight of Africans and Indians. Thus the A.N.C. National Executive Committee saw the multiple repercussions which could be expected from the Group Areas Act (1950).[7] It was, they claimed, '. . . intended to

---

[1] George Champion, the Provincial President of the A.N.C., Selby Msimang, his secretary, later an active member of the Liberal Party, and Chief Albert Lutuli, at this point a prominent member of the Provincial Executive, all felt strongly against close co-operation with the Indians. (Benson, *The African Patriots*, p. 153.)

[2] Yengwa's moderation was stressed by one of the Treason Trial defence lawyers, A. P. O'Dowd (author's interview, London, 5 Oct. 1965). It is also implied in Nokwe, 'The Great Smear', p. 8.

[3] Benson, *The African Patriots*, p. 155.

[4] Webb and Kirkwood, *The Durban Riots*, part I, p. 5.   [6] ibid., p. 6.

[5] Benson, *The African Patriots*, p. 154: '. . . the Durban riots met with smug complacency from the authorities. Only the A.N.C., the Indian Congress, the Native Locations Advisory Boards, and a handful of academic, liberal, and left-wing whites, drew attention to the grievousness of the situation and to the underlying causes—poverty, lack of homes, inadequate transport, lack of opportunity.'

[7] The Group Areas Act provided machinery to streamline residential segregation. Generally speaking, licences to conduct a business would be granted only within one's own residential area. Consequently large numbers of Indian traders found not only their homes but their livelihoods threatened. See Muriel Horrell, *Action, Reaction and Counteraction* (Johannesburg, S.A.I.R.R., 1963), p. 8.

ruin the Indian community economically and to divide the African people into tribal sections thereby weakening their political solidarity in their fight for national liberation.'[1]

Reciprocity between the Africans and the Indians had been achieved only slowly, and months after the Durban riots the relationship remained a fragile one. But on 1 May 1950, the Transvaal Indian Congress supported the A.N.C.'s call for a one-day stoppage of work in Johannesburg. Their contribution to the national strike of 26 June 1950 was a valuable one. In Durban, they bore the brunt of the protest, and their response on this occasion did much to temper A.N.C. suspicions.[2] Such common involvement in strike action underlined the Africans' and Indians' dependence on one another.[3] It also expressed a growing amity, and helped to create further unity.

Co-operation between the A.N.C. and Coloured political organizations developed later than that between the A.N.C. and the Indians. Naturally Coloured politics tended to be concentrated in the Cape, where by far the largest number of Coloureds lived.[4] In addition, politically-articulate Coloureds were divided among themselves in a way in which their opposite numbers in the African and Indian communities were not.[5] However, the impact of the Nationalist victory on the Coloured community had been particularly harsh.[6] Previously a comparatively privileged racial group, they were uniquely affected

[1] Draft Report of the National Executive Committee of the A.N.C. to the 38th Annual Conference to be held at Bloemfontein on 15–17 Dec. 1950, p. 2, mim., P.A.S.

[2] Benson, *The African Patriots*, p. 165.

[3] Sampson, *Treason Cage*, p. 85: 'The Indians and Africans needed each other: on the crudest level, the Indians needed the African numbers, and the Africans needed Indian organisation and money and the international connections of the Indian people.' See also Carter, *The Politics of Inequality*, pp. 365–6.

[4] According to the 1951 Population Census, there were at that time 1,103,016 Coloureds in South Africa; of these, 981,802 lived in Cape Province. Figures taken from R. Farquharson, *Interim Report of the Marginal Mines Research Unit* (Johannesburg, Univ. of the Witwatersrand, March 1963), P.A.S.

[5] e.g., the Non-European Unity Movement attracted a number of Coloureds to its anti-collaborationist platform; this was especially the case after the Government set up the Coloured Advisory Council in 1943. But the Coloured People's National Union continued to advocate co-operation with the Government, an attitude made less tenable when *apartheid* measures were extended to the Coloureds after 1948. Carter, *The Politics of Inequality*, pp. 360–1.

[6] Previously the Coloureds had enjoyed considerable advantages over the Africans and Indians. Apart from their limited political rights, their culture was substantially the 'white' culture, and the majority of them spoke Afrikaans. Even if they could not pass as 'white', their lives could be comparatively privileged (van den Berghe, *South Africa*, pp. 40–2).

by the Population Registration Act (1950), which provided for the rigid classification of people into racial groups.[1] A threat of a different kind to Coloureds was the Nationalists' well-known wish to remove Coloured voters from the common roll.[2] The African People's Organization (A.P.O.) took up the cause of the Coloured vote. With the A.N.C. and the S.A.I.C., they sponsored a Cape Town meeting from which grew a Franchise Action Committee. This Committee was responsible for a one-day strike in April 1951—a protest which received widespread support from Africans and Coloureds in Cape Town and Port Elizabeth.[3] Meanwhile, even the Coloured People's National Union, which had previously co-operated with the Government, had joined in a number of interracial demonstrations on the issue of the vote.[4]

The Youth Leaguers, in particular, were in a dilemma regarding members of the Communist Party within the A.N.C.[5] With the Programme of Action, they had encouraged recognition of the necessity for the A.N.C. to employ strike action—what David Bopape had called their 'atomic weapon'.[6] Yet they knew that to match the earlier spontaneous mass protests like the Alexandra Bus Boycott[7] and the Squatters' Movement[8] they needed the kind of organizing ability which the communist J. B. Marks, for example, had shown during the 1946 Mine Workers' Strike.[9] For a number of prominent Leaguers, the strike scheduled for 1 May 1950 provided a turning-point. Hotly opposed to what they regarded as a communist take-over of plans for the protest, which was to have been jointly arranged, the Leaguers were forced to sober reconsideration by factors such as the

[1] Under the terms of this Act, Coloureds were classified as 'white' or 'coloured'. Decisions were based on whether or not the Coloured person appeared white or was generally accepted as white. Such a method of classification meant that members of the same family could be divided into different racial categories (Horrell, *Legislation and Race Relations*, p. 11).

[2] See above, p. 48.　　　[3] Roux, *Time Longer than Rope*, p. 385.

[4] Walker, *A History of Southern Africa*, pp. 822–3.

[5] See above, p. 70.　　　[6] Benson, *The African Patriots*, p. 151.

[7] According to Roux, the Alexandra bus strike in August 1943 was 'a spontaneous mass protest, unprepared and owing little or nothing to political leadership'. By comparison the second strike in November 1944 was well organized. The two strikes forced the bus companies to revert to the original fare, which they had sought to increase (Roux, *Time Longer than Rope*, pp. 318–19).

[8] In April 1944 several thousand homeless Africans left Orlando and camped on near-by vacant municipal land. Their building of Shanty Town provoked the Johannesburg municipality into more constructive efforts to solve the acute problems of non-white housing (ibid., p. 322).

[9] Benson, *The African Patriots*, p. 127.

police brutality which broke up the strike in Johannesburg, and Parliament's comparative lack of concern at the number of casualties.[1] Before mutual recriminations could destroy their tenuous unity, Moses Kotane, Walter Sisulu, Nelson Mandela, and Oliver Tambo were working to salvage the relationship.[2] And it was during these post-mortems, that Mandela, for example, came to accept that Kotane was 'really a nationalist'.[3] Thus the communists demonstrated that they too could adopt and further nationalist aims and this was crucial in converting the virulent nationalist Leaguers to a new tolerance of the communist element within the A.N.C.

In addition, Youth League activists and other A.N.C. leaders were influenced by the way in which African communists showed themselves committed to the African nationalist cause. As President of the Cape A.N.C., Z. K. Matthews had to deal with complaints from people that the communists were gaining more and more influence.[4] Objections were not raised so much because of the ways in which communists engineered plans, but rather 'in terms of "These fellows are always the first to attend meetings, they are always the first to hand out leaflets." '[5] But it was this degree of committal which impressed not only older men such as Z. K. Matthews and Lutuli, but also the younger ones like Sisulu and Mandela.[6] Mandela explained his own conversion to the acceptance of communist help during the course of the Rivonia Trial in 1961. He said:

... for many decades communists were the only political group in South Africa who were prepared to treat Africans as human beings and their equals; who were prepared to eat with us; talk with us, live with us, and work with us. They were the only political group which was prepared to work with the Africans for the attainment of political rights and a stake in society.[7]

The A.N.C.'s differences with the Communist Party could be, and

---

[1] ibid., p. 164.   [2] ibid.   [3] ibid.

[4] G.M.C. interview with Z. K. Matthews, 19 Mar. 1964, p. 16, P.A.S.

[5] ibid., p. 17. See also Lutuli's view: 'If there is any danger of their [the communists] using Congress for their own ends and infiltrating into "key positions" it can only be the result of apathy among non-Communists.'(*Let My People Go*, p. 137.)

[6] A. P. O'Dowd, one of the defence lawyers during the Treason Trial, made this point about Sisulu in an interview with the author, London, 7 Oct. 1965. It was also an argument stressed by Joe Matthews, who was a Youth Leaguer like Mandela and Tambo (author's interview, London, 5 Oct. 1965).

[7] Mandela, *No Easy Walk*, p. 181.

needed to be, postponed. In Lutuli's words: 'We leave our differing political theories to one side until the day of liberation, and in the meantime we are co-operating in a defined area, in the cause of liberation.'[1] For Mandela also, co-operation was proof only of an immediate goal in common, 'the removal of White supremacy'. He denied that joint action meant 'a complete community of interests'.[2] Rather, the short-term objections of both coincided.[3]

Usually, moderate Congressmen were more readily persuaded to co-operate with communists than were the Leaguers. But there were exceptions. The Rev. J. Skomolo, for instance, was appalled by the loss of life and property involved in the May Day strike. With the 26 June Day of Protest (1950) in the offing he wrote in distress to Z. K. Matthews, President of the Cape Congress:

> Before these wounds are healed we are again formulating another strike. The nation is not ready. If we are to be at the mercy of the Communist party, take it from me, the Congress hasn't got another year to live. The Engine [sic] and brain of the Congress cannot be the communist influence.[4]

This was a view more likely to be heard in the Cape, where there was, in the early fifties, even an attempt to expel communists from the A.N.C.[5] But it was in the Transvaal that R. V. Selope Thema formed a National-minded Bloc within Congress.[6] Thema had been prominent in the anti-pass demonstration in 1919, and again as recently as 1945. But as Editor of *Bantu World* he now cut a more conservative figure, and objected to Marks's election as President of the Transvaal Congress.[7]

The distrust which Skomolo and Thema evinced was rare among the moderate element of the A.N.C.; it was, however, general among white liberals in the post-war years.[8] It would be less than just to suggest that white liberals had no sympathy with A.N.C. tolerance of

---

[1] Luthuli, *Let My People Go*, p. 137.

[2] Mandela, *No Easy Walk*, p. 179.

[3] ibid., p. 181.

[4] Letter dated 16 June 1950, mim., P.A.S. The Secretary of the Kimberley Branch of the A.N.C. expressed a similar opinion in a letter to Z. K. Matthews. He feared the strikes, called without proper consultation, would 'only drive away the people from the Congress because they are sure to fail and the people lose confidence in the leaders'. Letter dated 19 June 1950, mim., P.A.S.

[5] G.M.C. interview with Z. K. Matthews, 19 Mar. 1964, P.A.S.

[6] Benson, *The African Patriots*, p. 169.

[7] Roux, *Time Longer than Rope*, pp. 297, 322; Benson, *The African Patriots*, p. 169.

[8] See below, pp. 115–6, 165.

communism. But their own intolerance was based on reasons which were unconvincing to non-whites because of their differing circumstances. White liberals insulted the moderates in the A.N.C. leadership by their witch-hunting.[1] Too frequently, their fears seemed based on the assumption that one or two communists were 'somehow automatically cleverer' than the non-communists who outnumbered them on a committee.[2] White liberals also pointed to the lack of political rights which existed in Communist countries. From their point of view, this was a powerful reason for their distrust of South African communists, black or white. To Africans who lacked political rights under a non-communist government it was hardly a meaningful argument let alone a persuasive one.[3]

The Nationalist Government's Suppression of Communism Act constituted a further force unifying the interests of the A.N.C. and the communists—and further alienating white liberals. The A.N.C. Executive understood that it had been communist participation in non-white politics which prompted the Nationalist move. In his report to the 1950 National Conference, the Secretary-General, Walter Sisulu, made this clear:

> Although the ... Act purports to be directed against Communism in general and the Communist Party of South Africa in particular, we are satisfied from a study of the provisions of this Act that it is primarily directed against the Africans and other oppressed people and is designed to frustrate all their attempts to work for the fulfillment of their legitimate demands and aspirations.[4]

Thus, when individual communists were subsequently 'named' under

---

[1] According to Mhaleni Njisane—an African sociologist from Natal, who was a member of the A.N.C. and of the Liberal Party in the fifties—Lutuli was offended by this attitude. He though that people who constantly accused the communists of having a controlling influence and predicted their eventual domination were seriously underestimating the political sense of the Africans within the A.N.C. (author's interview, London, 23 Sept. 1965). Nokwe points out the irony of those whites, who saw Lutuli as a 'front man', at the same time expressing their confidence in him and their admiration of his policies (author's interview, Dar es Salaam, 15 Nov. 1965).

[2] Author's interview with Joe Matthews, London, 5 Oct. 1965.　　[3] ibid.

[4] Draft Report of the National Executive Committee of the A.N.C. to the 38th Annual Conference to be held at Bloemfontein on 15–17 Dec. 1950, P.A.S. During the Rivonia trial, Mandela spoke of the many Africans who tended to equate freedom with communism: 'They are supported in this belief by a legislature which brands all exponents of democratic government and African freedom as communists. ...' (*No Easy Walk*, p. 181; also Kuper, *Passive Resistance*, p. 71.)

the terms of the Act, they became, in A.N.C. eyes, martyrs to the cause of racial equality as much as to the cause of 'international communism'. Non-communists and communists were more closely identified, too, when the former were tried and punished under the Act for their participation in the Defiance Campaign.[1] It was not until the early sixties, that the terms of the Act were made to embrace white liberals—a development which then won them new favour in the eyes of the non-whites.

iv

The planning of the Defiance Campaign provides a convenient means of examining the different elements in A.N.C. leadership and philosophy in 1952. The Campaign was organized by the A.N.C. and the S.A.I.C.; the organizers planned to involve Africans, Indians, and Coloureds in protests against specific laws deemed to be 'unjust', for example, the Pass Laws, the Group Areas Act, and the Voters' Representation Act. Protests were most commonly to be acts of defiance against Pass Laws and the contravening of *apartheid* regulations in public buildings, like railway stations and post offices. It was hoped that the Government would respond by repealing the particular laws singled out for attack.[2]

The conduct of the volunteers clearly owed much to the technique of passive resistance developed by Mahatma Gandhi in the Indian Nationalists' struggle against Britain, a technique previously employed in South Africa by the Indians in 1946.[3] In ideological terms, the Defiance Campaign appears to have been stimulated by non-white nationalism. But neither the use of Ghandi's techniques nor nationalist aims were incompatible with liberalism. And the Campaign had all the appearance of a liberal challenge.[4] Campaign leaders used concepts and language derived from the Western liberal

[1] Mandela, *No Easy Walk*, p. 181.

[2] Report of the Joint Planning Council of the A.N.C. and the S.A.I.C., reprinted as Appendix C in Kuper, *Passive Resistance*, pp. 248–56.

[3] It seems doubtful that those who planned the Defiance Campaign were influenced by Gandhi to the extent which van den Berghe claims. See his *South Africa*, pp. 158, 161.

[4] This is a view supported by Leo Kuper. In his study of the 1952 Campaign he concludes that 'the immediate aims, and the assumptions underlying the resistance movement, are consistent with the spirit of liberalism'. He concedes, however, that the ultimate objectives of the participants ... will vary with their political outlook—liberal, Marxist or nationalist.' (*Passive Resistance*, p. 45.)

tradition. Moreover, the Campaign had an indubitably liberal purpose; the abolition of laws discriminating on grounds of race.[1]

For many the choice of method—that of non-violent passive resistance—was primarily a strategical decision, the appropriate method for the existing situation.[2] But whatever the variety of reasons for choosing this particular strategy, it was a method guaranteed to give the Campaign an appearance of moderation. For the Joint Planning Council—and for the A.N.C.—there were overwhelming practical reasons for rejecting at that stage the use of economic pressure through boycott or strike action. Such action would have served to divide the non-white races, whereas the campaign was in part intended to be an expression of their unity.[3] In addition, strike action would ultimately depend on African trade unions, which were generally weak; it would fail to involve the rural areas which the Council was anxious to include;[4] and the success of strike action required a disciplined response on a mass scale.[5] This last was something which in their existing state the Congresses could not guarantee; indeed, it was hoped that the Campaign would engender mass support.[6]

Moreover, previous strikes, most recently that of 1 May 1950, had revealed the likelihood of violence developing from strike action. Such strikes also demonstrated the overwhelming physical power of the Government. Thus violence was likely to be fruitless as well as hazardous and costly. Non-white leaders were forced none the less to acknowledge that with any non-white protest violence was an ever-

---

[1] The reaction of white liberals is discussed below, pp. 83 ff.

[2] In July 1951, a Conference of the National Executives of the A.N.C. and the S.A.I.C., as well as representatives from the Franchise Action Council, appointed a Joint Planning Council to outline plans for the Campaign (Kuper, *Passive Resistance*, p. 99). The Council's Report made clear the pragmatic base on which their recommendations had been made: 'With regard to the form of struggle best suited to our conditions we have been constrained to bear in mind the political and economic set-up of our country, the relationship of the rural to the urban population, the development of the trade union movement ... the economic status of the various sections of the non-white people and the level of organization of the National Liberatory movements.' (Ibid., p. 250.)

[3] ibid., p. 196.

[4] The Council realized it was imperative to gain support from the rural areas since the labour reserve was here. For this reason they included in the six laws against which they planned to protest, two which especially affected non-white in rural areas—the Population Registration Act and the Stock Limitation laws.

[5] Kuper, *Passive Resistance*, p. 196.

[6] Sampson, *Treason Cage*, p. 86; also Mandela, *No Easy Walk*, p. 22.

present possibility.[1] But in a project aimed at gaining wide non-white support, while at the same time giving minimum offence to the white community,[2] violence was an eventuality to be deliberately avoided—or at least, to be postponed for as long as possible.[3]

One of the most articulate spokesmen for the principle, as com-compared with the strategy, of non-violent passive resistance was the newly-elected President of the Natal Provincial Congress, Chief Albert Lutuli. Elaborating his reasons for rejecting violence, Lutuli sounded the impeccable white liberal. 'To refrain from violence is the sign of the civilized man as compared with the brute. The more truly civilized an individual is, the more likely he is to find peaceful methods of fighting for the things in which he believes. . . .'[4] Since white liberals in South Africa had customarily advocated the extension of the vote for all 'civilized' men, it is significant that Lutuli should see the use of non-violence as proof of civilization.

When Lutuli rejected violence on principle he may have represented only a minority view among A.N.C. leaders. But it seems likely that one of the reasons for adopting non-violence was that, as a body, Congress had traditionally been peaceable, in fact conciliatory, in its approach. And the Council aimed to capitalize on the strong liberal element in the rank and file of the A.N.C. The Campaign would scarcely have engendered such strong support at the grass-roots level—or even the initial sanction of the A.N.C. Conference in December 1951—but for the categorical rejection of violence implicit in the technique of passive resistance.

If the actual choice of method was largely the outcome of strategic

[1] Duma Nokwe made this point about the constant threat of violence in an interview with the author, Dar es Salaam, 15 Nov. 1965. Lutuli implies a similar awareness. Of violence, he says, 'It will do neither them nor us any good, and if they get it, it will not be from Congress. It will be simply the result of unendurable provocation, of trading for too long on a patience which has its limits. If the whites continue at present, nobody will give the signal for mass violence. Nobody will need to.' (*Let My People Go*, p. 103.) During the course of the Campaign, Joe Matthews wrote to his father, Z. K. Matthews, from the centre of resistance in the Eastern Cape. Speaking of the resisters in Natal, he said, 'I only hope it will be possible to keep down the spirit of Chaka and infuse the spirit of Ghandi among the Zulu masses. . . .' (Letter dated 3 Sept. 1952, mim., P.A.S.)

[2] Kuper, *Passive Resistance*, p. 43.

[3] Late in June 1952 Joe Matthews explained to his father that the planning for the third stage of the Campaign had been completed. He said it was clear such action would lead to violence which would not help the cause of the resisters. (Letter, n.d., mim., P.A.S.)

[4] Mary Benson, *Chief Albert Lutuli of South Africa* (Cape Town, O.U.P., 1963), p. 21.

considerations, the Campaigners proceeded with stated aims and in a manner entirely consistent with the tenets of Western liberal democracy. Their initial approach to the Government was in a letter to the Prime Minister—a letter which records the essentially liberal spirit in which they made their demands. Writing on behalf of the A.N.C., Moroka and Sisulu emphasized that the Africans had previously used 'every constitutional method' to press their 'legitimate demands', in particular, 'their inherent right to be directly represented in Parliament, Provincial and the Municipal Councils and in all Councils of the State'.[1] But consecutive governments had continued, they said to deprive them of 'fundamental human rights enjoyed in all democratic communities . . .' and rejected the A.N.C.'s 'offer of co-operation'.[2] They made no immediate claim for these full democratic rights, but instead asked for the repeal of six discriminatory laws. They sought to stress that they were not being anti-white, nor challenging the legal system as a whole: 'The struggle which our people are about to begin is not directed against any race or national group but against the unjust laws . . .'[3]

The Government's rejection of these claims was complete. They joined issue with the A.N.C. over the question of the 'inherent right' of the Bantu. In their view the differences between the races were 'permanent and not man-made'.[4] And they saw the non-whites' overtures, not as 'a genuine offer of co-operation, but an attempt to embark on the first steps towards supplanting European rule in the course of time.'[5] Special reference was made to the A.N.C.'s objective of full political rights; non-white majority rule, which would be the outcome, was quite unacceptable to the Nationalists, as it was to most of the white community. Those who threatened white rule were characterized as a minority willing to sacrifice the best interests of the masses in order to satisfy their 'political ambitions'.[6] Thus the Government's reply to the A.N.C. said:

It should be understood clearly that the Government will under no circumstances entertain the idea of giving administrative or executive or legislative powers over Europeans, or within an European community, to Bantu men and women, or to other smaller non-European groups.[7]

[1] Kuper, *Passive Resistance*, Appendix B, p. 233.
[2] ibid., pp. 233–4.   [3] ibid., p. 235.
[4] In a letter from the Office of the Prime Minister, dated 29 Jan. 1952, reprinted in Kuper, *Passive Resistance*, Appendix B, pp. 235–9.
[5] ibid., p. 237.   [6] ibid.   [7] ibid., p. 236.

In a second letter, Moroka and Sisulu did not move a fraction out-side their original frame of reference. They reiterated that the Africans wanted 'fundamental human rights in the land of their birth'. They were, they considered, 'left with no alternative' but to embark on the Defiance Campaign.[1]

As Lutuli later pointed out, this exchange of letters underlined the lack of 'a common language' between the non-white leaders and the Government.[2] The views expressed were fundamentally at odds. The idiom which the A.N.C. used was that of liberalism. As Leo Kuper explains in his *Passive Resistance in South Africa*, Congress was proceeding

... on the basis of a liberal humanitarian creed, which asserts the dignity of the human personality, the belief that all men are born equal, the conviction that the human being is educable, and the assumption that history is the story of the unfolding of freedom.[3]

As a consequence, they were able to evoke sympathy from those abroad who shared their values; they were also to compel a number of those whites in South Africa who regarded themselves as liberals to adjust their assumptions or modify their principles.

[1] Letter dated 11 Feb. 1952, reprinted in Kuper, *Passive Resistance*, Appendix B, pp. 239–41.
[2] *Let My People Go*, p. 105.
[3] Kuper, *Passive Resistance*, p. 109.

CHAPTER IV

The Defiance Campaign and its effects on whites and non-whites

i

The non-white Defiance Campaign which began on 26 June 1952 marked the opening of a new and critical phase in the history of political liberalism in South Africa. The Campaign and its aftermath together with the parliamentary election of 1953 caused a major re-alignment of liberal forces in South Africa. A group of white liberals who were profoundly influenced by the events of this period now made explicit their dissent from United Party colour policy. Yet the prime importance of maintaining non-Nationalist unity in the face of the forthcoming election prevented the formation of a separate liberal party until after the Nationalists had been returned to power. At the same time, liberals and liberal views underwent revaluation within the A.N.C. But even before the election—and the U.P. defeat—Congress leaders had become more radical than they were before the Defiance Campaign. Thus, as white liberals searched for a means to bridge the gap between white and non-white, that gap itself was widening.

ii

The Defiance Campaign was of great importance in producing an identifiable and unified body of white liberals in South Africa. The Campaign as a whole, its aims, its progress, the reaction which it provoked, was a challenge without precedent to those whites who professed to hold liberal views about colour. There was much about the actual conduct of the Campaign which sustained the earlier impression of moderation. The first of the resisters submitted themselves for arrest on 26 June 1952.[1] In general, the acts of defiance were

---

[1] Kuper, *Passive Resistance*, p. 122. This date had special significance for the A.N.C., since 26 June 1950 had been the date of Congress's first general strike. Later, on the same date, the Congress of the People was held in 1955, and, in 1957, an A.N.C. protest was staged against pass laws and a campaign launched for a minimum wage of a pound a day. 26 June had, by then, become at least in

distinguished by their deliberately non-violent character. In Johannes-burg, for instance, the first volunteers entered Boksburg location illegally only after the local magistrate had been officially informed by letter that 'they would deliberately court imprisonment. . . .'[1] By mid December, 8,057 volunteers[2] had been taken into custody as a result of their contravening pass laws or violating *apartheid* regula-tions. There was a studious forbearance in the volunteers' reaction to their arrest and trial, and also the imprisonment which many of them suffered.[3]

The clearest challenge to the *status quo* came from the Eastern Cape.[4] The number of arrests made there exceeded the total number of arrests made in all other Campaign centres in the Union.[5] Different explanations, complementary, rather than contradictory, have been offered for this prominence. It seems likely that the homogeneity of the Africans in the area made it easier to organize the volunteers effectively.[6] In addition, the Xhosa of the area had been strongly in-fluenced by Christian missionaries and their faith appears to have helped stimulate the local enthusiasm for the Campaign.[7] Significant, also, was the fact that the Cape Province was the one area in the Union where, until 1936, Africans had been entitled to the franchise. In that year they were removed from the common roll. Limited though their political rights had been, their exercise had built up a unique political awareness and an attachment to parliamentary government. Moreover, in the Eastern Cape relations between whites and Africans had been customarily more easygoing than elsewhere.[8] Influx control and pass laws, for instance, had never been strictly enforced by the local authorities. It seems reasonable to suppose that

---

the view of Congress leaders 'the people's day, born of travail and tempered in the heat of struggle'. (Alfred Hutchinson in *Fighting Talk*, July 1957.)

[1] Kuper, *Passive Resistance*, p. 125.

[2] This figure is taken from the Survey prepared for the National Action Com-mittee, dated 16 Dec. 1952, mim., P.A.S.

[3] Kuper, *Passive Resistance*, p. 126; Sampson, *Treason Cage*, p. 88.

[4] Carter, *The Politics of Inequality*, p. 376.

[5] See Survey prepared for the National Action Committee, dated 16 Dec. 1952, mim., P.A.S.

[6] An opinion expressed by Robert Resha, in an interview with the author, Adelaide, 8 Oct. 1966. In contrast, Resha argued, one difficulty of organization which the Transvaal leaders faced was how to cope with the tribal differences of migrant workers.

[7] Kuper, *Passive Resistance*, pp. 146–9; Benson, *The African Patriots*, p. 184.

[8] Benson, op cit., p. 187.

the fervour shown by the volunteers in towns like East London and Port Elizabeth was directly related to their fear of losing existing rights and privileges.[1]

Gwendolen Carter claims that the Defiance Campaign had practically no effect in awakening sympathy among Europeans.[2] But it certainly divided those interested in a liberal policy towards non-whites more sharply from their fellow-whites. It is true these liberals appeared to most Congress leaders to be playing the same theme as the rest of the whites—or only banal variations of that theme.[3] None the less, it seems likely that the frustration of being identified with the majority of whites *did* encourage white liberals to think in terms of a separate Liberal Party.[4]

Among white liberals, there was a distinctive reaction to the use of non-violent passive resistance. Both the leaders of the Institute of Race Relations and the Native Representatives appreciated the dilemma in which politically articulate non-whites were placed. True, before the Campaign had begun, the Institute attempted to discourage the A.N.C. from continuing with their plans.[5] But this was in anticipation of the particularly disruptive effects of violence in a multiracial society rather than a want of sympathy for the predicament of non-whites. In the same statement the Institute leaders said:

> It should be realised . . . that with the abolition of the Native Representative Council the African people have no adequate legitimate channel through which to express their grievances and needs and that public demonstrations carried out in an orderly manner are a recognised legitimate method of expressing public opinion and the only effective means of expression open to Africans.[6]

[1] Julius Lewin, 'The Rise of Congress in South Africa', in *Political Quarterly*, 24 (1953), 303.

[2] Carter, *The Politics of Inequality*, p. 373.

[3] e.g. after the Campaign had begun, the Institute of Race Relations offered to act as an intermediary with the Government. Joe Matthews wrote to his father: 'The Insitute . . . has again appealed to the government to call the leaders, with them as middle-man. They do not know how much they annoy us by these attempts. The impression they give is that the Congress will agree to negotiate if they say so.' Letter dated 5 Aug. 1952, mim., P.A.S.

[4] Lutuli considered that the Liberal Party, in particular, was 'very much the child of these times' (*Let My People Go*, p. 125).

[5] See the Statement issued to the Press on 14 Mar. 1952, and reprinted in *Race Relations News*, xiv, 4 (Apr. 1952), 37.

[6] ibid.; cf. a later Statement (of August 1952) in which the Institute leaders conceded that because there was 'no real avenue of approach and expression', there was 'no other course of action for Non-Europeans to adopt save passive resistance' (*Race Relations News*, xiv, 10 (Oct. 1952), 111–12).

G

The impact of the Defiance Campaign on the thinking of liberal whites can be gauged by a signed statement which appeared in the journal *Forum*, in October 1952. Included among the group of prominent citizens who signed this statement were some who committed themselves to the Liberal Association four months later, and subsequently helped form the Liberal Party in May 1953.[1] According to the signatories, the Campaign was a 'challenge to those who hold the reins of government; and . . . not less, a challenge to all who participate in the exercise of political power, i.e. the whole white community.'[2] Their 'immediate short-term programme of reform' was for the repeal of 'mischievous measures' such as the Group Areas Act (1950), the Suppression of Communism Act (1950), and the pass laws (1952).[3] The principles on which the Liberal Party was to be founded were clearly forecast in the *Forum* statement, which said:

We believe that it is imperative that South Africa now adopt a policy that will attract the support of educated, politically conscious, non-Europeans, by offering them a reasonable status in our common society. This can be done by a revival of the liberal tradition which prevailed for so many years with such successful results in the Cape Colony. That tradition, an integral part of South African history, was based on firm principle, namely *equal rights for all civilized people and equal opportunities for all men and women to become civilized.*[4]

The riots in the Eastern Cape in October and November 1952 were another important catalyst of liberal white opinion—and illiberal white opinion. Those whites with liberal views on colour had previously been in an isolated and minority position among whites when urban rioting occurred. After the Durban riots in 1949, for example, two officers of the Institute of Race Relations, Maurice Webb and Kenneth Kirkwood, published a report on the Commission and its findings.[5] They revealed a sympathetic, though not uncritical, understanding of the complex causes of the riots, and of the far-reaching changes which would be needed to prevent a recurrence. Again, after the May riots in 1950, both the Native Representatives and the Institute leaders recommended that the Government arrange a national convention to plan a mutually acceptable non-white policy.[6]

[1] e.g. Margaret Ballinger, W. C. Ballinger, Julius Lewin, Leo Marquard, Donald Molteno, Alan Paton.
[2] *Forum* (Oct. 1952).   [3] ibid.
[4] ibid. See above, p. 5, also below, pp. 112, 117.
[5] Webb and Kirkwood, *The Durban Riots and After.* See above, p. 71.
[6] Horrell, *Action, Reaction and Counteraction*, p. 10.

The Institute's request included a precondition that non-white leaders be included in such a convention.[1] Not surprisingly, liberals such as these reacted to the riots in the Eastern Cape in a distinctive way.

The riots coincided in time and place with the local staging of the Defiance Campaign. With the aid of Government publicity and white newspapers, the two events were immediately associated in the minds of a large proportion of the white population.[2] A startling and telling instance of this was the publicity given by white newspapers in general, and Government spokesmen in particular, to the deaths—not of twenty-six Africans—but of six whites.[3] One of these was a nun, Sister Aidan, a social worker among the non-whites, who was brutally beaten to death. The A.N.C. Youth Leaguer, Joe Matthews, commented bitterly: 'There seems to be a feeling that the death of six Europeans is the most vital political event that has occurred in South Africa.'[4]

Unlike most other whites, white liberals refused to oversimplify the causes of the riots; they also refused to judge the non-whites *en masse*. The President of the Institute exhibited a tolerance typical of these liberals in his explanation to the Institute's members:

> The political consciousness of the educated and otherwise sophisticated African has begun to permeate the masses of the African people at least in European areas. While the former are determined not to acquiesce in laws which derogate from human dignity and to demand citizen rights, the latter are rendered unhappy and sullen by the misery of inadequate housing, high food prices and the tensions caused by political and administrative measures.[5]

Two other developments—each related to the Defiance Campaign—must have helped to edge white liberals towards action on the colour question. Both events represented a particular challenge because they involved whites committing themselves unequivocally to the non-white cause. The first was the founding of the Congress of Democrats (C.O.D.). In November 1952, Oliver Tambo, a Youth Leaguer, and Yusuf Cachalia, a leading figure in the South African

---

[1] ibid.
[2] See Kuper's analysis of the variety (and lack of variety) of white responses to the Defiance Campaign in *Passive Resistance in South Africa*, pp. 154–80.
[3] Figures taken from Horrell, *Action, Reaction and Counteraction*, p. 12.
[4] In a letter to Z. K. Matthews, 13 Nov. 1952, mim., P.A.S.
[5] *Race Relations News*, xiv, 12 (Dec. 1952), 136; also Margaret Ballinger, *Ass. Debates*, vol. 81, 11 Feb. 1953, col. 1048.

Indian Congress, called a meeting in Darragh Hall in Johannesburg.[1] It was a unique occasion. They had invited all those whites to attend who had seemed sympathetic to their aims in staging the Defiance Campaign. To the diverse group that gathered as a result, they suggested that the whites establish 'a parallel white organization' to work in the closest possible co-operation with the A.N.C. and the S.A.I.C.[2] Here was an ideal with great appeal to the white communists who had been associated with the Congresses, and it was from these that the C.O.D. gained the bulk of its initial support. In addition, the move was backed by the Springbok Legion, the left-wing ex-servicemen's organization, whose leader, Cecil Williams, had encouraged Tambo and Cachalia in their plan.[3]

Here was immediately a reason for some liberals refusing to join. Margaret Ballinger, for example, whose decision was no doubt influential, would not commit herself to a group which was, in her view, so obviously communist.[4] And the fear—perhaps jealousy—of the communists which persisted among white liberals, both inside and outside the Liberal Party, suggest this was a powerful deterrent for a number of those who had gone to the Darragh Hall meeting with high hopes. There were those, too, who avoided the C.O.D. because it was planned as a 'parallel' organization; if they committed themselves it would be to a multiracial group, rather than to a white one.[5] In addition, the Congress of Democrats immediately made it clear that it stood for universal adult suffrage.[6] For a number of different reasons, this was a policy unacceptable to most white liberals in the early fifties. To some the principle of a qualified vote was sacrosanct; it was desirable in principle. To others the qualified vote was undesirable in principle but necessary in the South African situation; manhood suffrage would mean the swamping of racial minorities, including the white minority. There were those, too, who were convinced that a franchise based, for example, on educational qualifications was tactically wisest since it would be more palatable to the

---

[1] *Advance*, 27 Nov. 1952.
[2] Author's interview with Duma Nokwe, Dar es Salaam, 15 Nov. 1965.
[3] *Advance*, 27 Nov. 1952.
[4] Author's interview with Margaret Ballinger, Cape Town, 9 Dec. 1965.
[5] Marion Friedmann claimed this was her main reason for bypassing the C.O.D. (author's interview, London, 23 Sept. 1965). She subsequently became a foundation member of the Liberal Party, and was a member of the Party's Transvaal Executive from 1953 to 1961.
[6] *Advance*, 27 Nov. 1952.

white community.[1] All of these arguments presupposed that a qualified vote was still a policy acceptable to non-whites.

Whatever the reasons for liberals declining to join the C.O.D.—and
the reasons were probably additive with most—the emergence of the
C.O.D. was a clear challenge to white liberals. It was a challenge
which C.O.D. spokesmen lost no opportunity in spelling out. In the
C.O.D. booklet, *The Threatened People*, which was issued soon after
their founding, they pinned down the liberal position with uncomfort-
able accuracy:

> Twenty or thirty years ago [it said] the offer of the hand of friendship
> of the White man, and the creation of Joint Committees to meet the
> Non-European on some equal footing was a timely and even revolutionary
> advance towards race co-operation. ... Today, if Europeans talk to
> Non-Europeans of co-operation, it must not be on terms deemed adequate
> by the Europeans alone, but on the realities of the aspirations of an articu-
> late Non-European political movement.[2]

The communist-run newspaper, *Advance*, was also a mouthpiece
for C.O.D. opinion and frequently indicted white liberals. In January
1953 they were condemned for refusing to adopt a policy 'other than
one of social reforms'.[3] In particular, the Institute of Race Relations
came under fire for its 'wishwashy [*sic*] position'. 'Without principles
to guide it [the correspondent wrote], the Institute (like all South
African Liberalism) has been reduced to impotency, not only unable
to influence events but quite incapable of assessing their true sign.'[4]

Suspected and abused, and in their view misunderstood, on so
many fronts, the white liberals were confronted in December 1952
with a practical and compelling instance of 'liberalism in action'.
In both Johannesburg and Cape Town, two small groups of whites
joined the resisters in acts of defiance.[5] The Germiston group in
Johannesburg caused the greater stir. The seven whites included
Patrick Duncan, the son of a former Governor-General of the Union,
and, to judge from his family background, scarcely then a young man
to identify himself lightly with an illegal action, let alone one so clearly
pro-African. After two weeks' imprisonment, Duncan paid a £100
fine—ironically, something an African volunteer would find hard to

---

[1] These different lines of reasoning were voiced during the debate on the
franchise at the Liberal Party's first National Conference, Johannesburg, 11–13
July 1953.
[2] *The Threatened People* (1954), P.A.S., p. 25.   [3] *Advance*, 8 Jan. 1953.
[4] ibid.   [5] Benson, *The African Patriots*, pp. 189–90.

do.[1] But he made his arrest and trial the occasion to voice what he considered the choice for liberal whites. It was, he said, 'urgently necessary' to work for a government which would 'attract the loyalty of all races. . . .'[2] He considered the 'latent power' of the largely African working-class of crucial importance in defeating 'embattled Afrikaner nationalism'. And he wanted this to be channelled not into the Communist Party, or a 'Pan-African Nationalist Party', but into a 'South African Party open to all races on a programme of emancipation'.[3]

In my view [he concluded] the future of South Africa depends on the success of this third alternative and my individual action was aimed at affirming this truth, at pointing the way to common action, and at the same time clearly dissociating myself from the colour bar.[4]

Duncan's reasoning was close to that of most white liberals. Because they shared his views, his active involvement emphasized their inaction. Indeed he had, by his commitment, offered a challenge not only to the Government, but to many of the liberals.

iii

While the Defiance Campaign and its aftermath drove white liberals to reappraise their position, they were confronted with the prospect of the forthcoming election. There was widespread optimism among non-Nationalist whites that the Government would be defeated. Consequently it was of prime strategic importance that the liberals avoid any move before the election which would hazard the United Party's chances. Such a consideration dictated the policy of the Cape Town Liberal Group during the months of the Defiance Campaign. Their concern to become an effective force on the colour issue was consistently overridden by the necessity of maintaining non-Nationalist unity.

In August 1952, for example, Wollheim stressed that they were in

---

[1] After fourteen days' hard labour, Duncan's bad leg was painful, and he was also troubled by a gastric ulcer. See 'Patrick Duncan', in Peter Benenson, *Persecution 1961* (Penguin Books, 1961), p. 73.

[2] This statement of Duncan's was included in a biographical piece in *The Times* (London), 29 Sept. 1960.

[3] ibid.

[4] ibid. See the comment by Miss Freda Troupe, another of the Germiston defiers: 'We face the appalling danger that the present racial breach will widen beyond all bridging. . . .' *Advance*, 11 Dec. 1952.

an 'extremely delicate situation in connection with the next election.
...'[1] Yet, at the same meeting, Professor Beinart was asked to draw
up a shadow constitution for a possible future Liberal Party. It was
clear, the Minute Secretary recorded, 'that members felt that the
Group might have to become politically aware at an earlier date
than was originally anticipated'.[2]

By December 1952, the Group numbered 126, and Dr. Wollheim
reported that similar organizations were 'springing up spontaneously
all over the country'. He referred principally to Johannesburg, where
Margaret Ballinger, and her husband William, both of them Members
of Parliament, had organized a 'study and research group which did
not wish at present to become active politically'; there, too, Julius
Lewin, an expert in native law at the University of the Witwatersrand,
led a group whose primary aim was to liberalize the United Party;
in addition, an advocate, Jack Unterhalter, and his supporters were
seeking contact 'with all sections of the population including African
and Indian Congresses and trade unions'.[3] Meanwhile, in Natal, there
were at least two such groups established—in Pietermaritzburg, and
at the University in Durban.[4] Yet this range of support did not
induce the Cape Town group to deviate from their original decision.
Early in December they still determined to avoid publicity until
after the 1953 election, and 'to recruit only by invitation'.[5]

In January 1953, however, a South African Liberal Association
was formed. Its aim was 'to co-ordinate various liberal activities
and movements all over the country', a move which Dr. Oscar
Wollheim emphasized was 'urgently necessary if they were to become
politically effective'.[6] The vexed question of strategy was reopened at
the Association's inaugural meeting held in Cape Town. Leo Marquard, the author and publisher, who had earlier signed the *Forum*

[1] Minutes of the Meeting of the S.A.L.G., Salt River, 28 Aug. 1952, mim.
P.A.S.

[2] ibid.

[3] Minutes of the Meeting of the S.A.L.G., Rondebosch, 8 Dec. 1952, mim.,
P.A.S.

[4] Evidence from Hans Meidner, a teacher at the University of Natal and
Chairman of the Liberal Party in Natal in the fifties (interviewed by the author,
Reading, England, 20 Sept. 1965).

[5] Minutes of the Meeting of the S.A.L.G., Rondebosch, 8 Dec. 1952, mim.,
P.A.S.

[6] Minutes of the A.G.M. of the South African Liberal Association (S.A.L.A.)
16–17 Jan. 1953, mim., P.A.S. Earlier, a decision to seek liaison with 'the
Ballinger group' had been taken at an informal discussion at Kenilworth, Cape
Province, on 17 Dec. 1952.

statement and was now Chairman of the new body, raised the fundamental question of whether the liberals should—or should not—form a new party: 'The issue before Liberals at present was whether to cut loose from their political alignments or to choose the lesser of two evils as between the two major political parties.'[1] Marquard's own reluctance to 'cut loose' seems to have had important grounds other than an unwillingness to embarrass the U.P. Apparently he doubted whether enough of the Association's supporters were convinced of the necessity for a new non-racial party; he obviously feared the repercussions if an attempt to form such a party were made prematurely. He spoke, for example, of the 'grave responsibility' of those who, by the formation of a new group, would raise hopes among whites and non-whites. And he was obviously concerned to take what he called 'like-minded' non-whites into 'the fullest partnership and co-operation' from the outset—a precondition which he acknowledged it would not be easy to fulfil.[2] After prolonged debate, the new Association's members agreed to postpone the immediate formation of a separate political party in view of the imminent election. Instead they undertook to work 'behind the scenes' in the hope that their views would have a leavening influence in United Party circles, sufficient to effect reform in the official Opposition's racial policy.[3]

There was, however, no liberal redirection of U.P. colour policy prior to the election. On the contrary, shortly after the Liberal Association was formed, United Party colour policy became freshly suspect from a liberal point of view. Late in January the Nationalist Government introduced two Bills designed to prevent any repetition of the Defiance Campaign. The terms of the Public Safety Bill empowered the Government to declare a state of emergency in the face of civil disobedience and the Criminal Law Amendment Bill, once enacted, would harshly circumscribe the rights to campaign in protest against laws.[4] While the Second Reading of the Public Safety Bill was in progress, the Government announced the election date.[5] Such timing, whether deliberate or not, served only to highlight the United Party's dilemma. With an election in the offing they could not risk appearing to disagree with the Nationalists that the overriding con-

---

[1] Minutes of the A.G.M. of the S.A.L.A., 16–17 Jan. 1953, mim., P.A.S.
[2] ibid.   [3] ibid.
[4] Horrell, *Legislation and Race Relations*, pp. 49–50.
[5] Carter, *The Politics of Inequality*, p. 161.

sideration was the preservation of law and order. In any case, they were urged to support the new legislation by their own supporters in the predominantly U.P. areas of the Eastern Cape where rioting had occurred.[1]

The parliamentary debate on the two police measures clarified the position of white liberals. Their view, voiced by the Native Representatives and Labour M.P.s, was a minority one, and quite distinct from that offered by U.P. members. In discussing the Public Safety Bill, for example, Margaret Ballinger stressed that she distinguished between the A.N.C. leaders whom she considered trustworthy, and the 'gangster element' on whom she blamed the riots.[2] The passive resistance campaign, she argued,

... represents the determination of an important section of the African population to endeavour to fix attention on those aspects of our policy to which they are opposed, on the ground that it has no other way of making a protest that will impress this country.[3]

In contrast, although U.P. members hastened to attribute the riots to bad government, and even made efforts to free 'the law-abiding non-European' from blame, they generally evinced a much more arbitrary view of the cause of the riots. The United Party M.P., Mr. H. G. Lawrence, for example, saw the New Brighton riots as 'a reversion to some kind of primitive, savage, barbaric blood-lust'.[4] The U.P. leader, J. G. N. Strauss, claimed that if his party were returned to power they would 'consult moderate and responsible leaders',[5] but he had difficulty in countering the Nationalists' questions about whom he considered 'moderate and responsible'.

The nature of its leadership was one of the important ways in which the A.N.C. had changed. And Dr. H. F. Verwoerd, as Minister of Native Affairs, pointed out how those whom the Nationalists had

[1] ibid., p. 164.
[2] *Ass. Debates*, vol. 81, 16 Feb. 1953, col. 1239.
[3] ibid., 11 Feb. 1953, col. 1048.
[4] ibid., col. 991. United Party M.P.s generally failed to see that the riots were the work of a minority element, deplored as much by the local residents and the A.N.C. leadership as by the whites. cf. the conclusion reached by D. H. Reader in his study of the area where the rioting occurred. The respectable in the municipal areas, he claims, refused to be involved. 'Bolted doors and silent streets were the order of the day in municipal housing during the disturbances, and many of the residents sought safety in flight or at the police station.' *The Black Man's Portion: History, Demography and Living Conditions in the Native Locations of East London, Cape Province* (Cape Town, O.U.P., 1961), p. 28.
[5] *Ass. Debates*, vol. 81, 27 Jan. 1953, col. 95.

once regarded as 'reliable' were no longer to be trusted.[1] He ignored the crucial role which the Nationalists themselves had played in transforming the A.N.C.; in describing what he obviously—and rightly—considered as a drastic change of outlook on the part of Lutuli, he showed no appreciation of the kind of pressures and sense of frustration to which Lutuli had responded by supporting the Defiance Campaign. Lutuli, he said, 'always used to be considered by my Department as a moderate person but . . . [he] now propagates a policy of equal rights and . . . is chairman of the A.N.C. . . .'[2] Dwelling, as they frequently did, on the A.N.C. policy of equal rights, Government spokesmen questioned the direction of the non-white policy of the U.P. Mr. A. Mentz, a Nationalist M.P., for instance threw down the gauntlet by pointing to the ambiguity of what he called an 'ultra-liberalistic section' within the U.P.[3] He added, 'The non-European question will have to be solved either by means of apartheid or by means of equality. . . .'[4] Challenges such as this hurled at the Opposition made explicit the choice which faced all South African whites.

That these were the only alternatives was further underlined by the United Party's eventual support for both punitive measures. It was less than three years since they had rejected the principle of the Suppression of Communism Bill.[5] Their volte-face over the Public Safety Bill and the Criminal Law Amendment Bill could be interpreted only as a withdrawal to a more conservative position on the colour question. They were careful to secure the Nationalists' guarantee that neither of the new laws would be used against white political opponents.[6] Such a bargain served only to increase the disillusion of the more liberal spirits in the Torch Commando, and to dampen their enthusiasm for the forthcoming election.[7] Members of the Liberal

---

[1] ibid., 30 Jan. 1953, col. 302. Government spokesmen pointed to instances of Congress leaders being repudiated because their views were relatively moderate, e.g. the Minister of Justice, Mr. C. R. Swart, mentioned Moroka's rejection for Presidency of the A.N.C. in 1952 (*Ass. Debates*, vol. 81, 10 Feb. 1953, col. 1272).

[2] *Ass. Debates*, vol. 81, 30 Jan. 1953, col. 302.

[3] ibid., 12 Feb. 1953, col. 1101.

[4] ibid.; also Mr. C. R. Swart: 'There is no middle course. Either we retain control of the affairs of this country and legislation in the hands of the Europeans or we do not retain it. . . .' ibid., col. 1141.

[5] See above, p. 47.

[6] Carter, *The Politics of Inequality*, p. 327. cf. the later statement (19 Feb.) by the Minister of Justice, Mr. C. R. Swart, that the Government was prepared to use the Public Safety Act against the Torch Commando if necessary (ibid., p. 164).

[7] Carter, *The Politics of Inequality*, p. 327.

Association were equally distressed—and just as hamstrung by the closeness of the election. The protests which they were anxious to lodge against the new police measures had to be made, they decided, as *individuals* rather than as a formal protest from the Association.[1] The most constructive tactical move they could make within the general strategy they had accepted was to contact any white groups with comparable values and aims. To this end, representatives of the Association had informal talks with Labour Party M.P.s.[2] Early in April they reported that the latter had agreed to 'co-operate as closely as possible', and in particular to promote the Association's principles in Parliament.[3]

Meanwhile, the United Party soft-pedalled the colour question during the election campaign. They did challenge the Nationalists over the issue of economic integration, but in view of their concession to the Government on the new punitive laws, and the conservatism of the majority of their supporters, they could offer no clear alternative to *apartheid*. Consequently, party spokesmen stressed those issues which had customarily been the source of widest support for the United Party. They emphasized 'white' issues such as the unity of the white races, language equality, economic development, and the cost of living—all issues over which it was hoped a majority of the electorate would be in agreement.[4]

Thus, prior to the 1953 election, the United Party, contrary to liberals' hopes, retreated on the colour question. And they did so at a time when relations across the colour line had deteriorated sharply as a result of the Defiance Campaign. This crisis for white liberals coincided with the practical necessity to support the United Party as the only moderate alternative to the Nationalists in the 1953 election. The most optimistic of the liberals could, and did, interpret the U.P. retreat as a strategic withdrawal designed to gain votes in the election. Only for a minority of liberals was it conclusive proof that the U.P. would never take an unequivocal stand in favour of the extension of rights to non-whites.

---

[1] Minutes of the S.A.L.A. Council Meeting, Cape Town, 5 Feb. 1953, mim., P.A.S.
[2] ibid.　　[3] ibid., 9 Apr. 1953.
[4] Carter, *The Politics of Inequality*, pp. 168–9.

iv

As the Defiance Campaign ground to a halt early in 1953, A.N.C. leaders reassessed their position. In doing so, they revealed themselves to be newly critical of those whites who, within their own world, were regarded as liberals. Here can be seen part of the process of liberalism among non-whites developing to mean something substantially different than it did among white liberals. Clouded by other issues, this is a distinction difficult to draw. But it is an important one for it does much to explain why attempts at interracial co-operation between black and white liberals in the mid fifties were not more fruitful.

As early as June 1949 the writer of an article in *Inkundla Ya Bantu*— the only newspaper fully owned and operated by Africans—had spoken of 'pangs of an independent existence' pulsating 'within the Liberal heart'.[1]

> The Liberals . . . are obviously at the crossroads. They can either march out of the [United] Party and stand on their own or they can wait and watch the process of internal decay within the United Party in the hope that they might ultimately capture the machinery of this organisation.[2]

To non-whites, the Defiance Campaign made this choice on the part of white liberals unavoidable. In particular, the United Party's reaction to the Campaign meant the liberals would have to choose to 'stand on their own'. Writing to his father over the months of the Defiance Campaign, Joe Matthews, who was one of the Campaign leaders in the Eastern Cape, made frequent reference to his disillusionment with the United Party. Strauss, he was convinced, 'would like to sidestep Congress and manufacture some good-boys [sic] outside the A.N.C.'[3] He referred, too, to the shifts in opinion among the whites:

> . . . I predicted that the country would gradually divide up into reactionaries behind the Nats [sic] and progressives of all shades behind the A.N.C. That is now reality or almost reality. The Whites will have to form a party that is prepared to make definite changes or join Congress.[4]

---

[1] *Inkundla Ya Bantu*, 11 June 1949.   [2] ibid.
[3] Letter dated 16 Sept. 1952, mim., P.A.S.
[4] ibid. Since Congress did not accept whites as members, Matthews was presumably referring to the possibility of whites who endorsed A.N.C. aims forming a parallel organization. It this sense, whites 'joined Congress' in November 1952, when the Congress of Democrats was formed. See above, p. 87.

No such realignment involving white liberals took place prior to the election. Yet in that period a number of them expressed views which in their own community differentiated them sharply from the Government and from the United Party.[1] It was over this issue of racial policy that the Liberal Party was to emerge immediately after the election—a radical move within the white world though much less startling to non-whites.[2] During the Defiance Campaign the non-white leaders had looked to people like the future founders of the Liberal Party to take an unequivocal stand against the Government. Instead, the misgivings they expressed at the time seemed to the Congress leaders only minor ones. *Apartheid*, which provided with increasing efficiency for all kinds of tangible segregation, guaranteed also that the non-whites were prevented from appreciating the issues over which the whites were divided. The comparative silence of white liberals was, to the non-whites, tantamount to collusion. To A.N.C. leaders the contrast between white liberals and the C.O.D. was an invidious one. Those radical whites, including a large number of communists, who subscribed to the C.O.D. identified themselves with the A.N.C. and with African nationalism in a way that white liberals were clearly not prepared to do.

Suspicion of betrayal by those whites who professed to be liberal was a major theme at the A.N.C. Cape Provincial Congress held on 14 February 1953. This was just two days after the United Party had supported the principle of the Public Safety Bill. The degree of frustration which the A.N.C. leadership obviously felt may well have derived partly from the fact that it had been in the Cape that relations between the races had in the past been least subject to regulation. Hope of anything more positive developing out of the Cape liberal tradition was finally gone. Dr. J. L. Z. Njongwe, Acting Provincial President in Z. K. Matthews's absence, spoke of 'The unmasking and exposing of whites in South Africa.'[3] This, he said, was the 'most striking and remarkable feature' of the Defiance Campaign.[4] The United Party was freshly suspect for conniving at the Government's new restrictive legislation clearly directed at the campaigners. But their reactions, Joe Matthews claimed, had 'never indicated a funda-

[1] See above, pp. 83 ff.
[2] See below, pp. 119–20.
[3] Presidential Address to the Cape Provincial Congress, 14 Feb. 1953, mim., P.A.S.
[4] ibid.

mental disagreement with the Nationalists over the policy of maintaining a slave system in the country.'[1]

More significantly, Joe Matthews warned the delegates against taking seriously 'the appeal of those who call themselves "Liberals" or "Friends" of the African people. . . .'[2] They were, he contended, a 'weak and an ineffective force in South African politics. . . .'[3] It was Dr. D. Mji, a Youth Leaguer newly elected to the National Executive, who was most outspoken. His charge was one, not of weakness, but of treachery.

Again, there has emerged, from the white camp, a large number of so-called liberals, who, shaken by the strength of the black man, are so afraid for their future, that they must now try to win the favour of our people, or try to be in such a position in relation to the struggle, so that they can be able to guide it along their own lines. . . . Liberals have for a very long time been the back-room boys of the African National Congress. Liberals, have, for a whole century, stumped the political growth of the African people. . . . Perhaps you wonder what I mean by 'LIBERAL'? A Liberal is an animal, commonly white in colour, though there are in the Liberal camp, found a few black cross-overs. A Liberal is a double dealer. . . . He (she) is mainly occupied in dividing our people, classifying them into civilised and uncivilised. . . . He (she) talks of a civilised voting standard for Africans and promises certain concessions and privileges for a certain type of African but collaborates with Malan to maintain the *status quo*.[4]

At first glance, Mji's rejection of the liberals seems complete. There is, however, clear evidence that he was rejecting the particular liberalism of South African whites. Certainly their liberalism had been characterized by a belief in the vote for every civilized man, a view which Mji derided. Moreover, he went on to condemn their gradualism:

I want to warn the African leaders that the temper of the common

---

[1] In a Political Review to the Cape Provincial Congress, 14 Feb. 1953, mim., P.A.S. In Matthews's opinion, the election would merely decide 'whether the Africans should be chastised with whips or scorpions. . . .' cf. the point made by Dr. D. Mji (President of the Traansvaal Youth League) to the same meeting: 'It must be clearly understood by our people that neither of the two major European political parties has any truly democratic designs for our people. The one differs from the other as a pick-pocket from a thief'. (Opening Address to the Cape Provincial Congress, 14 Feb. 1953, mim., P.A.S.)

[2] Political Review presented to the Cape Provincial Congress of the A.N.C., 14 Feb. 1953.

[3] ibid.

[4] Opening Address to the Cape Provincial Congress.

man is against all that Liberalism stands for; The people want full equality now! The people want to participate fully in shaping the destiny of their country; These [sic] they do not conceive as coming about ... through gradualistic make-shifts which must take them another one hundred years. They want freedom now. FREEDOM IN OUR LIFETIME.[1]

The gravamen of Mji's charge against the white liberals was their pace as much as their direction. In his own mind, the term 'liberalism' was synonymous with dilatory, compromising methods—'gradualistic make-shifts',[2] he called them.

The sense of urgency expressed in the cry 'FREEDOM IN OUR LIFE-TIME' was a central part of Congress philosophy as tempered by the Defiance Campaign. And with the accent so frequently on timing, it is easy—and misleading—to overlook that the aims which A.N.C. leaders were so anxious to attain were, in general terms at least, compatible with liberalism. More than once Mji had spoken of 'so-called liberals', implying that South African liberals were not liberals at all. This distinction does more than highlight the number of ways in which the term 'liberal' has been used and abused in South Africa —and elsewhere. It increases the weight of other evidence that liberal views were by no means antipathetic to Congress members.

The imperative note sounded by Mji was characteristic of the nationalism clearly evident in the period. And one of the main reasons why it becomes more and more difficult to trace easily the strands of liberalism within Congress philosophy is that where African leaders were directly concerned with ideology they were usually thinking and talking about nationalism. This had been true earlier. The clearest manifestation of it had been the emergence of the A.N.C. Youth League in the mid forties.[3] The experiences of the Defiance Campaign increased immeasurably the sense of nationalism among Africans in South Africa. This had been the intention of those who had planned the Campaign,[4] and there were clear signs that they had succeeded. Leaders later commented on the emergence of a 'conscious national pride',[5] and on 'the high degree of political consciousness' which had been engendered[6]—both facets of nationalism.

But this central concern with the growth of nationalism did not

[1] ibid.   [2] ibid.   [3] See above, p. 36.
[4] See the Statement taken from Chief Albert J. Luthuli in the case R. v. Adams and Others, n.d., mim., P.A.S., p. 6.
[5] Dr. J. L. Z. Njongwe in his Presidential Address to the Cape Provincial Congress, 14 Feb. 1953, mim., P.A.S.
[6] Nelson Mandela in Liberation (Nov. 1953), p. 16.

necessarily exclude liberal principles from A.N.C. philosophy—
although it implied a fundamental challenge to liberalism as South
African whites understood and practised it. 'The attainment of a
democratic government in South Africa, must', insisted Njongwe,
'be based on African Nationalism.'[1] He went on to say that to
Africans, democratic government meant 'the attainment of full
citizenship rights for all, irrespective of race, sex or creed'.[2] Clearly
the black concept of what constituted 'democratic government' was
crucially at odds with white interpretations, including that of the
white liberals. Herein lay a further cause for the difficulties in
communication which black and white liberals had in the mid
fifties—in the period before political opinion polarized so sharply
along racial lines that the clearly dominant philosophy on both sides
was nationalism, a black nationalism and a white nationalism. In the
early fifties, however, A.N.C. leaders—including some of the most
intensely nationalistic—retained their interest in some of the ideals
of liberal democracy. They also frequently expressed their acceptance of multiracialism.

> We accept and know [said Njongwe, for example] that the European,
> Indian and Coloured people are South Africans, no less than the Africans
> themselves . . . we shall not be a party to the development of racial arro-
> gance on the part of the African people. If my people developed racial
> arrogance and *herrenvolkism*, I would fight this menace just as we are now
> fighting Afrikaner Nationalism.[3]

Much of what African nationalists said did not run contrary to
the opinions of many of the consciously liberal-minded among the
non-whites. But there was, during the Defiance Campaign, a deliberate move against those Africans whom it was felt had become too

[1] In his Presidential Address to the Cape Provincial Congress, 14 Feb. 1953.
[2] ibid. Njongwe had earlier made reference to the fact that A.N.C. leaders
considered that the growth of African nationalism and a multiracial state were
completely compatible: 'We stand and [sic] fall on building a South African
Nation out of a multiracial society. . . .' (In his Opening Address to the Natal
Provincial Conference, 1 Nov. 1952, which was reproduced in *Afrika*, the
newsletter of the A.N.C. and Natal Indian Congress, No. 3, 7 Nov. 1952, mim.,
P.A.S.)
[3] In his Opening Address to the Natal Provincial Conference, 1 Nov. 1952.
Njongwe, however, conceded that anti-white feeling was likely to grow in the face
of white intransigence. cf. Joe Matthew's comment to Z. K. Matthews in August
1952: 'At the moment there is no bitterness towards Europeans—but things like
canes and the cat will engender such bitterness as will take years to eradicate.'
(Letter dated 5 Aug. 1952, mim., P.A.S.)

closely identified with white liberals and their views. In October 1952 Joe Matthews wrote to his father of the 'political infants' who thought 'sweet-reasonableness' would influence Malan.[1] Among those guilty of this palpably soft-minded liberal view were, in Matthews's opinion, Dr. Silas Molema and Dr. William Nkomo.[2] Later in the year, an Executive circular to Cape branches spoke of 'pleading, cowardly . . . leaders who were always ready to compromise after they had been flattered by taking tea with the rulers of the people. . . .' 'SAVE US [it later added] FROM THE TEA DRINKING LEADERS.'[3]

Within Congress then, the Campaign served to weed out, as Njongwe put it, 'political scorpions and opportunists'.[4] Special hostility was reserved for the ardent liberal and President of Congress, Dr. James Moroka. On trial for his part in the Campaign, Moroka arranged to be defended by separate counsel. This was a move contrary to the prearranged resolution for the volunteers to stand trial as a group.[5] In addition, his lawyer pleaded in mitigation that Moroka's ancestors had helped the Voortrekkers.[6] Whatever Moroka's motives, these tactics were interpreted by most other Congress leaders, and in particular by the Youth Leaguers,[7] as constituting a gross betrayal. It was for this reason that Moroka lost the Presidency at the A.N.C. elections of December 1952.[8]

Moroka was succeeded by Albert Lutuli, previously Natal Provincial President. Lutuli's deposition as chief of the Umvoti Mission Reserve had been in the strongest contrast to Moroka's failure. Faced by the Government with the alternative of giving up all political activity or resigning from the Chieftainship, Lutuli had refused to do

[1] Letter dated 2 Oct. 1952, mim., P.A.S.

[2] ibid. Molema, despite the comparative caution of his views, continued to hold the office of Treasurer of the National Executive of the A.N.C. until he was banned in 1955. (Benson, *The African Patriots*, pp. 195, 225.) Nkomo had been one of those first interested in the A.N.C. Youth League, but he subsequently modified his views and eventually became primarily interested in Moral Rearmament. (ibid., p. 102.) He was, he claimed, expelled from the A.N.C. by Mandela in 1953 (author's interview, Pretoria, 2 Dec. 1965).

[3] Circular Letter to all Congress Branches of the Province from the Office of the Cape Province Working Committee of the A.N.C., n.d., mim., P.A.S.

[4] Presidential Address to the Cape Provincial Congress, 14 Feb. 1953, mim., P.A.S.

[5] Benson, *The African Patriots*, p. 191.

[6] A point made by Jordan Ngubane in 'Change in Congress Leadership', *Indian Opinion*, 2 Jan. 1953.

[7] The Youth League's view was emphasized by Dr. S. Molema in an interview with G.M.C., Mafeking, 4 Mar. 1964.

[8] Sampson, *Treason Cage*, p. 91.

H

either. He had subsequently lost his Chieftainship.[1] As Ngubane pointed out at the time, in an article in *Indian Opinion*, 'his heroic stand immediately made him the symbol of African resistance to apartheid tyranny.'[2]

No one embodies better than Lutuli the new kind of liberalism which had emerged in Congress ranks by the early 1950s. In a sense there was, as Xuma contended, 'no such thing as a moderate African.[3] And the Defiance Campaign had served in the Government's view to expose older leaders of Congress like Lutuli and Matthews. It had been specifically on the grounds that these men were no longer 'moderate' that Verwoerd, as Minister of Native Affairs, had rejected a United Party proposal to negotiate with the 'moderate' leaders of the A.N.C.[4] Lutuli's active involvement in the Campaign, as well as his refusal to relent in the face of the Native Affairs Department ultimatum had placed him beyond the pale.[5] Z. K. Matthews, for his part, had committed the unforgivable crime in Nationalist eyes; while abroad on a lecture tour in North America, he had made the most of his opportunity to publicize the evils of *apartheid* and bring the South African problem to world attention.[6]

These were reasons for the Nationalists to reject out of hand men of the stamp of Lutuli and Matthews. But there were other factors which served to make it difficult for them to find common ground with white liberals who, at first glance, appeared to share a number of their premises. This is particularly evident in the case of Lutuli himself. By the conclusion of the Defiance Campaign, his views were crucially at odds with those of white liberals in a number of ways.[7] First, he had publicly rejected a gradual extension of rights as well as the methods of petition and deputation, both still acceptable to

[1] This series of events is recorded by Lutuli in his autobiography, *Let My People Go*, pp. 108–12.

[2] *Indian Opinion* 2 Jan., 1953. cf. Nadine Gordimer's comment: 'Chief Luthuli had gone into the campaign a country chief; he came out a public figure' (in 'Chief Luthuli', *Atlantic Monthly* (Apr. 1959), p. 37).

[3] *Advance*, 20 Nov. 1952.   [4] *Ass. Debates*, vol. 81, 30 Jan. 1953, col. 302.

[5] ibid.   [6] ibid.

[7] The crucial effect which the decision to join the Defiance Campaign had on Lutuli has been stressed by M. B. Yengwa, who was Secretary of the Natal A.N.C. under Lutuli's Presidency. Lutuli was, he said, 'transformed into a different man altogether. Before that he was conscious of being Chief and used to say that he couldn't do this or that or it might interfere with his job. Afterwards, it was not that he was irresponsible, but he was prepared to damn the consequences as long as he was advancing the cause of the movement.' Benson, *Chief Albert Lutuli of South Africa*, p. 19.

white liberals. Thirty years of his life had been spent, he said, 'knocking in vain, patiently, moderately and modestly' at a door which was 'closed and barred'.[1] He publicly identified himself with 'the new spirit' of his people which he felt had found 'an effective and legitimate way of expression in the non-violent Passive Resistance Campaign.'[2] This was a view in sharpest contrast to the way in which liberal-minded whites had responded to the Campaign. Their pleas to the Government for reconsideration of *apartheid* were almost invariably prefaced by a condemnation of non-violent passive resistance.

In addition, white liberals active in the early months of 1953 feared the communist influence in the A.N.C. Here, too, Lutuli's view sharply diverged from theirs. He accepted that eventually a conflict would develop between the conservative and communist camps within Congress. But it was an issue that could—and must—be postponed.[3] Meanwhile, he was willing to accept help from anyone who would subscribe to the A.N.C.'s immediate aims. This was an attitude which clearly distinguished him from those, for example, who were to found the Liberal Party. For most of that group, anti-communism was a cardinal principle.[4]

Lutuli's interpretation of Christianity—and its obligations—was also markedly different from that of almost all the liberal-minded whites. He expressed to Anthony Sampson his disappointment that so few white liberals and Church leaders had identified themselves with Congress.

I can't appreciate [he said] *why* the Church leaders seem to hesitate to support our liberal movement. . . . Our movement is based on Christian philosophy, but the Church is *hostile* to us. Only are a few, like Huddleston and Reeves and Blaxall, don't see things the same and share our troubles with us.[5]

The different circumstances in which an African political leader had to work had forced Lutuli to face up to the implications of his faith, a stock-taking which most white Christians were able to post-

[1] This was part of Lutuli's public statement made after he was dismissed from the Chieftainship in November 1952. The entire speech is reprinted in Appendix A of *Let My People Go*, pp. 206–10.

[2] ibid., p. 207.

[3] ibid., pp. 137–8: 'Resistance movements cannot afford the luxury of McCarthyism . . .' (p. 138).

[4] See below, p. 115–6.

[5] Sampson, *Treason Cage*, p. 195.

pone indefinitely. Some of them no doubt agreed with Lutuli that it was beholden upon Christians to oppose laws and conditions 'that tend to debase human personality. . . .'[1] But they could not—and would not—see their choice as the clear-cut one which Lutuli felt it to be.

Just how far Lutuli's position was removed from that of most white Christians in South Africa—and elsewhere for that matter—is suggested in the public statement which he made after his dismissal from the Chieftainship in 1952. He spoke of his belief in the technique of non-violent passive resistance as 'the only non-revolutionary legitimate and humane way that could be used by people denied . . . effective constitutional means to further aspirations.'[2]

> What the future has in store for me I do not know. It might be ridicule, imprisonment, concentration camp, flogging, banishment and even death. . . .
>
> My very painful concern at times is that of the welfare of my family but I try even in this regard, in a spirit of trust and surrender to God's will as I see it, to say 'God will provide'.
>
> It is inevitable that in working for Freedom some individuals and some families must take the lead and suffer: The Road to Freedom is via The CROSS.[3]

It was not until the early sixties that liberal whites were forced to confront such possibilities.[4] Until then the question of the inevitability of suffering had not appeared as an issue about which white liberals needed to decide. Consequently, the acceptance of physical suffering as the price of liberal principles was another factor which sharply divided Congress from white liberals in the months after the Defiance Campaign.

Lutuli's election as President of the A.N.C. in December 1952 was more than a question of expediency. It strongly suggests that liberal views *as they had developed among Africans* were still acceptable to Congress. Among comment which followed Lutuli's election was that of Joe Matthews: 'We are all pleased that Lutuli has been chosen to take the lead. He is level-headed and fearless. . . .'[5] It seems especially significant that this should be the opinion not of an older Congressman—like Joe Matthews's father to whom he was writing—

---

[1] Luthuli, *Let My People Go*, p. 209.
[2] ibid., p. 209.   [3] ibid.
[4] White members of the Liberal Party were detained and imprisoned during the 1960 Emergency. See below, p. 215.
[5] Letter dated 3 Jan. 1953, mim., P.A.S.

but the view of a young and active Youth Leaguer, one of the group whose ardent nationalism made Congress appear radical to the whites.

Congress stock-taking, unlike that of white liberals, had taken place prior to the election of 1953. The degree of disillusionment which A.N.C. leaders felt over white politics in general, and white liberals in particular, drove them to the conclusion that the outcome of the 1953 election was irrelevant to furthering the Congress cause.[1] In this they differed crucially from white liberals to whom the prospective election remained at least a strategic priority. Following the Nationalists' return to power Lutuli denied that the election had been important to non-whites:

In effect the white electorate as a whole voted for the Nationalist policy because the Opposition also stood for the fundamental policy of denying non-white people full democratic rights; and its belief in segregation is consonant with apartheid and white domination.[2]

In Lutuli's view it was clearly impossible to advocate the extension of rights to non-whites, as white liberals did, and continue to support the United Party. Thus Lutuli—and the A.N.C.—called white liberals to account as they reviewed their position after the United Party's defeat. Now they were to consider again the question of forming a separate liberal party.

[1] Non-white leaders did disagree on the importance of the election. To some the U.P. still represented the lesser of two evils. To the more radical, a second Nationalist victory would hasten polarization and, they hoped, promote their cause. Carter, *The Politics of Inequality*, pp. 172–3, 215–17.

[2] ibid., p. 217.

CHAPTER V

The 1953 election and the realignment of white liberals

i

The return of the Nationalist Government to power in April 1953 destroyed the tenuous unity of non-Nationalist whites. The realignment which followed resulted in the formation of a Liberal Party, a non-racial party based on the principles of Cape liberalism and committed to the use of 'democratic and constitutional means'.[1] This attempt to bridge the gap between white and non-white was rejected with scorn by the A.N.C. and its allies. Meanwhile, not all liberals were equally disillusioned with the United Party, and rather than join the Liberal Party, a number chose to remain loyal to the United Party in the hope of eventually converting the Opposition to a liberal colour policy. These liberals, who were to form a ginger group, remained within the ranks of the U.P. until 1959. Until then, in their view, the United Party was, at least potentially, a liberal party.

ii

The election of 15 April 1953 returned the Government to power. The years 1948–53 had seen a steady increase in their electoral support. In 1950, the six members elected to the new seats for South-West Africa were all Nationalists. In 1951, a fusion between the Nationalists and the Afrikaner Party guaranteed the Government the support of the nine M.P.s then representing the Afrikaner Party. Thus, in 1953, the United Party lost eight seats compared with 1948, but the Government had gained twenty-four.[2] Although the United Party won a clear majority of votes, the Nationalists now held ninety-four seats in contrast to the U.P.'s fifty-seven and the Labour Party's five.[3]

The United Democratic Front had failed in its purpose of ousting

[1] Statement issued to the Press, 9 May 1953, mim., P.A.S. See below, p. 112.
[2] Figures taken from Chart 1 (showing election results 1910–53) in Carter, *The Politics of Inequality*, pp. 448–9.
[3] ibid.

the Government and in the wake of defeat the alliance collapsed. The U.P. had been heavily defeated in spite of the extensive help which the Torch Commando had provided during the campaign. The Commando was most directly affected by the breakdown of non-Nationalist unity; with electoral defeat it disintegrated almost immediately.[1] It had been the closeness of the 1953 election and the widespread hope of defeating the Government which had inspired support for the Torch Commando. There was little hope of sustaining mass support for such a movement until the next election in five years' time. The Commando lacked the cohesive characteristics of a well-established political party like the U.P., and could not survive the defeat of its main purpose.[2]

The short history of the Torch Commando, particularly its failure and collapse, provided instructive lessons for white liberals. It illustrated the limitations and relative impotence of a pressure group. One clear instance of such weakness had been the Commando's failure to persuade the U.P. to oppose the police measures devised by the Nationalists to counter the non-white Defiance Campaign; the Commando had been immobilized by their previous commitment to the United Democratic Front.[3] Mindful of this, the liberals could see possible advantage in forming an independent political party, rather than remaining a pressure group. Also, the Torchmen's limited airing of the colour question had helped to increase public awareness of the issue;[4] a liberal party might well capitalize on this interest, which the Torch Commando had chosen not to exploit.[5]

Perhaps most important of all, white liberals had noted the Commando's failure to develop a distinctive non-white policy. There had been some censure on this score from potential supporters of the Commando—presumably, too, potential supporters of a Liberal Party. For example, after Coloured ex-servicement had been debarred by a Torch Commando decision from taking part in the parade organized to commemorate El Alamein, a 'Disgusted European Ex-Serviceman' wrote to the *Cape Times* with the question,

---

[1] The second National Congress of the Torch Commando met in Johannesburg on 12 June 1953, to discuss the Commando's future. Gwendolen Carter comments 'The very closeness of the vote, and the limited regional support for continuation, indicated that in fact Torch was very nearly, if not quite, dead.' *The Politics of Inequality*, p. 329.
[2] ibid., p. 308.   [3] See above, p. 60.
[4] Carter, *The Politics of Inequality*, p. 328.
[5] See above, pp. 57–2.

'Is this much-vaunted democracy of the Torch-bearers but a thin veneer hiding the stinkwood of racialism?'[1] At the same time, the Nationalists, so much more conscious of the urgency of the colour question than most Torchmen, had laughed the latter to scorn for their enigmatic statements on the issue. An editorial in *Die Burger*, for example, drew attention to the absence of an unambiguous native policy in the Torch Commando's programme. The editor commented, 'the Torch must have a wick or it will not burn long.'[2] He stressed 'The only clear alternative to the National Party policy of apartheid is Liberalism.'[3] It was because some liberals at least agreed with such a view that they decided to form a new Liberal Party, based on a programme of equal rights regardless of colour. Thus, although the Liberal Party did not grow directly out of the Torch Commando, there are important connections between the two. The most obvious is that a number of leading Torchmen found a new and more congenial means for expressing their liberal views in the party founded on 9 May 1953.[4]

Other South Africans read different political lessons from the history of the Torch Commando. The Federal Party, formed at the same time as the Liberal Party, was just as much a reaction to the fate of the Commando. This new party was based on two cardinal principles—the inviolability of the Constitution and the rights of 'English' Natal to act independently if the Government were to threaten the entrenched clauses.[5] The Federal Party's native policy was little different from that of the U.P. They were chiefly concerned with the equality of the white races and the issue of provincial rights. In this, they harked back to questions prominent at the time of Union, rather than to the newly pressing issue of non-white rights. The emergence of such a party had grim overtones for the success of the Liberal Party which was primarily concerned with the rights of non-whites.

iii

Hoping for a United Party victory, the Liberal Association had agreed, before the election in 1953, to postpone further debate on

[1] *Cape Times*, 12 Oct. 1951.
[2] *Die Burger*, 4 Oct. 1951.
[3] ibid.   [4] See below, p. 110.
[5] The initial statement of principles made by the Union Federal Party is reprinted in Appendix IV of Carter, *The Politics of Inequality*, pp. 476–8.

the desirability of founding a liberal party.[1] At a post-election meeting on 18 April 1953, the question of the Association's future was automatically raised again. Dr. Wollheim suggested to the Council that many United Party members were 'thinking that they might just as well have been defeated on an honest liberal programme as on the compromise which they had adopted.'[2] Even in this new situation, however, there was no clear agreement on the necessity of forming a liberal party. In fact, discussion of the question revealed fundamental differences which had previously been overlaid by members of the Association pinning their hopes on the election. Leslie Rubin, a lawyer who was, at this time, a candidate for a Native Representative's seat in the Senate, claimed that 'people all over the country. were in favour of 'the immediate formation of a political party'.[3] Others agreed with him that the Council ought to act immediately, But Wollheim spoke of the possibility of the United Party being split by a Nationalist appeal to the right-wing of the U.P. to break with the liberals within the party.[4] Such an eventuality would in fact mean that the fragmented United Party would then become a liberal party, as many liberals had hoped. Donald Molteno, however, stressed that the Association's members still shared fundamental values with non-Nationalist whites, and, in this sense, the United Party's defeat was no cause for forming a separate party. He wanted to preserve a united front against the Government 'as long as the sacrifice in other directions was not too great.'[5]

When the issue was next discussed by the Council on 29 April there was a clear division concerning the purpose of the Association's annual general meeting, scheduled for 8–9 May.[6] Those who wanted that meeting to discuss the formation of a political party were defeated. Instead, the Council agreed that after their A.G.M. they would publicize the Liberal Association's existence and seek support for their aims.[7] Before the week-end of 8–9 May, however, Wollheim and Rubin, acting without consulting the Council,[8] issued a press statement which said that the Council intended discussing the issue of

[1] See above, pp. 94–5.
[2] Minutes of the Meeting of the S.A.L.A. Council, Cape Town, 18 Apr. 1953, mim., P.A.S.
[3] ibid.   [4] ibid.   [5] ibid.
[6] Minutes of the Meeting of the S.A.L.A. Council, Cape Town, 29 Apr. 1953, mim., P.A.S.
[7] ibid.
[8] G.M.C. interview with Colin Eglin, Cape Town, 24 Jan. 1964.

forming a party.[1] They thus precipitated a fresh airing of the question and the debate of 8–9 May concluded with the founding of a separate Liberal Party, despite the continued reluctance of some members of the Council. A prolonged discussion on 8 May was followed by a vote in which fifteen delegates supported the formation of a party and five opposed it.[2] The vote had failed to win the overwhelming majority required by the constitution to convert the Association into a party. However, when the discussion was reopened the following day, a second vote was taken. Three people had apparently changed their minds overnight, which may indicate their dilemma and uncertainty. This time the vote was eighteen to two, and consequently the South African Liberal Association became the South African Liberal Party.[3]

At this crucial meeting, there had been a number of different arguments in favour of further delay.[4] Prominent among these was the view that the time should be taken to capitalize on the existence of a liberal minority within the United Party. This continuing hope that the U.P. could still be converted into a party representing liberal views on colour meant that a number of those who regarded themselves as liberals remained United Party supporters in the fifties.[5] It was not until 1959 that their position became quite untenable and they left the U.P. to form the Progressive Party.[6] Meanwhile, throughout the fifties, white liberals were divided between the Liberal Party and the United Party, a fact which severely limited their effectiveness.

The motives of those who chose to support the formation of a Liberal Party were various. In the Transvaal, the idea of a new party had wide support because Association members considered it urgent to provide an alternative to the influence of the communists among the non-whites. Thus the Transvaal delegates came to the decisive Council meeting with a clear mandate to form a political party.[7] In these circumstances, other delegates, including Margaret Ballinger, feared that if a party were not formed the liberals in Johannesburg would act unilaterally. Most reluctant to see the party begin on anything other than a national basis, they were also anxious that it

---

[1] *Cape Times*, 6 May.
[2] Minutes of the Meeting of the S.A.L.A. Council, Cape Town, 8–9 May 1953, mim., P.A.S.
[3] ibid.   [4] ibid.   [5] See below, pp. 121 ff.
[6] See below, p. 190.
[7] Minutes of the Meeting of the S.A.L.A. Council, Cape Town, 8–9 May 1953, mim., P.A.S.

should be firmly based on the principles which they upheld. Such people saw themselves as the defenders as well as the heirs of the Cape liberal tradition.[1] A dominant figure in the Transvaal, and one likely to play a leading role in a Transvaal-based party, was Jock Isacowitz. Previously a founder of the Springbok Legion, a soldiers' organization established during the war under 'left-wing' leadership, Isacowitz was an admitted ex-communist. The prospect of his assuming control of a new Liberal Party was particularly galling to people like Margaret Ballinger and those whose views she represented —for example, Ellen Hellmann, prominent in the Institute of Race Relations and widely regarded as an expert on the colour question, and Arthur Keppel-Jones, then Professor of History at the University of Natal.

On the other hand, Peter Brown, a wealthy young farmer who led the Natal delegation, and who in the early sixties was to become National Chairman of the Party, was less apprehensive; in fact, it was the respect which he knew a number of the Natal liberals had for Isacowitz's work in the Transvaal,[2] as well as the sizeable backing that existed in the Natal groups for the formation of a party, which influenced him to support the move, although he had come to the meeting without a clear mandate. He and H. Selby Msimang, who had been a founding member of the African National Congress in 1912 and more recently Secretary of the A.N.C. in Natal, were also anxious that a new Liberal Party should precede any other break-away from the United Party, such as the Natal Federalists were threatening.[3] Msimang was the sole African delegate to the Council, but his presence as an equal underlined the Association's concern to represent itself as a non-racial organization. It was this common interest, despite different motives, which finally led to the Liberal Association's decision to form a Liberal Party.

iv

The Cape liberal tradition was clearly embodied in the ideals which the new Liberal Party planned to promote. Donald Molteno voiced a feeling general among the liberals when he spoke at the party's first public meeting in Cape Town in June 1953: 'The Cape

[1] G.M.C. interview with Margaret Ballinger, Cape Town, 18 Jan. 1964.
[2] G.M.C. interview with Peter Brown, Durban, 29 Jan. 1964.
[3] ibid. See above, p. 108.

institutions are founded on liberalism . . . it does work, it has worked and I am inspired with the faith that it will work again . . .'[1] In particular, there was an insistence on the need to assert the civil and political liberties of individuals. The early leaders, such as Oscar Wollheim, Alan Paton, Margaret Ballinger, and Leo Marquard, were concerned with individual injustices which they believed could and should be remedied by the extension of constitutional rights. Once established, these individual liberties would be adequately safeguarded by the observance of the rule of law and the existence of an independent judiciary. Initially, the Liberals were preoccupied with political and civil rights, and economic questions were, by comparison, neglected.[2] As a result of the Liberals' involvement with non-whites' economic hardship during the fifties, this emphasis was to change. Meanwhile, the prime concern with civil and political liberty was well reflected in the Press announcement of the party's inauguration. This was a statement which their ideological forefathers, Cape liberals such as William Schreiner, James Rose Innes, and Alfred and Winifred Hoernlé, would have approved without reservation. The party was to be based, the Liberals agreed, on the following principles:

1. The essential dignity of every human being irrespective of race, colour or creed, and the maintenance of his fundamental rights;
2. The right of every human being to develop to the fullest extent of which he is capable consistent with the rights of others;
3. The maintenance of the rule of law;
4. That no person be debarred from participating in the government and other democratic processes of the country by reason only of race, colour or creed, and that political rights based on a common franchise roll be extended to all suitably qualified persons.[3]

It was in stating this last principle that the Liberals most clearly dissociated themselves from the United Party. They had made equal rights regardless of race the basis of their party platform. With the exception of the Communist Party, banned in 1950, no political party in South Africa had previously endorsed the extension of full political rights to non-whites.

Care was taken to establish immediately that the party would employ 'only democratic and constitutional means' to implement

[1] *Advance*, 25 June 1953.
[2] A point emphasized by Patrick van Rensburg, *Guilty Land* (Penguin Books, 1962), p. 140.
[3] Statement issued to the Press, 9 May 1953, mim., P.A.S.

their principles, and would oppose 'all forms of totalitarianism such as communism and fascism'.[1] The early Liberals had come to their task of bridge-building from the white side of the gulf and they showed a predilection for traditionally white strategies. The principles and weapons were those forged by their background and education. Of prime importance in the Liberals' choice of method was their belief in the value and effectiveness of parliamentary democracy. They did not question that the South African system was, despite its drastically limited electorate, a parliamentary democracy. It was the Liberals' intention to make their democracy more genuinely representative. Conscious here of precedent, they no doubt were influenced by the fact that parliamentary democracy seemed to have worked in the extension of political and civil liberties in other countries. The British example, in particular, gave them reason to think that a new political party was a fruitful way to best effect change within the existing system: the Labour Party in Britain had flourished after its adherents' earlier attempt to work in co-operation with the Liberals. In South Africa, parliament had since Union been generally an effective medium of change. Even the Nationalists under Malan had rejected the extreme form of Afrikaner nationalism represented by Kruger, and deliberately chosen to continue to work through parliament. Within this framework, it did not appear necessary, let alone wise, to opt out of the parliamentary system. As it was, they had adopted a position which Peter Hjul, later Chairman of the party in the Cape, emphasized was 'extremely radical in the South African context as far as the whites were concerned'.[2] To declare, as they did by the formation of a new party, that the United Party was an inadequate parliamentary Opposition, was, by their standards, a momentous step.

A further reason for determining to use democratic and constitutional means was that, at this point, the Liberals (like Congress leaders at the time) were primarily concerned with the extension of *civil and political liberties*. These had been, in the past, secured and guaranteed by parliamentary legislation. Furthermore, those nonwhite rights which had recently been removed through Nationalist initiative, had been removed through the *parliamentary process*. And United Party connivance had been crucial to the Nationalists' success—for instance, in the case of the punitive measures following the Defiance Campaign. To the Liberals, it was not the parliamentary

[1] ibid.   [2] G.M.C. interview with Peter Hjul, Cape Town, 26 Jan. 1964.

system that appeared to have failed, but the United Party. What was *most* needed, so it seemed, was a new party to work within the parliamentary process.

Furthermore, the Liberals trusted to constitutional means because they retained faith in man's rationality and the power of logical argument. Such a faith underlay the Liberals' determination to use methods of consultation, free discussion and negotiation. It was a faith implicit in the open letter which Mr. Alan Paton, the party's first Vice-President, wrote to mark the party's founding. It was, he claimed, 'time for all good and sensible people' to act, and he recommended the extension of the franchise as 'the only reasonable and practical method' of building a common society.[1] At the party's first public meeting, Mr. H. J. Hanson, Q.C., a member of the National Executive, stressed that the 'realization of non-European national aspirations' was 'inevitable', and could be arrived at 'by goodwill and concessions and by constitutional means'.[2] The Liberals' optimism was derived from, and confirmed by, the experience of their nineteenth-century forerunners; rationality and right principles would triumph. This confidence was expressed with characteristic liberal sanguinity by Julius Lewin in 1953:

No laws, however harsh, [he said] and no government, however tyrannical, will succeed in putting an end to protest and resistance against flagrant injustice by men and women of all races. Ever since the early nineteenth century, prevailing policies in South Africa have always been challenged by some people in South Africa. That tradition will not die out. It may take a long time but the dominant race is destined to discover that there are some things in life that lie too deep for law. The recognition and acceptance of common humanity regardless of race is among the certainties of the future.[3]

In referring to his belief in 'common humanity regardless of race' Lewin expressed an outlook characteristic of all liberals.

The expectation which Lewin voiced was reinforced by what appeared to Liberals as a number of good omens, visible in the

---

[1] Letter of Alan Paton on the Occasion of the Launching of the Party in Cape Town, May 1953, mim., P.A.S.

[2] *Johannesburg Star*, 5 June 1953; cf. T. W. Price, 'The Liberal Party Replies' in *Liberation* (Sept. 1953), p. 13. '[The Liberal Party] believes that by argument, much organisation, and ceaseless constitutional action it can arrive at the objective of true freedom for all—and that without any storming of bastilles, barricade mounting or waving of tattered banners.'

[3] Julius Lewin, 'The Rise of Congress in South Africa', in *Political Quarterly*, xxiv (July 1953), 306.

particular time and circumstances in which they formed their party. Aware, for example, of the development of independent non-white nations *outside* South Africa, as well as the international sanction given to this trend by the United Nations Charter, the Liberals shared the conviction aired by Edgar Brookes that 'white man's overlordship' had passed in a multiracial world.[1] This was, of course, as much cause for hope to ardent African nationalists as it was to liberals, black and white, but all of them were prone to overlook the complexities of the change. White liberals did not realize that, as Congress opinion hardened in response to *apartheid* measures in the fifties, the whites were to develop a nationalism of their own, a new solidarity to supersede the old division of Boer and Briton.

The Liberal Party's insistence on securing civil and political liberty by parliamentary means was not only consistent with tradition; it also avoided the intractable question of possible alternatives. The relative impotence of pressure groups had been revealed by the earlier provincial liberal groups and the Liberal Association.[2] Even to condone, let alone organize and participate in, passive resistance or strike action, ran the risk of estrangement from the white community, and it was essential to maintain at least the whites' tolerance if the Liberals were to eventually be effective bridge-builders between white and non-white.[3] Moreover, the Liberals had a strong—and sensible—fear of violence. They recognized that it was not only literally destructive of people's lives and life-earnings, but that it would serve, as it had done during the riots of October and November 1952,[4] to alienate further white from non-white, to increase suspicion, fear, and hostility to the point where the gulf between white and non-white would prove fixed and permanently impassable, and where the liberal voice could not be heard at all across that gulf.

Standing as they did for the extension of freedom, Liberals were naturally hostile to the idea of a totalitarian system which they

[1] Edgar H. Brookes, *South Africa in a Changing World* (Cape Town, O.U.P., 1953), pp. 36ff. 'We have [he said] no hope of preserving white racial dominance. It is not a question of whether it will fall, but of when.' ibid., p. 136.

[2] See above, pp. 62, 91–2.

[3] The analogy of 'bridge-building' was frequently used by Liberal leaders. Margaret Ballinger spoke of the Party's main function being 'to build bridges between Europeans and non-Europeans' (*Johannesburg Star*, 13 May 1953). cf. Alan Paton's comment at the Liberal Party's first public meeting: 'We are not extremists but, in fact, stand between the extremes of Afrikaner nationalism and of Native nationalism' (*Johannesburg Star*, 5 June 1953).

[4] See above, pp. 86–7.

readily identified with South African communists. At the time the Liberal Party was founded, the cold war showed no sign of abating and the distrust of communists which South African Liberals evinced was widely shared in the Western world. There was, too, tactical wisdom in dissociating themselves from communists. It seems they would have done so anyway, on ideological grounds, but the virulence of the Government's charges against the Torch Commando on this score underlined the importance of such a defensive move.[1] Moreover, under the Suppression of Communism Act, the definition of 'statutory' communism was so broad that all Government opponents ran the risk of being identified as communists.[2] Such an eventuality would be fatal to any political party competing for votes.

Despite the Liberals' unity on general principles and methods which it was appropriate for the party to employ, a fundamental disagreement was soon apparent. The issue was universal adult suffrage. In framing a franchise policy it became evident that there were Liberals of different kinds within the party. The extent of these differences was revealed during the party's First National Conference held in Johannesburg in July 1953. Some delegates had joined the party assuming that universal adult suffrage was its ultimate aim; a qualified franchise would be acceptable only as a temporary measure.[3] To others, however, the qualified franchise was a cardinal principle. Generally this group argued for the Cape liberal principle of the 'vote for all civilized people';[4] some of them clearly doubted whether universal suffrage should be introduced into a multiracial society.[5] Those who upheld a permanently qualified franchise considered their liberalism adequately expressed by guaranteeing that there would be no discrimination in the process of qualifying to vote.[6]

This cleavage of opinion was finally bridged only by the practical necessity to present a united front, and a united front which would

---

[1] According to one Nationalist M.P., Mr. D. J. Van den Heever, the Commando was 'a combination of S.A.P.—Torchmen which can only result in a Left dictatorship in South Africa.' *Ass. Debates*, vol. 78, 25 Apr. 1952, col. 4412. cf. Malan's allegations made at the Orange Free State Congress of the National Party in September 1951 (*Cape Times*, 12 Sept. 1951).

[2] See above, p. 47.

[3] e.g. Dr. O. Wollheim, Prof. Price, Mrs. Philip, Mr. Hans Meidner. See Minutes of the First National Conference of the Liberal Party of South Africa, Johannesburg, 11–13 July 1953, mim., P.A.S., pp. 5, 8, 9.

[4] Margaret Ballinger, as reported in the Minutes, p. 10.

[5] e.g. Mr. B. A. Maharaj, Mr. L. Rubin, Mrs. M. Ballinger, ibid., pp. 5, 8, 10.

[6] e.g. Mr. W. Stanford, ibid., p. 7.

win the maximum degree of support from the white electorate. Arguments of exigency prevailed. Senator Ballinger's contention that the party was interested in winning political power was not disputed.[1] Nor was the claim of the Cape delegate, Mr. G. Sergeant, that the Liberals' task was to appeal to moderates on both sides of the colour line. His plea to delegates to avoid 'panicking the European electorate' met with a ready response.[2] The official statement which emerged from the First Party Conference made no reference to the Liberal Party's ultimate objective with regard to the franchise. It read:

> The aim of the Liberal Party of South Africa is to achieve the responsible participation of all South Africans in the government and other democratic processes of the country and to this end aims to provide compulsory education for all South Africans and the extension of the right of franchise to all adult persons who have received such education.[3]

Tension on this issue persisted. The question was reopened at the party's 1954 National Congress. But a motion that the party should stand for a permanently qualified franchise was defeated by a vote of twenth-nine for and fifty-one against.[4] In a new policy statement, the Liberals established the principle of universal adult suffrage, but the resolution emphasized the probable necessity of progressive stages of enfranchisement.[5] This additional clause was a concession to the vigorous minority which continued to oppose universal enfranchisement. It enabled the party's view of the franchise to be interpreted as widely as possible—a decided tactical advantage when the Liberals still sought, without alienating non-whites, to make an impact in white society.

v

From the beginning the Liberals were well aware of the immense difficulties of their winning the non-white sympathy and support so crucial for their party's success as a multiracial body. Theirs might be 'the great middle way' as one enthusiast described it,[6] but it was immensely difficult to plot such a path. To adopt plans sufficiently moderate to retain hope of wide white support was to immediately increase the suspicion and hostility already existing among non-whites.

---

[1] Minutes of the First National Conference of the Liberal Party, p. 8.
[2] ibid., p. 9.   [3] ibid., p. 13.
[4] Summary of the Minutes of the National Congress of the L.P., Durban, 10–12 July 1954.
[5] ibid.
[6] T. W. Price, 'The Liberal Party Replies', in *Liberation* (Sept. 1953), p. 13.

I

Alternately, to respond with less equivocation to non-white pressures was to instantly alienate themselves from the white community. As Jordan Ngubane, the prominent African journalist and member of the party, explained:

> We must at the very outset face the fact that to say a man is a liberal, is politically speaking in this country not to pay him a compliment. The non-European regards the word Liberal as virtually synonymous with traitor or spy. Whether we like it or not we have a frightful reputation to live down.[1]

This 'reputation' was not helped by the traditional paternalism which marked the attitude of so many of the early Liberals. It was an attitude fundamental, almost natural, to the outlook of many of them, so much so that it was often unconscious in them.[2] But it was an approach guaranteed to arouse the animosity of the very people the Liberals were most anxious to meet on the best terms—the leaders of the A.N.C. One of the most consistently moderate of these, Z. K. Matthews, typified the Congress leaders' reaction to the early overtures from the Liberals: 'The question is whether they [the Liberals] have enough strength and enough ability to overcome the reluctance of the average liberal white South African to work *with* instead of *for* the African.'[3] The paternalism which continued to characterize the attitudes of many white Liberals was a constant source of irritation to the non-whites, particularly to that minority who were politically articulate and socially sophisticated.[4] But much of the Liberals' contact with non-whites had been with those who were in superficial but obvious ways their inferiors—economically poorer, less well-educated—people in need of assistance. And it was inevitable that, in such circumstances, they should act *in loco parentis*. If they were to help build a common society, they had first to acknowledge the realities of illiteracy, poverty, and ignorance. As Maurice Webb had warned in 1945, while President of the Institute of Race Relations, it was no good the liberals pretending that race did not matter and

---

[1] Ngubane, *An African Explains Apartheid*, p. 193.

[2] Alfred Hoernlé had earlier identified this particular pitfall to which liberals were subject: 'The greatest moral danger in the very heart of the liberal spirit itself is that, in the relation of the well-meaning superior to stricken inferior, it is so apt to become paternalism and condescension.' *South African Native Policy and the Liberal Spirit*, p. 150.

[3] In the *Saturday Review of Literature*, 2 May 1953, quoted in Sampson, *Treason Cage*, p. 102.

[4] A point made by several A.N.C. leaders whom the author interviewed, e.g. Joe Matthews, Robert Resha, Duma Nokwe.

that after all, they were all brothers, for in doing so they would overlook the basic fact that brothers were 'far from being all alike'.[1]

The principles and methods which the Liberal Party adopted in 1953 were consistent with those of the A.N.C. in the mid forties. They were not compatible with the outlook of the A.N.C. in 1953. At this time, the chief stumbling-block preventing effective co-operation between the Liberals and non-whites was the party's commitment to constitutional and parliamentary means. This was a qualification guaranteed to arouse hostility. The Liberals' chosen methods were largely denied to non-whites. At least officially, the African National Congress had agreed to boycott their minimal representation in the South African parliament.[2] They were left only with the choice of passive resistance, strike, and boycott, all strategies which in 1953 the Liberals rejected as unconstitutional.[3] Moreover, the kinds of bans imposed on Congress leaders as a result of their role in the Defiance Campaign were an ever-present threat to any non-white contemplating extra-parliamentary but non-violent protests.[4]

The Liberals' strategies were not available to the A.N.C. leadership. Lutuli had made this point with obvious chagrin at the time of the Defiance Campaign in 1952: 'It is suggested that we should use constitutional means, but nobody has indicated what constitutional means we may use to gain our freedom.'[5] Nelson Mandela, the Defiance Campaign leader, also took issue with the Liberals here. Such a strategy could, he argued, 'only have a basis in reality for those people who enjoy democratic and constitutional rights.'[6]

The theory [he said] that we can sit down with folded arms and wait for a future parliament to legislate for the 'essential dignity of every human being irrespective of race, colour and creed' is a crass perversion of elementary principles of political struggle.[7]

[1] Maurice Webb, *In Quest of South Africa*, presidential address delivered to the S.A.I.R.R., Cape Town, 17 Jan. 1945; reprinted as *New Africa Pamphlet*, No. 8 (Johannesburg, S.A.I.R.R., 1945), p. 14.

[2] See above, p. 33–4.

[3] cf. Margaret Ballinger's reference to the Defiance Campaign as an 'unparliamentary outbreak', at the first Liberal Party meeting in the Cape, reported in *Advance*, 25 June 1953.

[4] See below, p. 150.   [5] Quoted in *Contact* (6 Sept. 1958).

[6] Searchlight on the Liberal Party', in *Liberation* (June 1953), p. 7.

[7] ibid., pp. 7–8. Speaking for the S.A.I.C., Dr. Yusuf Dadoo agreed: 'the only effective way of fighting the policies of the present government was by extra parliamentary methods on the basis of the greatest possible co-operation of the whites and non-whites in opposing Nationalist policies and actions at every step.' *Advance*, 14 May 1953.

Like other Congress leaders, Mandela deeply resented the Liberals' paternalism and their refusal to allow A.N.C. leaders to co-operate as equals in the struggle for their rights.

Spokesmen for the Congress of Democrats were particularly vitriolic. The parliamentary arena was barred to most C.O.D. leaders under the terms of the Suppression of Communism Act (1950). In this, as in other ways, the C.O.D. and the Liberal Party were antipathetic. The only whites collaborating closely with non-whites, the C.O.D. openly scorned the Liberal Party's approach as a hopeless compromise.

> To talk of using only 'parliamentary' methods [their spokesman said] is to treat the movement for political rights in this country as one of whites alone; for this community alone has parliamentary power. . . . There can [he predicted] be no political future for a party which sets itself resolutely against extra-parliamentary activity and thus withdraws itself from the entire political life of four-fifths of the people in the country.[1]

This criticism was cruelly accurate. To be consistent with their declared objectives the Liberals could not withdraw themselves 'from the entire political life' of the non-whites. The question remained. How far could they—and should they—co-operate with the A.N.C. and the S.A.I.C.?

The Liberal Party's initial overtures to the Congresses inevitably sounded paternal, and worse, patronizing. The Liberals seemed to call in question the maturity and status of the Congresses. The party's initial Press statement on 'Relations with Non-European Organizations' was hotly criticized.[2] The C.O.D. scorned the party's expression of 'profound sympathy with the aspirations of all non-European peoples for economic, social, education and political advance. . . .'[3] They wanted to see total identification with the non-whites, not merely 'profound sympathy'.[4]

A year later, in July 1954, the Liberals modified this policy which had exposed them to ridicule from the very people they wished to champion. They made it clear that they were not interested in competing for non-white members, and would regard simultaneous membership of any Congress and the Liberal Party as 'compatible'.[5]

---

[1] *The Threatened People*, p. 16.
[2] Relations with Non-European Organizations—policy adopted at National Congress, July 1953, mim., P.A.S.
[3] ibid.   [4] 'Speaking for the Natives', in *Fighting Talk* (July 1953).
[5] Relations with Non-European Organizations—policy adopted at National Congress, July 1954, mim., P.A.S.

They stressed that they wanted to see non-white political organizations expand under their chosen leaders. And they added an assurance about their 'sincere desire to co-operate with the African National Congress, the South African Indian Congress and other representative bodies of Non-European political opinion. . . .'[1]

Initially, the Liberal Party was predominantly white. Although there was a small African membership within the first months of the party's inception and these members could participate fully in party councils, they were not eligible to vote or stand for any municipal, provincial or parliamentary office. In any case, the whole conception of a political party in which non-whites could share real power and influence with whites was so alien to South Africans that even the more radical elements in the party were forced to concede that they were 'for present purposes, though not in intention, a White-created, White-dominated and White-led party' and would 'probably remain so for some time.'[2]

Nevertheless, the Liberals' stand called into question the whole structure of South African society, underpinned as this was by the traditional practice of white supremacy. The Liberals felt they had thrown down the gauntlet to white South Africa. In particular, they had challenged the Nationalist Government. The editor of *Die Transvaler*, organ of the Transvaal Nationalist Party, stressed that the Liberal path left 'no dividing lines'. 'The final result . . . [he warned] will be that the European will disappear into a Black sea and that all the great spiritual values which make life worthwhile for him will go under with him.'[3]

vi

The U.P. leader, Mr. J. G. N. Strauss, greeted the appearance of a Liberal Party with the reassurance that the '[colour] problem could be solved only as it developed from generation to generation.'[4] In addition, he emphasized that the 'United Party stood steadfastly for European leadership in South Africa while doing justice to the reasonable aspirations of non-Europeans.'[5] The liberal minority who

[1] ibid.
[2] C. W. M. Gell in a letter to Wollheim, dated 13 Dec. 1953, P.A.S.
[3] *Die Transvaler*, 8 June 1953.
[4] *Cape Times*, 13 May 1953.
[5] ibid.

had chosen to remain within the United Party rather than join the Liberal Party must have chafed under such complacency. Indeed the Opposition's defeat in the 1953 election revealed serious tensions within the United Party. Yet, despite these, the U.P. remained an 'umbrella' party until 1959. It continued to provide political shelter for those whose liberalism applied largely, if not exclusively, to the white racial issue; but it included as well a minority who persistently pushed for a liberal restatement of U.P. policy towards non-whites.[1] How and why was this strained unity preserved? What does the persistence of such an alliance reveal about the character of liberalism in the United Party in the period 1953–9?

Faced with increased Nationalist power (even if in seats rather than votes), United Party leaders as well as the 'progressive'[2] back-benchers saw the political wilderness threatening a splintered Opposition. The possibility of such splintering if they should fail to close ranks on some middle-ground was given substance by the revolt of Bailey Bekker and four other right-wingers in October 1953.[3] These men were critical of Strauss's leadership of the party; they had judged him and found him wanting a more conservative, more Nationalist-like non-white policy.[4] But their overriding concern was the future unity of the white races, and it was with this aim uppermost in their minds that they formed the Conservative Party in August 1954.[5] Paradoxically, this party which chose to call itself 'conserva-

[1] One member of this group was R. A. F. Swart, elected as a United Party M.P. in 1953. Swart recalls that in 1953 there were already 'two definite wings' on race relations in the U.P., at least among the Party's M.P.s. Invariably, 'on discussions on bills on race relations there was a very clear division in the caucus which then needed a formula to present some sort of united team in Parliament.' G. M. C. interview with R. A. F. Swart, Durban, 31 Mar. 1964.

[2] I have chosen to use 'progressive' to describe the liberal element in the U.P. between 1953 and 1959 which supported the extension of non-white rights. It was this group which left the Party in 1959 to form the Progressive Party. To refer to them as 'liberals' in discussing their role in the mid fifties may have led to some confusion since, in this period, the U.P. as a whole continued to support a number of liberal principles relating to white rights, rather than non-white rights.

[3] Bekker and four other U.P. members were expelled from the Party in October 1953. A sixth member who shared their views resigned from caucus in January 1954 to join the 'independent wing' of the United Party. In August 1954 Bekker announced the formation of a new party, soon afterwards named the Conservative Party. See *A Survey of Race Relations in South Africa 1953–1954* (Johannesburg, S.A.I.R.R., 1954), pp. 3–4.

[4] ibid.; also Carter, *The Politics of Inequality*, p.354.

[5] The Conservatives' priorities are suggested by their statement of Fundamental Principles (reprinted in Appendix IV of Carter, ibid., pp. 478–80). The Party's

tive' was founded on what, fifty years before, had been accepted as a liberal principle. In the early twentieth century, the liberal solution of the South African problem had been the reconciliation of the white races through the granting of self-government. The exit of such a group from the United Party in 1954 must have been encouraging to the 'progressives'; once again, in a negative way, it indicated a strengthening of the liberal element in the U.P.

There were other important practical considerations sustaining party unity. The emergence of the Liberal Party could not be ignored. No United Party M.P. defected to the Liberal Party but the new party might well draw electoral support from the U.P. In this regard the presence of a 'progressive' element within the U.P. might be a valuable counter-attraction. By contrast, after the 1958 election and another U.P. defeat, there was clearly a strong feeling in the party that the ginger group had been a serious liability rather than an asset.

The reluctance of the 'progressives' to dissociate themselves from the party had several additional causes. Certainly, at first they were conscious of their own lack of political experience; this was especially so since a number of them had been first elected in 1953.[1] New M.P.s like Ray Swart, Zach de Beer, Jan Steytler, Helen Suzman, and Townley Williams were, by their own admission, 'very junior in the political field'.[2] To leave the party as the older Bernard Friedman did in 1955,[3] was, as Ray Swart understated, 'quite a big step to take'.[4] Moreover, the United Party was Hofmeyr's old party and the accepted medium through which whites could express liberal views on the colour question.[5] Perhaps the most important factor, however, in preventing their earlier exit from the U.P. was their hope that they could gradually convert the party to their point of view.[6] Such optimism was later recalled by Colin Eglin, who was in 1953 a U.P. member of the Cape Provincial Council. As a member of the Liberal

---

principles were to be based 'on a true South Africanism, founded on the sentiments of the moderates of both European language groups in South Africa.' The six Conservatives eventually split on the constitutional issue in the crucial vote of 28 February, 1956 and three of them joined the Nationalists, ibid., p. 141.

[1] Twelve United Party M.P.s resigned to support the Progressive Party in November 1959 (*Africa Digest*, vii, 2 (1959)). Of these, 9 had been elected to the Assembly in 1953, and 2 in 1958.

[2] G.M.C. interview with R. A. F. Swart, Durban, 31 Mar. 1964.

[3] See below, p. 125.

[4] G.M.C. interview with R. A. F. Swart, Durban, 31 Mar. 1964.

[5] See above, pp. 11, 15–16.

[6] G.M.C. interview with R. A. F. Swart, Durban, 31 Mar. 1964.

Association he had supported the formation of the Liberal Party, but he then chose to stay within the U.P. fold:

I thought that the time was most inappropriate for the formation of the party in the sense that I think the '53 election saw the high water mark of Liberal opinion within the United Party. . . . The fact that you'd had the Torch Commando working in close association with the United Party had tended to give it an infusion of modern thought, if not liberal thought. . . . My view at that stage, having worked within the United Party, was, that if ever there was a chance of moving the United Party in a more liberal direction, that opportunity presented itself as a result of the '53 election.[1]

In retrospect it may seem that the 'progressives' were foolish or, at best, short-sighted to have nurtured the hope that the United Party could be made after their own image. But their illusions were nourished by the same kind of reasoning which had so long delayed the formation of a separate Liberal Party. As R. A. F. Swart, one of those who left the U.P. in 1959 had pointed out, it was only gradually that they came to realize how far they were from the mainstream of U.P. policy.[2] And, as this realization dawned, they were finding increasingly that they held principles in common with each other, making them a distinct group within the party, a group which might even survive if they attempted a separate existence.[3]

But at first it had still seemed to those with liberal views on the colour issue, that they could adequately demonstrate their commitment within the ranks of the United Party. To such people, the U.P. still represented distinctly, in fact, fundamentally, different values from those of the Nationalists. There was much—apart from expediency—to bind them together. Not the least important of such ideological ties was the constitutional question. It was this rather than any other issue which dominated the political struggle in the first three years after the 1953 election. The Nationalists' determination to win victory on the Coloured vote was undiminished. Furthermore, where the maintenance of white supremacy appeared to be at stake, the Government was fully prepared to disregard the spirit, if not the letter of the law. They were quite prepared to be revolutionary in their 'conservatism'. In such a situation none of the

---

[1] G.M.C. interview with Colin Eglin, Cape Town, 24 Jan. 1964. Eglin restated this view in an interview with the author, Cape Town, 13 Dec. 1965.
[2] G.M.C. interview with R. A. F. Swart, Durban, 31 Mar. 1964.
[3] ibid.

'progressives' was likely to dissociate himself from the United Party's objections as to the means by which the Government planned to achieve their purpose. But a number of them sought, in addition, assurances about the Coloured policy which a future U.P. government would adopt. Seven of them in fact resigned their seats on this score. The six who were persuaded into returning did so only after making it clear to caucus that they accepted the party line on one condition: that the U.P., if returned to power, would restore the Coloured voters to the common roll.[1] Only Bernard Friedman refused to compromise. Having resigned his seat in 1955, he fought and lost a by-election, a fate which the other 'progressives' no doubt noted.[2] Those rebels who did not follow Friedman out of the party were eventually able to see their 1955 ultimatum on the Coloured question accepted as party policy prior to the 1958 election. Such success, even if qualified and delayed, must have seemed a vindication of their belief that the U.P. could be redeemed.

The 'progressives' and their supporters outside Parliament must also have been encouraged by the restatement of United Party racial policy issued after the party's National Congress late in 1954.[3] They had been directly involved in the protracted discussions at regional and provincial level prior to the party's National Congress in November 1954.[4] And in the official policy which emerged from that meeting there was considerable cause for liberal optimism. The statement acknowledged that 'a large and permanently detribalized Native urban population' had become 'an integral part of the South African economy' and that this made imperative 'the better co-ordination of European and Native interests in the social, economic and political life of the country.'[5] Here was cause for hope to those who believed, as the 'progressives' within the party (and the Liberals outside) did, that economic interdependence would eventually have to lead to an extension of political liberties. The U.P. statement even conceded that political rights were 'an inevitable historical corollary to an increase in economic power'.[6] This assurance was, however, followed by significant provisos. A 'long period of training in the ways of democracy and especially in its responsibilities' lay ahead of the African, the statement said, and, in addition, any granting or extension of

[1] Carter, *The Politics of Inequality*, p. 144.   [2] ibid.
[3] Carter, *The Politics of Inequality*, p. 140.
[4] *A Survey of Race Relations in South Africa 1953–1954* (Johannesburg, S.A.I.R.R., 1954), p. 3.
[5] Carter, *The Politics of Inequality*, p. 284.   [6] ibid.

political rights must depend on 'an established and decisive majority of the present electorate.'[1]

Qualifications such as these did not deflate the hopes of the 'progressive' element within the party. One of the most powerful factors sustaining their support of the United Party was the belief that industrialization must inevitably mean an extension of rights to non-whites as it had seemed to bring to the industrialized working classes in Europe, especially in England. John Cope, a United Party M.P., who remained loyal to the Opposition until he supported the 'progressive' breakaway in 1959, expressed this faith in a book published in 1952. He claimed: 'The most important development of the years 1930–1950, overshadowing all other developments and inexorably determining the future of South Africa was the beginning of the great industrial revolution.'[2] The relevance of such development to the colour question he explained in these terms: 'Jan Hofmeyr saw that all these economic trends in the country as well as in the towns, must inevitably promote the liberal forces for which he stood.'[3]

In the forties, the U.P. had publicly acknowledged that economic integration was inevitable.[4] Smuts had subsequently appointed the Fagan Commission; their findings were to be the blueprint by which the United Party Government would cope with the increasing urbanization of non-whites. With their election defeat in 1948, the U.P. lost the opportunity to implement the recommendations of the Fagan Report. But their apparent willingness to modify party policy on account of the effects of industrialization was a source of encouragement to the 'progressives' in the fifties. Also because the U.P. was identified with 'big business' in South Africa, it seemed logical to suppose that a liberalization of colour policy on account of the imperatives of industrialization would stem from the United Party.

Yet, as Herbert Blumer demonstrates,[5] industrialization was not inevitably the agent of liberal change which the progressives believed. Industrialization in a multiracial society will stimulate important changes such as urbanization, increased opportunities for non-whites and new cash incomes.[6] But it will not automatically modify the

---

[1] ibid.

[2] Jan H. Hofmeyr, *South Africa*, 2nd edn., ed. J. B. Cope (London, Ernest Benn, 1952), p. 231.

[3] ibid., p. 237.   [4] See above, pp. 24–5.

[5] 'Industrialization and Race Relations', in Guy Hunter (ed.), *Industrialization and Race Relations*, pp. 220–53.

[6] ibid., p. 250.

pattern of race relations. If that racial mould is well-established, as it was in South Africa, before extensive industrialization the existing racial order will not necessarily disintegrate.[1]

However, the Report made by the Tomlinson Commission in March 1956 provided the 'progressives' with what seemed conclusive proof of their reasoning. The Government had depended on the Commission to provide incontrovertible evidence that a policy of *apartheid* was practicable. When the Commission failed to do this— or at least, concluded that it was possible only on conditions which the Government would not—or could not—meet,[2] non-Nationalists in general, and the United Party in particular, were jubilant.[3] Although the U.P. was denied access to a full copy of the Report (which, in itself, was no doubt cause of grievance over Government arbitrariness), they were given ample opportunity to detect and attack what they regarded as the fallacies of some of the Report's conclusions. In addition, they were able to indict the Nationalists for their failure to accept fully the Commissioners' suggestions, for the White Paper which the Government issued soon afterwards made it clear that they had no intention of fully implementing the Commission's

[1] ibid., p. 253. Blumer concludes: 'Industrialization will continue to be an incitant to change, without providing the definition of how the change is to be met. It will contribute to the reshuffling of people without determining the racial alignments into which people will fall. . . . In general, it will move along with, respond to, and reflect the current of racial transformation in which it happens to be caught.'

[2] The Government rejected a number of the Commissioners' key recommendations. They disagreed, for instance, that non-whites should be permitted to purchase land as individuals, that white industrialists should be allowed to invest in the reserves, and that the Government should at that point commit themselves to a long-range plan. D. Hobart Houghton, *The Tomlinson Report: A Summary of the Findings and Recommendations in the Tomlinson Commission Report* (Johannesburg, S.A.I.R.R., 1956), pp. 75–6.

[3] e.g. Mr. Douglas Mitchell, leader of the U.P. in Natal, claimed that the Tomlinson Report had 'blown apartheid to bits' (*P.D.* No. 33, 4 Sept. 1956). Tantalus, in the *Sunday Express* (1 Apr. 1956) voiced the view popular among non-Nationalists: 'It was not a desire to cure the rotting ulcer of the Reserves which inspired the Nationalist Government to appoint this [Tomlinson] Commission. It wanted to prove a political theory' (*P.D.* No. 13, 5 Apr. 1956). cf. the terse comment made in the *Friend* (27 Apr. 1956): 'Apartheid as a policy is dead.' The editorial continued: 'What remains? Perhaps it would be best if Dr. Verwoerd and Mr. Strydom now stopped prattling about 'separate development' and 'the Bantu's own areas' and stuck simply to 'baaskap apartheid' which means 'keeping the Native in his place and no nonsense about rights and privileges'. Then at least the country would know where the Nationalist leadership stands and the world would know where South Africa stands.' (*P.D.* No. 17, 3 May 1956.)

recommendations.[1] If theoretical *apartheid* had been finally proved a myth, as the United Party argued was the case, the chief bastion of support for Nationalist non-white policy had collapsed. They were *bound*—by U.P. and 'progressive' logic at least—to accept the fact of permanent economic integration.

In fact, however, the Nationalists were undaunted by the Commission's conclusion that the best they could hope for finally was partial territorial separation.[2] The controversy which the Tomlinson Report had provoked had, far from weakening the Government, only strengthened the Nationalists' resolution to implement those aspects of *apartheid* which they judged to be practicable. The Report's forecast of further increases in the urbanization of non-whites seemed all the more reason to press ahead meanwhile with laws to minimize interracial contact, and where such contact was unavoidable, delineate clearly the regulations which would govern it.

The concessions which the more radical element in the Opposition won from the U.P. in the mid fifties may appear as paltry gains. But the 'progressives' judged that it had been partly their pressure which had led party leaders to contemplate and approve changes in a liberal direction. There were, as well, other omens of a liberal shift. As the Nationalists extended the application of *apartheid* in the mid fifties, non-Nationalists reacted violently to Government threats to liberal institutions such as schools, universities, and churches. As a consequence those years were marked by a barrage of liberal protest, both at home and abroad. All of this encouraged the 'progressive' element within the U.P., as well as like-minded whites outside the party, to judge that they were on the side of the big battalions. Furthermore, they assumed that the big battalions always win.

[1] A précis of the Government White Paper is included as Appendix B in D. Hobart Houghton, *The Tomlinson Report: A Summary.*

[2] e.g. *Die Transvaler* defended the Government (4 Apr. 1956): 'In principle, the report is a confirmation of the general direction pursued constantly by the Government. In details, it ought to be regarded as a guide which can assist the Government in the jotting out of practical policy movements. The Government conceived it thus and thus it will be used' (*P.D.* No. 17, 3 May 1956).

CHAPTER VI

The Nationalist attack on liberal institutions

i

Before 1953 *apartheid* legislation had directly affected the lives of non-whites rather than whites. Although English-speakers in particular had felt their rights threatened by the constitutional issue, their freedom was not so obviously endangered as was that of non-whites by laws like the Population Registration Act and the Group Areas Act. After the Nationalists were returned to power in 1953, however, the Government found it necessary to infringe the autonomy of 'white' institutions in the cause of *apartheid*. The institutions chiefly affected were schools, universities, and churches. Such institutions, where they were English-speaking, had traditionally upheld liberal values. They thus represented, at the very least, the *ideal* of equality for non-whites and consequently threatened the success of *apartheid*.

With this extension of *apartheid*, resistance against the Government broadened to include Afrikaner Nationalists who generally challenged not the theory of *apartheid*, but the method of its practical application. The agitation of older opponents increased; vigorous protest came from the 'progressive' minority of the U.P. and the Liberals, who wanted to extend rights to non-whites, as well as from non-Nationalist whites who were not primarily concerned with non-white rights, but rather, for example, with the principle of minimum Government interference. In addition, hostile opinion from abroad was focused on South Africa to an extent without precedent. Such a proliferation of protest in the mid fifties encouraged non-Nationalist whites to believe again that the Government would be defeated in the next election due in 1958.

ii

Immediately after the Nationalists' victory in 1953, the Prime Minister, Dr. D. F. Malan, launched an attack on what he deemed liberal opposition. Since he and his Government regarded as 'liberal' all those who advocated racial equality, he condemned, without any distinction, the United Nations, Communist Russia, 'semi-Communist India', and the British Labour Party.[1] The racial equality which they all championed would, Malan claimed, 'inevitably' mean the destruction of the white races in South Africa. Malan's determination to avert this 'national suicide' was displayed in his attitude towards the 'growing and audacious liberalism' within South Africa itself.[2] Here he made particular reference to the communists as well as to those involved in the Defiance Campaign. The latter had challenged the basic structure of South African society by their protest against 'all discriminatory laws, even the oldest and most traditional. . . .'[3] Malan concluded: 'This impossible position can be rectified only by a strong Government unhampered internally by irreconcilable viewpoints.'[4] One such 'irreconcilable' view was that represented by liberals and liberal institutions in South Africa. And the Government was clearly determined to erase the liberal viewpoint.

To implement this general aim, the Nationalists introduced the concept of Bantu Education and its logical counterpart, the segregation of universities.[5] The Bantu Education Act was passed in the Assembly in September 1953.[6] The Act centralized African education under the control of the Native Affairs Department. The Minister of Native Affairs was given wide powers to decide such matters as the nature of the syllabus and the media of instruction. Government spokesmen emphasized repeatedly that these were to be related to the children's environment and the purpose of such education was to be strictly vocational.[7] For example, Mr. W. A. Maree (who was to be made Minister of Bantu Education when the position was created in 1958) explained in 1953: '. . . the fundamental idea will be that functionally the Native must fill a role in the community different to that of the European, and . . . that the Native has a different cultural background from the white man . . .'[8]

Such a move was a direct outcome of the Nationalists' determination to apply *apartheid* in all areas of life. In particular, the existing

[1] *South Africa*, 18 Apr. 1953, quoted in the Africa Bureau's *Information Digest* (April–May 1953), p. 20.
[2] ibid.   [3] ibid.   [4] ibid.   [5] See below, pp. 133 ff.
[6] *Ass. Debates*, vol. 83, 29 Sept. 1953, col. 4426.
[7] Muriel Horrell, *A Decade of Bantu Education* (Johannesburg, S.A.I.R.R. 1964), pp. 5–6, 9–11.
[8] *Ass. Debates*, vol. 83, 17 Sept. 1953, col. 3613.

provisions for African education had been unsatisfactory because, as Dr. H. F. Verwoerd, the Minister of Native Affairs, pointed out, the 'education . . . [an African] received . . . made him feel he was not a member of the Bantu community but a member of a wider community.'[1] Maree explained the Government's case. There was no middle way:

. . . there are in South Africa today actually only two courses open . . . there are only two possible trends of policy which can be followed in regard to the Natives in general. One is the trend of liberalism, which means uniform development. On the other hand, there is the trend adopted by the Nationalists, which means development in their own sphere. On the one hand one has liberalism which means nothing but intermingling; on the other hand one has nationalism which means segregation.[2]

Maree went on to stress: 'Native education is at present nothing less than an instrument in the hands of liberalism.'[3] Such liberalism was at variance with Government policy; in particular, it fostered an ambition for political rights which would remain unfulfilled. Verwoerd was quite explicit: '. . . if the Native in South Africa today in any kind of school in existence is being taught to expect that he will live his adult life under a policy of equal rights, he is making a big mistake.'[4]

The principle of Bantu Education, quite apart from the manner of its implementation, was contradictory to any liberal view of education; it was unacceptable to all non-Nationalist whites. They refused to accept the idea that the type of education one received should differ according to race. Even the Eiselen Commission (whose report provided the basis for the Act)[5] had questioned the Nationalists' assumption that there were innate differences between the ability of white and non-white. United Party M.P.s stressed that the basic principles of education must be the same for all races.[6] For those

[1] ibid., col. 3577.   [2] ibid., col. 3611–12.   [3] ibid., col. 3612.
[4] ibid., col. 3586. cf. the comment made by Mr. M. D. C. de Wet Nel: 'Native education will no longer be a loose cog in the life of the Bantu as the position is today. . . .' Ass. Debates, vol. 83, 23 Sept. 1953, col. 4044.
[5] The Commission on Native Education had been appointed in 1949 with Dr. W. W. M. Eiselen, Secretary for Native Affairs, as chairman. The Commissioners submitted their Report on 18 Apr. 1951. Carter, The Politics of Inequality, p. 102.
[6] e.g. Mr. T. O. Williams: 'There is only one educational road whatever the colour of a man's skin.' Ass. Debates, vol. 83, 23 Sept. 1953, col. 4093; also Dr. A. Jonker, ibid., 17 Sept. 1953, col. 3651.

liberals primarily concerned with non-white rights rather than white ones the plan to educate the non-whites for permanent inferiority was fundamentally offensive. The Liberal Party had been founded in 1953 on the principle of equal rights regardless of race.[1] In particular, the Liberals sought political rights for non-whites. This could only be accomplished, in their view, by following the precedent established by the Cape liberals—that of granting the franchise to all those who had reached a minimum education level.

Furthermore, the Government's plan involved the centralization of African education which had previously been under the control of the provinces. To those customarily conscious of provincial rights, such as the English-speakers in Natal, the Nationalists' move was as much a threat to white rights as to non-white.[2] Hostility towards the Bantu Education Act was, in this regard, at least as much a fear of an extension of Afrikaner dominance, as it was indignation over the threatened deprivation of non-white rights. Thus the most conservative of the United Party M.P.s had common cause with the 'progressives' within the party. Such a consensus strengthened temporarily the bonds which existed between non-Nationalist whites with very different views on colour.

The 'English' churches in South Africa made strong allies for such opponents of Bantu Education. They were singled out for attack by the Government for spreading 'liberalistic' views among non-whites.[3] As the chief agencies of African education prior to 1953, they had been concerned to promote Christian values as well as to provide a general education for non-whites. In sharpest contrast to the teachings of the Dutch Reformed Churches, the other Christian denominations in South Africa had customarily taught that 'all men were equal in the sight of God'. Such religious teaching had obviously provided the groundwork for the political ideals of some of the liberals.

The Nationalists' plan to assume direction of Bantu Education posed church leaders with an unprecedented challenge. If they failed to comply with the terms of the Act they faced severe penalties.[4] They were thus faced with the basic question of whether an inferior education was better than no education at all. Without exception they protested at the Government's action and underlying intentions and expressed resentment, too, at their loss of independence.[5] But the

[1] See above, p. 112.
[2] e.g. Mr. D. Mitchell, *Ass. Debates*, 17 Sept. 1953, cols. 3599ff.
[3] Mr. W. A. Maree, *Ass. Debates*, 17 Sept. 1953, col. 3612.
[4] Horrell, *A Decade of Bantu Education*, pp. 21–3.   [5] ibid., pp. 24–34.

majority of them, with bad conscience perhaps, but with good reason, complied with the Nationalists' conditions.[1]

Those who refused to do so—most notably members of the Roman Catholic and Anglican hierarchies—were vilified by the Nationalist Government. In the struggle which followed they defended their principles eloquently and dramatically, and thus provided fresh hope for the liberal cause in the fifties. In particular, the Anglican priest, Trevor Huddleston, whose identification with non-whites and their problems was the ideal of the most ardent of the white liberals, made a striking appeal to opinion overseas. His book, *Naught for Your Comfort*,[2] publicized abroad in the fifties the quality of non-white living conditions in South Africa. And, with other new factors, was responsible for the mounting volume of overseas criticism.[3]

iii

The Nationalist attack on liberal views did not stop with schools. And just as the Bantu Education Act embroiled the 'English' churches, so the prospect of university *apartheid* engaged the 'English' universities in a struggle against the Government. The Nationalists' intention to segregate universities was first announced in May 1955.[4] A Separate Universities Education Bill was tabled in March 1957. No warning had been given that private interests as well as public policy would be affected and the Government was forced to redraft the Bill. In its revised form, the Bill did not prohibit the 'open' universities from admitting non-whites; rather, the students themselves were liable to prosecution if they did not comply with the terms of the proposed law.[5] Such a revision was no doubt due to the hostility which the initial Bill had provoked; yet the modification in no way affected the Nationalists' purpose of segregating universities.

The new Bill was reintroduced in the House of Assembly in April 1957. It envisaged university colleges for the tertiary education of all non-whites. Separate colleges would be provided for Africans, Coloureds, and Indians; in the case of the Africans, colleges would be

---

[1] ibid.
[2] Trevor Huddleston, *Naught for Your Comfort*, 1st edn., 1956 (London, Fontana, 1960).
[3] See below, pp. 137, 141, 144, 146, 182.
[4] *A Survey of Race Relations in South Africa 1956–1957* (Johannesburg, S.A.I.R.R.), p. 197.
[5] ibid., p. 203.

K

tribal in character. In this way, the Nationalists planned to discourage non-whites from developing ambitions to be part of an integrated society; non-whites' training at university level was to be strictly vocational with a view to their future role among those of the same race.[1]

Previously, South African universities had been free to choose whom they accepted as students. Three universities had enrolled non-whites—the University of Cape Town, the University of the Witwatersrand, and the University of Natal, although in Natal non-white students had attended separate classes in separate buildings.[2] Under the terms of the Separate Universities Education Bill, these universities would lose their autonomy with regard to whom they taught. The Government's motives were clarified by Mr. D. J. Mostert during the Second Reading of the Bill: 'We do not have the slightest intention of harming academic freedom, but we have the deliberate purpose of saving academic freedom from the disastrous influence of liberalism which is using the university as a breeding place.'[3] But the 'English' universities were not easily mollified.[4] In response to their vigorous protest, the Minister of Education, Arts, and Science, the Hon. J. H. Viljoen emphasized that the Government had the right to interfere 'as the national interest' demanded it.[5] He spoke in ominous terms:

... it must be remembered that the degree of autonomy which the universities have today was accorded them by the State and can therefore be amended by the State. . . . The State has now decided on a certain policy of great national importance with regard to the relationship between White and non-White, and that policy does not stop at the borders of the universities . . . there can be no *imperium in imperio*.[6]

Here was a concept of the role of the State fundamentally different from that held by all liberals. In their view, the State existed to safeguard the rights of the individual which were paramount. The

[1] ibid., pp. 199–201. University colleges for Africans were to be under the control of the Minister of Native Affairs; colleges for other non-whites were the responsibility of the Minister of Education, Arts and Science.

[2] See *The Open Universities in South Africa*, a report published on behalf of the Conference of representatives of the University of Cape Town and the University of the Witwatersrand, Johannesburg, held in Cape Town on 9, 10, and 11 Jan. 1957 (Johannesburg, Witwatersrand Univ. Press, 1957), p. 2.

[3] *Ass. Debates*, vol. 95, 27 May 1957, col. 6795.

[4] Horrell, *A Decade of Bantu Education*, pp. 125–6; also *A Survey of Race Relations in South Africa 1956–1957*, pp. 201–2, 206–7.

[5] *Ass. Debates*, vol. 95, 27 May 1957, col. 6771.   [6] ibid., col. 6770.

Nationalists, by contrast, argued that the interests of the State were supreme. Such a claim had the strongest totalitarian implications and represented the gravest threat to liberty.

Statements such as Viljoen's were repeatedly challenged by United Party members, who doggedly defended the principle of academic freedom. The universities to be affected also took up cudgels against the Nationalists. Members of staff, as well as the students, through their official body, the National Union of South African Students, protested against the Government's latest move to apply *apartheid* to the open universities.[1] English-language newspapers gave consistent and favourable coverage to such demonstrations and protests, which were sustained for the years during which the measure was under public, as well as parliamentary, debate.[2]

The grounds on which these opponents criticized the Government's scheme for university *apartheid* were liberal ones. More often than not, however, concern was shown for the white rights which were in jeopardy rather than for non-white rights. Most non-Nationalists had yet to realize that if they condoned the infringement of non-white rights they automatically infringed their own freedom. Official objections to university *apartheid* were raised because some were 'opposed in principle to legislative enforcement of academic segregation on racial grounds.'[3] Protests were lodged, too, because the anti-segregationists argued that the separate academic facilities which the Nationalists planned for non-whites 'could not be equal to those provided in an open university'.[4] Protests on these grounds enjoyed the support even of those who were firmly opposed to the extension of political rights to non-whites. Theirs was clearly not a liberalism which meant they were willing to apply a liberal solution to the colour problem. It seems likely that one of the chief reasons (if not the main one) why the protesters chose university autonomy and academic freedom as the most important ground to be defended was precisely because this was all that some of them were concerned with.

[1] Horrell, *A Decade of Bantu Education*, pp. 126–8.
[2] e.g. the *Rand Daily Mail* (22 Jan. 1957) reported that a deputation representing the S.R.C.s of 'Wits' and Cape Town University had unsuccessfully sought an interview with the Minister of Education (*P.D.* No. 2, 28 Jan. 1957); the *Cape Argus* (23 Feb. 1957) reported wide public support for the principle of academic non-segregation at the two 'open' universities among a group of prominent citizens, which included leaders of commerce and industry, former judges, publishers, and writers (*P.D.* No. 8, 7 Mar. 1957).
[3] *The Open Universities in South Africa*, p. 2.   [4] ibid., p. 5.

Tactically, it was a wise choice of emphasis. It not only ensured the widest opposition to the Government from non-Nationalists. It also guaranteed the support of the Afrikaans universities. Numbers of those who taught in the 'English' universities were accustomed to despise Afrikaner culture in general, and the status of Afrikaner academics in particular. But they could not afford to scorn potential allies in their struggle against university *apartheid*. The staff and students of Afrikaans universities might well be willing to oppose the Government on the issue of their autonomy;[1] they would be unlikely to do so on the issue of non-white rights.

Tactics aside, however, it seems that the principle of academic freedom held top priority in the minds of most of the anti-segregationists in the 'English' universities. So anxious were they to make their position unmistakably clear that they defended (at least by implication) the closed universities' right to exclude students on grounds of colour. Representatives of the Universities of Cape Town and the Witwatersrand who conferred in Cape Town in January 1957 endorsed this reasoning in their Report:

> If the closed universities do not wish to become open, they are insisting upon the conditions which they prefer. They should not be compelled to change their policies. It is their own free choice; we would not support any suggestion that they should be coerced into a change.[2]

The universities were primarily concerned with their own particular interests. Misgivings on this score were expressed by the writer of the Education League pamphlet, *Open Minds in Open Universities*, published in 1956. It was not, the writer argued, primarily a 'trade union' struggle in which the universities were fighting to defend their independence:[3]

> The preservation of individual liberties is the fundamental issue posed by the present threat to the open universities. This is why their threat is also a real threat to every person in South Africa who values democratic freedom. This is why the freedom of the universities is part and parcel of the freedom of South Africans.[4]

[1] e.g. Prof. J. C. Coetzee, Rector of Potchefstroom, stressed the importance of academic independence for all universities, including the proposed non-white colleges. *Die Transvaler*, 3 Apr. 1958 (*P.D.* No. 18, 8 May 1958); also Horrell, *A Decade of Bantu Education*, p. 128.

[2] *The Open Universities in South Africa*, p. 35.

[3] *Open Minds in Open Universities* (Johannesburg, Education League, 1956), p. 8.

[4] ibid.

The Liberal Party supported such a view. Party spokesmen defended the principle of academic freedom, but in their view, any distinction made between white rights and non-white rights was dangerously misleading. Margaret Ballinger made this clear in the Assembly:

Every thinking person amongst the European population is opposed to this measure, for at last they are beginning to realize, with these attacks on the highest institutions of the country—first, the church and now the universities—what apartheid as visualized by the Nationalist Government really means. *It means the undermining of everybody's freedom* [author's italic].[1]

Here Mrs. Ballinger emphasized the Liberal Party's conviction that the Nationalists were intent on the destruction of the liberal state.

Opposition to the Government appeared to be advancing on all fronts. Non-Nationalists were greatly encouraged by the nature and extent of overseas reaction to the proposed segregation of South African universities. Vigorous protests were mounted by university teachers in Britain—a fact of particular significance to those who taught in 'English' universities in South Africa and felt themselves to be much more akin to their fellow academics in Britain than they were to their fellow South Africans, the Afrikaner Nationalists. Their hopes were naturally raised and sustained by the publicity given to their cause by such groups as the British Committee on Science and Freedom. The issue was thoroughly aired in the Committee's Bulletin[2] and discussed at a public protest meeting which they organized.[3] It was at this meeting that the idea of an 'academic boycott' of South African universities was mooted.[4] At the time, in November 1957, this was seen as possible pressure to hasten inevitable success, rather than as the desperate and futile gesture it became when put into effect in the sixties.

What appeared to Nationalists and non-Nationalists alike as a flood of overseas criticism was due in no small measure to the efforts of the National Union of South African Students. Not unexpectedly, this student organization, with branches in the English-speaking universities, was more inclined than the staff to be radical in their opposition to the Government. The campaign which they waged evoked an

[1] *Ass. Debates*, vol. 95, 27 May 1957, col. 6811.
[2] e.g. the issue of *Science and Freedom* (No. 9, August 1957) entitled *Apartheid: The Threat to South Africa's Universities*, which included a message from Trevor Huddleston, and articles by liberal educationists Edgar Brookes and A. van der Sandt Centlivres (then Chancellor of the University of Cape Town).
[3] *The Times* (London), 4 Nov. 1957 (*Africa Digest*, v, 3 (1957)).   [4] ibid.

enthusiastic response among students—and academics—abroad. By March 1957 they had already received expressions of sympathy and support from the National Union of Students in America, as well as from official university sources in the West Indies, Canada, Australia, New Zealand, England, Sweden, Nigeria, Holland, Germany, and Italy.[1] At the same time, the President of the N.U.S.A.S., Mr. E. M. Wentzel, made an appeal to the Nationalist Prime Minister. The gravamen of his protest was that the universities were being coerced into supporting the racialist doctrine of *apartheid*.[2] He referred to the way in which German universities had by their capitulation to the Nazis, 'contributed materially to the growth of Nazism'. 'This [he said] must not be allowed to happen in South Africa. . . .'[3]

Opposition to the segregation of the universities initially appeared to be effective, for the issue was protracted. After the Separate University Education Bill was passed at the Second Reading in May 1957, it was referred to a Select Committee and subsequently to a Commission of Inquiry.[4] Such delay, and further opportunity to voice their protests, raised the hopes of non-Nationalists. The general election of 16 April 1958 took place with the issue unresolved. The Government's opponents trusted that the controversy would have weakened the Nationalists' position; in fact, they were returned to power with an increased majority.[5] In their strengthened position, they introduced the Extension of University Education Bill into the House on 13 August 1958. This Bill incorporated the recommendations of the Majority Report of the Commissioners.[6] It was debated during the first session of parliament in 1959, during which time the Opposition continually forced divisions and the Government repeatedly employed the guillotine.[7] The Extension of University Education Bill was finally enacted on 11 June 1959, four years after the Nationalists had made public their plans for university *apartheid*.[8] As the Government had sought from the beginning, the Act provided for the establishment of university colleges for non-whites. Non-white

[1] *Rand Daily Mail*, 15 Mar. 1957.
[2] *Cape Argus*, 13 Mar. 1957 (*P.D.* No. 10, 21 Mar. 1957).
[3] *Cape Times*, 14 Mar. 1957 (*P.D.* No. 10, 21 Mar. 1957).
[4] *A Survey of Race Relations in South Africa 1957–1958*, p. 194.
[5] See below, p. 187.
[6] *A Survey of Race Relations in South Africa 1957–1958*, pp. 194–201. A Minority Report submitted by 5 of the 13 Commissioners was disregarded by the Government. ibid., p. 200.
[7] *A Survey of Race Relations in South Africa 1958–1959*, pp. 266–7.
[8] See above, p. 133.

students already enrolled at 'white' universities could complete their courses. In future, no non-white student was permitted to attend the hitherto open universities without Ministerial consent.[1]

iv

In the meantime, anti-Government protest had reached fever-pitch over the Native Laws Amendment Bill introduced in February 1957. Intended to simplify and consolidate existing regulations governing the movements of urban Africans, the Bill constituted a further attack on liberal institutions. After revision,[2] the terms of the Bill provided that where such bodies as hospitals, churches, and welfare organizations were situated in 'white' areas, permission must be sought from the Minister of Native Affairs before these institutions could continue to operate. Provided that the local authority agreed, the Minister could debar Africans (other than employees) from these institutions, if he considered their presence constituted a 'nuisance'.[3] Such regulations would clearly mean manifold restrictions of liberties and the prospect antagonized a wide range of critics.[4]

The United Party was immediately involved because the proposed law was further evidence that the Nationalists would not accept economic integration as permanent.[5] It provided stricter controls on the influx of migratory labour and increased the power of local authorities to deal arbitrarily with non-white urban workers whose situation contravened the regulations. These provisions caused 'progressives' within the United Party—as well as more conservative U.P. members—to challenge afresh the feasibility of *apartheid*. On behalf of the U.P., Mrs. Helen Suzman argued: 'The whole trend of economic development in this country is away from the migratory system of labour and towards stabilization and nothing . . . will stop this progress.'[6] The Government had a ready reply to such a case. Mr. J. C. Greyling asked on their behalf: 'What is the reply of the United Party? What is going to be their reply one day when the Native comes along, as he must come and will come, and asks the White man in South Africa for the vote, for the right

[1] *A Survey of Race Relations in South Africa 1958–1959*, p. 266.
[2] *A Survey of Race Relations in South Africa 1956–1957*, p. 25.
[3] ibid., pp. 25–7.   [4] ibid., pp. 31–5.   [5] See above, pp. 24–5, 43–4.
[6] *Ass. Debates*, vol. 94, 21 Mar. 1957, col. 3297.

to own land?'[1] Here they raised the issue of the ultimate result of economic integration—a result which only 'progressives' like Mrs. Suzman would welcome, and one which was unacceptable to most U.P. supporters.

Other opposition sprang from the Government's intention to restrict severely opportunities for interracial contact; the Minister of Bantu Administration and Development was to be granted wide powers to prohibit any kind of interracial meeting in the 'white' areas of town.[2] Here the independence of such bodies as the Institute of Race Relations was threatened.[3] The prospect of bans on interracial meetings struck an especially heavy blow to the Liberal Party; party spokesmen saw immediately the threat to their existence as a multiracial party.[4] The editor of *Contact*, the unofficial party paper,[5] wrote:

. . . [the law's] implications are so far-reaching that it is almost impossible to imagine all the opportunities which it provides for interference in the narrow field of liberty which still lies open to us . . . [the law] strikes at the very roots of everything in which . . . [a member of the Liberal Party] believes most strongly.[6]

The 'church clause' provoked particularly widespread and vigorous opposition.[7] Part of Clause 29(c) of the original Bill made it compulsory for churches in white areas to apply for permission to the

[1] ibid., 3 Apr. 1957, col. 3968.

[2] Horrell, *Legislation and Race Relations*, p. 53. Restrictions on interracial contact were essential for the success of *apartheid*. *Die Transvaler* (27 Feb. 1957) explained why: 'It is not so much the destruction of the feeling of difference and otherness which is the great danger for the preservation of the European and his civilization in this multiracial land. As long as liberalistic bishops and canons, professors, students and politicians can freely attend church and hold meetings and socials, together, apartheid will be infringed in its marrow.' Quoted in Carter, *The Politics of Inequality*, p. 118.

[3] A point made by the 'progressive' U.P. member, John Cope, *Ass. Debates*, vol. 94, 21 Mar. 1957, col. 3307. The Institute's reaction is described in *A Survey of Race Relations in South Africa 1956–1957*, pp. 12, 16–17. In July 1957 the President and Director wrote to all members: '. . . more people are seeing the situation, not as a matter of just dealing between White and non-White, but in its proper perspective as a matter of individual liberty.' ibid., p. 16.

[4] e.g. Senator W. Ballinger's comment:'It is fairly obvious to all that the Liberal Party is one of the targets in Verwoerd's Bill' (*Star*, 7 Mar. 1957, in *Africa Digest*, iv, 5 (1957)); also Alan Paton, 'Freedom of Human Association is at Stake', *Rand Daily Mail*, 30 Apr. 1957.

[5] See Publicity Commission Report in Minutes of the National Congress of the L.P., Johannesburg, 4–6 Apr. 1959, mim., P.A.S.

[6] *Contact* (Mar. 1957).

[7] *A Survey of Race Relations in South Africa 1956–1957*, pp. 18–19.

Minister of Native Affairs in order to hold services which non-whites would attend.[1] If permission were not sought—and granted—the church concerned was liable to prosecution. Opposition to this aspect of the Bill was so extensive that the clause was modified twice.[2] In its final form, it left the offending African, rather than the church concerned, liable to prosecution.

Church leaders were not satisfied by this sop to the autonomy of liberal institutions.[3] The 'English' churches, which had been initially aroused over the Bantu Education Act, were challenged afresh. Prominent among the dissenting Church leaders was the Anglican Bishop of Johannesburg, the Right Rev. Ambrose Reeves. His stand made excellent copy for the English press in South Africa, as well as overseas newspapers.[4] But it did not force the Government to concede any vital ground. On the contrary, such hostility, especially from abroad, increased their determination to defend their isolated position. The Bill was finally enacted on 24 May 1957. Its provisions were enforced five days later.

V

Some—but not all—of those who opposed the *apartheid* legislation of the mid fifties saw clearly how far white rights and non-white rights were inextricably interwoven. One protest group which came to a gradual acknowledgement of this fact was the Black Sash, a women's organization which emerged in May 1955.[5] The group's aims were not new. The Black Sashers were initially concerned with the preservation of the Constitution and with promoting the unity of the white

---

[1] ibid., pp. 17–18.   [2] ibid., pp. 19–22.

[3] ibid., pp. 23–25; also *Rand Daily Mail*, 15 July 1957—a pastoral letter from the Bishop of Johannesburg, the Right Revd. Ambrose Reeves, had been read in all Anglican churches in the Johannesburg diocese on Sunday 14 July 1957. It had included the following: '. . . if at any time the Minister decides to implement this ["church"] clause in any, or all, of the churches in our diocese, in regard to any religious service or church function, we call on our clergy and people to disobey this direction.'

[4] The widespread interest—and protest—which the 'church clause' aroused is indicated by the coverage given to the issue in *Africa Digest* at the time, e.g. v, 2–3 (1957).

[5] Called at first the Women's Defence of the Constitution League, the group was formed on the initiative of a handful of women, who met in Johannesburg on 25 May 1955. The name of the League was changed to that of 'The Black Sash' by an agreement reached at the League's national congress in April 1956. See Mirabel Rogers, *The Black Sash* (Johannesburg, Rotonews, 1956), p. 227.

races in South Africa. In addition they sought to protect civil liberties and 'the principles of parliamentary democracy'.[1] They were, in all of this, influenced by their recollections of fascism in the thirties and forties, and they interpreted the Nationalist manoeuvres as 'echoes of the jackboot'.[2] Such views were clearly similar to those which the United Party had traditionally upheld. They were principles guaranteed to gain wide support among non-Nationalist whites.

In contrast with their aims, Black Sash tactics were novel. Their most characteristic—and arresting—method of protest was to stand in public places in silent vigil, wearing their black sashes. In so doing, they provoked the Government and Nationalist sympathizers to the limits of their patience, not least because of the traditional Afrikaner view of the proper place of the second sex.[3]

The Black Sash failed to do more than irritate the Government over the constitutional question. Yet by the time the Nationalists secured the removal of the Coloured voters from the common roll in November 1956, the Sashers had already found new purposes. They had decided to become a fact-finding educative group, as well as to continue their vigilance and vocal protest against threats to individual rights.[4] It rapidly became clear to the Sashers that the infringement of such rights during the fifties was having its chief impact on the non-whites rather than on the whites. And the women found themselves drawn increasingly to defend non-white rather than white rights. The Government's plan to introduce passes for African women met with dogged resistance from the Black Sashers;[5] so, too, did the Nationalist Bill to establish separate universities.[6] As they became involved in social welfare work among Africans who lived and worked in the cities and towns, they soon became conversant with—or, at least,

[1] Eulalie Stott emphasized that these were initial aims of the Black Sash in a discussion recorded in *The Black Sash*, ix, 2 (May–July 1965), 25.

[2] The National President, Jean Sinclair, in 'Ten Years of Endeavour', in *The Black Sash*, ibid., p. 1.

[3] e.g., the remark made by Dawie, the political commentator of *Die Burger* 11 Feb. 1956). 'Their method [he said, referring to the Sashers] combines the highly unfeminine quality of silence with the extremely feminine quality of nagging troublesomeness.' (*P.D.* No. 6, 16 Feb. 1956).

[4] *A Survey of Race Relations in South Africa 1955–1956*, p. 5.

[5] e.g. the Western Cape divisions of the Black Sash was one of the sponsors of an 'Association to Abolish Passes for African Women' formed in 1957. *A Survey of Race Relations in South Africa 1956–1957*, p. 72.

[6] The official statement of the Black Sash against the Government's move to segregate universities appeared in *The Black Sash*, iii, 16 (Mar. 1959), 10–11.

aware of—the intricacies of the laws affecting non-whites.[1] And they saw a need to help those whose jobs and families were threatened by the multiple influx control regulations. As a result of this a series of advice offices were set up: the first, known initially as the Bail Fund Office, was established in the Western Cape Region in 1958.[2] In this way the Sashers hoped to help non-whites secure justice in the courts over the pass laws.

However, this change of direction was marked by a decline in membership. These defections were due in part, no doubt, to the waning of the initial enthusiasm of some of the Sashers, particularly in view of their failure to achieve their primary objective. But others were disillusioned not so much by this failure, as by the changing character of the organization itself. Theirs had been a concern not *primarily* for white rights, but *exclusively* for white rights.[3] This exodus enabled the Black Sash to endorse publicly the cause of constitutional rights for non-whites. One result of their direct involvement with non-whites and their disabilities was what one of them described as 'a realization of the fatal infirmities in the South African Constitution'.[4] At their 1958 national conference the Sashers emphasized that the Constitution was inadequate to 'fulfil the needs of our multi-racial society', and they determined to work for a new constitution, which would more effectively safeguard the rights of *all* races.[5]

The emergence and survival of such a group gave hope to all Government opponents. The Sashers themselves were heartened by their own sense of purpose[6] and also by those successes, which, even if relatively limited, seemed directly attributable to their efforts.[7] Again, not the least reason for trusting that the tide would turn against the Government was the way in which news of Black Sash activities

[1] Margaret Roberts, 'Women Who Care', in *The Black Sash*, ix, 2 (May–July 1965), 12.
[2] Noel Robb, 'The Athlone Advice Office', ibid., pp. 18–19.
[3] Author's interview with Jean Sinclair, Black Sash Office, Johannesburg, 8 Dec. 1965.
[4] Margaret Roberts, 'Women Who Care', p. 14.
[5] *A Survey of Race Relations in South Africa 1957–1958*, p. 20.
[6] e.g. Margaret Roberts, Cape Western Regional Chairman in the sixties, recalls that it was 'an immense relief to be able to do something positive, to dissociate oneself from the nation's Gadarene gallop—to dig one's heels in on the edge of the slippery slope and run up a flag, even though it had to be a solemn black one. . . .' 'Women Who Care', p. 14.
[7] e.g. their dogged resistance to the 'church clause' seemed to help render it null and void, and they were able successfully to defend the non-racial municipal franchise in the Cape. ibid., p. 12.

was reported overseas. As the editor of the Johannesburg *Star* pointed out: 'Their gesture . . . has gained the attention of the whole civilized world in a way no other form of protest could have done.'[1]

vi

Perhaps no aspect of the proliferation of protest was more encouraging to the anti-Nationalists than the growth of dissension within Nationalist ranks. Criticisms of Government policy were expressed with increasing frequency by prominent Afrikaner churchmen and university teachers. One of the first to challenge the Government was Professor B. B. Keet of the Stellenbosch Theological Seminary. In his book *Whither South Africa?* published in 1956 he argued that total *apartheid* was an impossibility and that the manner of its partial implementation could not be reconciled with Christian principles.[2] A year later he was willing to uphold these views in an address to the South African Institute of Race Relations, a move which seriously antagonized the Government press.[3]

But criticisms from within Nationalist ranks were more generally made about method and timing rather than about principle. On the issue of university segregation, for example, the editor of *Die Burger* welcomed the postponement of the Bill in May 1957. The Government had, he considered, laid unwise emphasis on exclusion of non-whites from open universities.[4] In addition, it ought to be acknowledged that there would be a long delay before the new non-white universities would be able 'to provide equal facilities in all respects. . . .'[5] A number of notable Afrikaners were prepared still to accept the possibility of total *apartheid*, but pressed the Government hard to move more quickly and effectively in the direction of territorial segregation. Among the advocates of this policy was Professor J. H. Chris Coetzee, who addressed the Afrikaanse Calvinistiese Bond congress in Potchefstroom in April 1957:

> Apartheid in the sense of a continuing horizontal separation with the European on top and the Bantu under the line of separation is increasingly untenable in practice. In approach and in practice we will have to change to

[1] 11 Nov. 1955. Mirabel Rogers records overseas reporting of Black Sash activities, e.g. in the Canadian *Montreal Star*, the London *Daily News* and *The Times* (*The Black Sash*, pp. 179, 187, 189).
[2] *Die Transvaler*, 26 Jan. 1956 (*P.D.* No. 4, 2 Feb. 1956).
[3] *P.D.* No. 26, 11 July 1957.
[4] *Die Burger*, 20 May 1957 (*P.D.* No. 20, 29 May 1957).   [5] ibid.

a situation where the dividing line will be a vertical one. It is based, literally and figuratively, on the territorial: a homeland and a fatherland of one's own for each.[1]

Views such as these were readily interpreted by non-Nationalists as a sign of an imminent split in the ranks of Nationalist support. This confirmed their hopes that the Government would be defeated in the 1958 general election.

vii

Formidable anti-Government forces appeared to exist in the months preceding the 1958 election. The possibility of change was elaborated by the political correspondent in the *Rand Daily Mail*. It appeared, he said, that 'the so-called traditional South African attitude to the Black–White racial problem is beginning, very slowly, to crumble under the strain of self-examination.'[2] He continued:

On either side of this central body of what is euphemistically called conservative opinion, unquestioned for so long, there are growing numbers of people who are breaking away, people who have faced up to and made their choice. . . . At last there are the beginnings of a proper polarisation of South African politics and a proper interplay of opinion is coming into being.[3]

The writer predicted that the process of polarization would eventually enable a liberal solution of the colour question to be found. Those who shared his optimism had, in fact, mistaken the shadow for the substance. In retrospect, it was clear that they had misinterpreted the evidence.

The Government's opponents, including liberals, misjudged the importance of division within the Nationalist camp. This 'revolt in Afrikaner intellectual thought'[4] spread still further after the 1958 election, but it did not threaten the Nationalists' hold on political power. Rather, its impact was absorbed by the Nationalist politicians and can be seen most directly in the Government's concept of territorial *apartheid* which the Nationalists had developed by 1959.[5] The significance of the 'English' churches' involvement was also misunderstood. True, the criticism of *apartheid* by prominent churchmen

---

[1] *Die Weste*, 4 Apr. 1957 (*P.D.* No. 14, 18 Apr. 1957).
[2] *Rand Daily Mail*, 13 Feb. 1958.   [3] ibid.
[4] *Golden City Post*, 6 July 1958 (*P.D.* No. 27, 10 July 1958).
[5] See below, p. 188.

in South Africa aroused liberal opinion abroad. But such criticism had precisely the opposite effect to that which the Government's opponents predicted. Not least because frequently the churchmen involved were Englishmen by birth, and not South Africans, the Nationalists were confirmed in their belief that the rest of the world did not understand their problem. Moreover, English-speakers slowly grew less hostile about what had previously seemed merely anti-Britishness on the part of Afrikaner Nationalists. In this way, overseas support for the liberal cause in South Africa, which liberals in particular had hoped would bring the Nationalists to their knees, eventually boomeranged back against them.[1]

The polarization which was taking place in South Africa in 1958 did not bring about the 'proper interplay of opinion' which the *Rand Daily Mail* correspondent had believed it would. The basic question in white politics in South Africa was already, in the fifties, not whether the whites would remain dominant, but by what means they could do so most effectively. Clear consensus on this shared necessity was to emerge after the 1958 election. The polarization which then took place did not produce a choice between the two major political parties based on alternative political principles. Rather, it revealed the extent of the United Party's agreement with the Nationalists' colour policy and the gulf which divided them both from those who advocated the extension of non-white rights.

[1] See below, p. 212.

CHAPTER VII

Further frustration for the African National Congress (1953–1955)

i

Before the election in 1953, the A.N.C. had drawn away from the principles espoused by white liberals in South Africa. They were committed to the use of means regarded as unconstitutional in the white world, and they had repudiated gradualism and a qualified franchise.[1] Thus, after the election, the gap between Congress and white liberals was as great as ever, despite the formation of a separate Liberal Party.[2] The aims and methods which the Liberal Party endorsed in 1953 made the term 'liberal' highly suspect among Congressmen. Congress leaders regarded themselves by this time as African nationalists. Even so, liberal principles persisted in the outlook of the A.N.C. leadership in the fifties and when they spoke of their fundamental aims they generally used the language of Western liberal democracy. Lutuli, for example, in his Presidential Address to the Natal A.N.C. late in 1953, spoke in these terms: 'Our Nationalism should be progressive and liberal and thus embrace a co-operation with other communities on the basis of equality and an intense desire for the universal enjoyment of democratic rights by all people in the country.'[3]

The A.N.C. were, however, denied the use of the constitutional and parliamentary means still open to white opponents of the Government. Moreover, in the face of the reprisals of the Nationalists following the Defiance Campaign, the strategy of passive resistance was no longer practicable.[4] Even the right to protest against unjust laws had been curtailed in the non-white world—a fact in sharpest contrast to the widespread and vociferous protests by whites in the same period.[5] In such circumstances the A.N.C.'s only source of strength,

---

[1] See above, pp. 31, 68–9.   [2] See above, p. 111.
[3] Presidential Address by the Provincial President read at the Annual Conference of Natal A.N.C., Ladysmith, 31 Oct.–1 Nov. 1953, mim., P.A.S.
[4] See above, p. 92.   [5] See above, ch. VI, *passim.*

and potential bargaining power, lay in their numbers. Had they possessed effective control over a large African majority, they would have been in a strong position to persuade the white minority to share political power. It thus became of paramount importance that they build a well-organized, well-disciplined mass movement.

In view of their aim, the most urgent task was to consolidate the sudden and considerable increase in membership. Between June 1952 when the Defiance Campaign began and December 1952, the paid-up membership had risen from 7,000 to 100,000.[1] J. L. Z. Njongwe—who had been outstanding in his leadership of the Campaign in the Port Elizabeth area[2]—claimed publicly in February 1953, that the A.N.C. had 'politicised the people and welded them into a single united people ready to struggle for freedom'.[3] In actual fact, no such unity had been created. While there was an unprecedented chance to capitalize on the enthusiasm of the non-whites, the Campaign had nevertheless highlighted a number of weaknesses in Congress organization. Unless these were remedied, the initiative, which the Congress leaders felt they had won, would soon be lost.[4]

The organizational difficulties with which Congress was confronted were, in part, the outcome of what the General-Secretary, Oliver Tambo, described in 1954 as the 'low political development' of the Africans.[5] The mass support which leaders hoped to gather was crucially dependent on whether they could train Africans in unfamiliar roles within the structure of the A.N.C. This involved, initially, training organizers who would provide steady leadership

[1] Kuper, *Passive Resistance*, p. 146.

[2] Njongwe's qualities as a leader are discussed briefly in Benson, *The African Patriots*, pp. 167–8.

[3] In his address (as Acting President) to the A.N.C. Cape Provincial Congress, 14 Feb. 1953, mim., P.A.S. On the same occasion Joe Matthews claimed that the Africans had built 'an unprecedented unity and confidence in themselves and their destiny'. In a Political Review presented to the Provincial Conference of the African National Congress (Cape) 14 Feb. 1953, mim., P.A.S.

[4] Njongwe referred to this gaining of the initiative in his Presidential Address to the Cape Provincial Congress, 14 Feb. 1953. Later in 1953, at the Transvaal Provincial Congress, Mandela's Presidential Address referred to this same renewed enthusiasm which the Campaign had generated (*No Easy Walk*, p. 22). cf. the Transvaal Executive's reference to the value of the Defiance Campaign, which had, they said, 'brought the organisation into physical contact with the broad masses of the people who had not heard of the African National Congress. . . .' Executive Committee Report to Transvaal Provincial Conference, Sophiatown, Johannesburg, 10–11 Oct. 1953, mim., P.A.S., p. 2.

[5] Report to the 42nd Annual Conference of the A.N.C. held in Durban, 16–19 Dec., 1954, mim., P.A.S., p. 13.

that was consistent with directives passed down the chain of command. It was also essential to train local leaders to handle branch funds in a responsible manner.[1] Many local leaders would have had little, if any, previous experience with financial matters of that sort—and the rank and file who paid their dues at local level would have had even less. Moreover, in the face of their own poverty, there must have been the constant temptation to embezzle funds. Problems of this order rarely faced white political parties; in the white world, the rules of political activity were well-established and more widely understood. Not so among Africans. Moreover, the A.N.C.'s difficulties were exaggerated in rural areas; yet, if Congress was to be a genuinely mass movement, they could not limit their canvassing to urban areas.[2]

As the Defiance Campaign ground to a halt, the A.N.C. implemented the 'Mandela Plan' in its earliest form in January 1953. This was intended to 'consolidate the Congress machinery' by more effective *local* organization and consistent co-operation between the different levels of leadership.[3] Yet, by the time the Cape Provincial Congress met in August 1953, there had been a drop of 40,000 in membership since the peak reached during the Defiance Campaign.[4] According to the General-Secretary's Report, the 'Mandela Plan' had made no appreciable difference to the poor co-ordination between branches and provincial headquarters not the least because there proved to be insufficient funds to pay the organizers.[5]

Basic organizational problems were again a feature of the Acting General Secretary's Report to the National Conference in December 1954 (a report which Oliver Tambo could not himself deliver to the Conference because he was under ban). In his view—and presumably

[1] Cf. the complaint made by T. E. Tshunungwa, the Cape Provincial Secretary, that branches were mishandling funds and, in particular, had failed to send the appropriate amounts to provincial and national headquarters (Cape Provincial Report, dated 16 Nov. 1955, mim., P.A.S.].
[2] Such a view is implicit in Tambo's comment on rural areas in his Report to the A.N.C. Annual Conference, Durban, 16–19 Dec. 1954, mim., P.A.S., p. 4: 'As far as the Africans are concerned the creation of an anti-fascist front means broadening the social basis of the National movement. There is a danger of the African National Congress becoming an urban-based and urban-orientated organization. It may tend to forget and ignore the vast potential represented by the peasants and farm labourers.'
[3] Mandela, *No Easy Walk*, p. 28.
[4] Secretarial Report to the Cape Provincial Conference, Cradock, 15–16 Aug. 1953, mim., P.A.S.
[5] ibid.

L

in the opinion of the National Executive on whose behalf he reported—the question of 'organizational problems' was 'the most urgent issue for consideration'.[1] Tambo spoke, too, of lack of proper co-ordination between branch and provincial level, of the failure of branch leaders to carry out instructions, and of their neglecting correspondence. Particularly where branch membership was large, local officials tended, he said, 'to become conceited and to regard themselves as chiefs and bosses and not as servants. . . .'[2]

The problems of efficient organization were made more difficult by the multiple effects of Government bans and punitive measures. Restrictions on leaders—imposed as they were with relative unexpectedness—made it, at the very least, hard to achieve continuous and consistent direction of Congress activities. As early as August 1952, key officials of the A.N.C. had been arrested under the terms of the Suppression of Communism Act.[3] By mid December thirty-seven Defiance leaders had been arrested, twenty of whom were given suspended sentences of nine months.[4] Furthermore, once the Public Safety Act and the Criminal Law Amendment Act came into operation in February 1953, those who engaged in protest against laws faced the possibility of three years' imprisonment, rather than the previous penalty of six months.[5] As sentences became increasingly severe they were bound to deter Africans from supporting the A.N.C. The extent of Government intimidation was not as great as it was to become in the late fifties, or after Congress was banned in March 1960, but already in the mid fifties it was an additional consideration which leaders had to take into account. African leaders knew, as Lutuli later conceded, that it was 'easier to raise one's voice in company with five thousand other [sic] than to court imprisonment with twenty others'.[6]

Congress leaders were, naturally enough, reluctant to admit—and

[1] Report to the 42nd Annual Conference of the A.N.C., held in Durban, 16–19 Dec. 1954, p. 11.
[2] ibid., p. 13.   [3] Kuper, *Passive Resistance*, pp. 193–4.
[4] Survey prepared for the National Action Committee, 16 Dec. 1952, mim., P.A.S.
[5] See above, p. 92. The provisions of the Public Safety Act were not invoked until a State of Emergency was declared in March 1960. But the terms of the Criminal Law Amendment Act applied immediately.
[6] Luthuli, *Let My People Go*, p.121. Cf. Roux's comment: 'People had been prepared to suffer imprisonment for weeks and in some cases for months. But they were not willing to risk imprisonment for years, with floggings in addition.' Roux, *Time Longer Than Rope*, p. 394.

certainly unwilling to advertise—that their fellow Africans could be intimidated. To dedicated nationalists like Mandela, Nokwe, Lutuli, and Resha, it was inconceivable that there could be any consideration which could legitimately outweigh the prime importance of winning an extension of non-white rights. Lutuli was typical in this regard, when he spoke of the 'tyrannical bans' which the Nationalists had imposed on him, and on M. B. Yengwa, the Provincial Secretary of the A.N.C. in Natal.[1] In a message to the Provincial Congress in Natal in October 1954, he assured the delegates that the bans would not 'in anyway weaken the bond of comradeship' in the 'noble struggle for the liberation of the Africans in the Fatherland.'[2] But the Nationalists' attempt to clip the wings of Congress did have serious practial consequences; Congress leadership was emasculated and ordinary members were intimidated.

These difficulties were acknowledged and analysed by Oliver Tambo in his Secretary-General's Report to the A.N.C. Annual Conference in Durban, in December 1954.[3] He referred to 'stringent and hostile conditions' necessitating 'an entirely new organizational footing.'[4]

... [the Government] are [he said] destroying our national organisation and trade unions by banning and deporting leaders of these organisations and by prohibiting public meetings and intimidating and terrorising both the speakers and the audience.[5]

The problems which the A.N.C. faced, he argued, were how to re-organize and function *under conditions of a fully-fledged police state in which we live*' [author's italic].[6] The Cape Provincial Secretary, T. E. Tshunungwa (who was also National Organizer of the A.N.C.) toured the Cape in August and September of 1955. In his efforts to explain why all the branches had lost 'big numbers' he wrote:

Apart from reports of people not having renewed their current year's membership, there are no new people joining the movement. On questioning the members about why the membership is so low, I have been told that

---

[1] In his message to the Natal Provincial Conference, 30 Oct. 1954, mim., P.A.S.
[2] ibid. cf. Z. K. Matthews: 'It is of course impossible for any Minister to ban anybody from the A.N.C. As far as the A.N.C. is concerned these sons of Africa are still members of our organisation with their names written indelibly not on bits of paper which can be confiscated but in the hearts of their people where they are beyond the reach of governmental influence.' In his Presidential Address to the Cape Provincial Conference, Port Elizabeth, 18–19 June 1955.
[3] See above, p. 149.
[4] Report to the A.N.C. Annual Conference, Durban, 16–19 Dec. 1954, p. 13.
[5] ibid.   [6] ibid., p. 11.

quite a number of people are scared of joining Congress. *Police intimidation is the order of the day* [author's italic].[1]

The Government's policy was not exclusively one of intimidation. They combined coercion with the prospect of increased material benefits. The Western Areas Removal Scheme (1954) entailed loss of freehold property rights for Africans, but it secured them better living conditions.[2] Likewise, the Bantu Education Act (1953) introduced strict Government control of all aspects of African schooling; but, at the same time, it apparently offered more Africans the chance to be educated.[3] Thus, the Government's canny blend of punishment and reward also made it difficult for the A.N.C. to secure the loyalty of a large African membership. Lutuli spoke with contempt of those who made 'freedom synonymous with meare [*sic*] happiness and the possession of material wealth.'[4] But the fact of the matter was that the A.N.C. was faced more and more with Africans ignoring Congress claims upon their loyalty in the face of the alternative advantages of a 'non-political' life—and the risks of active involvement in Congress.

It had always been hard for Congress to demonstrate how crucial local support was to the success of a mass organization. It was equally difficult to show rank-and-file members and non-members how the A.N.C. and its ideals were relevant to their particular circumstances. Congress could offer only an abstraction, the possibility of future political rights. Meanwhile, the most they could guarantee was a sense of collective identity. Tambo bemoaned the fact that payment of the Congress annual subscription guaranteed only nominal support.[5]

Members should [he insisted] be given political education and made to understand that *they* are the Congress; that *they* have to fight for their

[1] Cape Provincial Report, 15 Nov. 1955, mim., P.A.S.
[2] Edward Feit, *South Africa: The Dynamics of the African National Congress* (London, O.U.P., 1962), p. 38.
[3] The proportion of children of school-going age which were attending school rose from 41 per cent in 1953 to an estimated 63 per cent in 1962. By then primary school accommodation was increasing at the rate of almost 6 per cent a year. The means of achieving this had been the Government's introduction of the 'double session', where the same teacher took two classes in succession. This meant, of course, that more children were being taught, but the time spent in school was shorter than previously. Horrell, *A Decade of Bantu Education*, pp. 49, 162–3.
[4] Presidential Address by the Provincial President read at the Annual Conference of Natal A.N.C., Ladysmith, 31 Oct.–1 Nov. 1953, mim., P.A.S.
[5] Report to the 42nd Annual Conference, Durban, 16–19 Dec. 1954.

freedom and emancipation; that they are responsible for the success, failure and growth of Congress. . . .[1]

Congress eventually acknowledged that they could only sustain and increase mass support for the A.N.C. by championing local issues which affected most immediately the material well-being of the Africans.[2] Yet it was only reluctantly that Congress leaders diverted their energies to what Lutuli described as 'Ambulance Work'.[3] It was, in his view, and that of those who shared the leadership with him, a *political* struggle in which they were engaged. But in their quest for mass support it would have been foolish not to capitalize on the effects of *apartheid* legislation. After 1953, such legislation affected, or threatened to affect, many more non-whites than previous Nationalist measures had done. As Sampson points out: 'To the simplest African people, the new catchword of apartheid was no longer an abstraction. It meant raids, removals, pass-books, passes for women and, most of all, police.'[4] Thus Congress leaders agreed to attempt redress of local and particular grievances as well as pursue their objective of full political rights. Such a decision meant additional strain on their limited resources; most important, their central purpose was, in such circumstances, too easily overlooked. Lutuli expressed this dilemma, and made clear his own priority to the Natal Provincial Congress in October 1954. He spoke bitterly against those who accused Congress

. . . of being unrealistic in its programme and of ignoring the immediate interests of Africans which, they allege, are limited to bread and butter politics such as fighting for adequate wages, better housing, etc. We do not [he said] accept this charge of neglecting these immediate needs of the people for our Congress programme enjoins local Congress officials to give immediate attention to the local needs of their areas. In our view, attention to these local needs need not cause the shelving of the fight for fundamental rights. The vote in all democratic states is the *only* key to Democratic Rights, privileges and obligations.[5]

Lutuli used several historical examples to illustrate his point. With the Uitlanders in Kruger's Republic, with the Jews in Nazi Germany,

[1] ibid.
[2] e.g. the Secretarial Report to the Cape Provincial Conference which acknowledged that 'the failure to tackle local problems' had 'inevitably and detrimentally affected' the A.N.C. (Cradock, 15–16 Aug. 1953, mim., P.A.S.).
[3] In his message to the Natal Provincial Conference 30 Oct. 1954.
[4] Sampson, *Treason Cage*, p. 96.
[5] Lutuli's message to the Natal Provincial Conference, 30 Oct. 1954.

and with Indians in South Africa, comparative wealth and economic status had been, he claimed, no guarantee against loss of political liberty.[1] This was a truth which 'progressives' within the United Party had still to grasp; as yet they trusted that increased prosperity would inevitably lead to an extension of political rights. The Nationalists, in contrast, fully understood Lutuli's reasoning—and the A.N.C.'s prime concern with full political rights. Their policy was designed to thwart Congress ambitions by a judicious mixture of intimidation and material benefits.

ii

Congress leaders appreciated the dangers of temporarily shelving their ultimate political goal. Confronted with declining membership, however, they were forced to seek mass support by planning campaigns on issues which were of immediate interest to non-whites. Two such issues presented themselves soon after the Nationalists' return to power. The Government announced that, under the terms of the Resettlement Act, they intended removing Africans from the Western Areas of Johannesburg to new non-white housing developments south-west of the city;[2] in addition, they introduced the concept and practice of Bantu Education.[3]

The major grounds of Congress resistance to both measures was essentially liberal.[4] On the issue of the Western Areas Removal Scheme, the A.N.C. chose to take their stand on the principle of freehold ownership of land.[5] Not all Africans who lived in the Western Areas owned land; many were tenants or subtenants. But in the new settlements of Meadowlands and Diepkloof, there would be 'no ownership of ground'.[6] In addition, the scheme was part of the Government's plan for rigid residential segregation,[7] a principle to which Congressmen were firmly opposed. Furthermore, to comply with the removals was to accept increased Government interference

[1] ibid.   [2] Feit, *South Africa*, pp. 37–8.   [3] See above, p. 130.
[4] Both protests were part of a 'Resist *Apartheid* Campaign' which was planned in May 1954. Feit, *South Africa*, pp. 37–8.
[5] This was a factor stressed in a set of *Discussion Notes on the Western Areas Scheme* (n.d., mim., P.A.S.), apparently drawn up for use by those responsible for publicizing the Western Areas Protest. A number of the issues involved are set out in the booklet *The Western Areas Removal Scheme: Facts and Viewpoints* (Johannesburg, S.A.I.R.R., 1953).
[6] Dr. H. F. Verwoerd, quoted in Carter, *The Politics of Inequality*, p. 91.
[7] Feit, *South Africa*, p. 37.

in their lives. They were jealous of the relative freedom of movement which regulations—or absence of regulations—allowed those living in the Western Areas, compared with the restrictions and degree of surveillance which governed non-whites in newer locations.

In accepting these as the primary motives of any protest, Congress leaders showed too simple an understanding of the complexities involved. They conceded afterwards, for instance, that they had taken too little account of how attractive the new accommodation appeared to those people who lived in the poorest conditions of Sophiatown.[1] And one of the reasons why it proved impossible to rally and sustain mass support was that the ways in which people's motives differed naturally tended to lessen the impact of the protest. As Edward Feit makes clear:

> Cross-currents existed among the different schools of thought. The man who objected in principle to removal might also be worried about the higher cost of living, and the man pleased to get a new house might also dislike the idea of removal without consultation.[2]

These 'cross-currents' would not have undermined the Congress campaign in the way they did had it not been for the absence of clear tactical direction from campaign leaders, a weakness in part caused, and certainly aggravated, by Government intimidation. Robert Resha, a prominent Transvaal Youth Leaguer and resident of Sophiatown, was in charge of the resistance to the move at the time the Government implemented their scheme in February 1955. His difficulties—all reasons for the failure of the protest—were multiple.[3] The Government won an immediate tactical advantage by putting forward the date scheduled for removals after several earlier changes of plan. Their simultaneous declaration of a State of Emergency made A.N.C. top-level planning hazardous, especially when the leadership was already partly paralysed by Government bans. The night before the removals began, a crowd which Resha estimated at 20,000 were gathered in Sophiatown. Here was, at least in potential, the mass support which Congress had sought. But at this point, with only a few hours before removals were to begin and with completely

---

[1] Evidence in the Report of the Secretariat on the Western Areas, quoted in Feit, *South Africa*, p. 44.

[2] Feit, *South Africa*, p. 38.

[3] The details included in this paragraph were gleaned from the author's interview with Robert Resha, Adelaide, 8 Oct. 1966. See also Feit, *South Africa*, pp. 42–6.

inadequate alternatives to offer would-be rebels, Congress' short-comings were painfully clear. Their impotence was equally apparent. Confronted with police 'supervision' of the removals, and the availability of army support in the case of any widespread resistance or, presumably, an overt call to such resistance, Congress was faced in the final analysis with the choice of encouraging violence. Such an alternative represented no real choice at all. And the A.N.C. failed to prevent the removals from beginning on 9 February 1955.[1] By the time the second removals began later in February those who had already moved were praising their new homes. This further weakened the position of the Congress campaigners.[2] They were forced to acknowledge failure: they had lacked both effective organization and tactics in the face of powerful opponents and the countervailing interests of their potential supporters.

The possibility of an outbreak of violence had haunted those who campaigned against the removals. Earlier, the question of the use of violence had been thoroughly aired among Congress leaders during the planning of the Defiance Campaign.[3] They had, at that point, determined, for various reasons, to studiously avoid violence. The riots in the Eastern Cape had proved only too well how right they had been to foresee that violence would be disastrous to their cause. And, generally speaking in the mid fifties, they redoubled their efforts to appear non-violent. There were still prominent Congressmen, such as Lutuli, Tambo and James Conco, for whom non-violence was a cardinal principle, a principle indicative of their staunch attachment to liberal principles.[4] Furthermore, those whose fundamental objection to the use of violence had earlier been made on grounds of expediency had now, in the mid fifties, additional grounds for their misgivings. It became increasingly evident that the

[1] Congress did arrange accommodation for fifty families who vacated their homes in Sophiatown rather than be moved to the new location of Meadowlands. But, as Feit points out, such accommodation was necessarily makeshift and the 'rescued' families had forfeited their chances of new homes in Meadowlands. ibid., p. 46.

[2] ibid.   [3] See above, pp. 79–80.

[4] Several people who had close contact with A.N.C. leaders during this period support this view. Michael Parkington, the lawyer for the Defence advocate in the Treason Trial, considered that Tambo, Lutuli, and Matthews were, without question, averse to violence between 1954 and 1956 (interview with Thomas Karis, 13 Feb. 1964, P.A.S.). A. P. O'Dowd, another of the defence team, judged Conco, Yengwa, and Tambo to be 'liberals' (author's interview, London, 7 Oct. 1965), and this view of Tambo was supported by Bishop Ambrose Reeves (author's interview, London, 12 Oct. 1965).

Government held an overwhelming advantage in terms of military strength, based as this was on a streamlined chain of command. Also, to endorse a policy of violence, in the face of the political immaturity of local A.N.C. leaders—a problem aggravated by Government decimation of the ranks of trained leaders—was to arm A.N.C. officials with a weapon which they did not understand. It was likely to misfire badly in such circumstances; among other things, it would polarize white and non-white opinion as the riots had done in 1952. Any violent clashes between Congress and the police were bound to encourage the more conservative non-whites to withdraw their support from Congress entirely, and at the same time, would increase the frustration—and harden the extremism—of the hot heads within Congress. Sampson argues:

> The urgent task, as the black leaders saw it was the maintenance of restraint and discipline, and the avoidance of any kind of violence which would give the police the pretext to effect a show-down of shooting. Any attempt at terrorism in the police-ridden cities ... could only lead to fiercer counter-terrorism. .... A disunited rising of an angry mob was much more of a nightmare to Congress than to the Government leaders who so freely invoked it as a danger.[1]

In staging their protest against Bantu Education in April 1955, Congress leaders were confronted with a similar situation to that which they had faced over the Western Areas Removal. Here again their fight for liberal principles was lost in the crush of conflicting interests and the Government's monopoly of power. Official protests lodged against the Bantu Education Bill were invariably framed in terms defending inalienable rights. Mandela's reaction to the Bill was characteristic of the general response of A.N.C. leaders. He made his position clear in his Presidential address to the Transvaal A.N.C., an address which, since he was banned, Robert Resha read on his behalf.[2] It was his contention and one universally shared by liberals, black and white, inside and outside South Africa, that the Minister of Native Affairs, Dr. H. F. Verwoerd, aimed to teach African children that they were by nature inferior to whites.[3] Spelling out the A.N.C. view, Mandela said:

> ... we declare our firm belief in the principles enunciated in the Universal Declaration of Human Rights that everyone has the right to education; that education should be directed to the full development of the human

[1] Sampson, *Treason Cage*, p. 96.
[2] Reprinted in Mandela, *No Easy Walk*, pp. 21-31.
[3] ibid., p. 26, See above, p. 131.

personality, and to the strengthening of respect for human rights and fundamental freedoms. It shall promote understanding, tolerance, and friendship among the nations, racial or religious groups and shall further the activities of the United Nations for the maintenance of peace. The parents shall have the right to choose the kind of education that should be given to their children.[1]

The official Congress stand was on basic liberal principles. But as the plans were devised for an A.N.C.-directed boycott of the new Government schools, it became clear that there were, in the minds of many of the Congress followers, other factors which were at least worthy of serious consideration. These, together with organizational difficulties as well as the nature of Government reprisals, put paid to the A.N.C.'s plans to defy the terms of the Act effectively. Certainly most urban Africans agreed with their leaders about the importance of education. J. C. de Ridder points out that it was 'the supreme desire of the vast majority of urban [African] parents to give their children the opportunity of an education. . . .'[2] He adds: 'Educational achievement is synonymous with success, and success spells more money.'[3] To non-whites living on the knife-edge of poverty, education, whatever its quality, appeared a guarantee of a job and hence of a regular income. Such people might object to the limited range of vocational training which Bantu Education offered, or to the Government's plan that Africans be taught in their tribal languages: such proposals limited their children's opportunities.[4] But they were unlikely to sacrifice even an inferior education if the alternative were no education at all. These people were put into a dilemma when the Government counter to the A.N.C. protest took the form of a denial of any kind of education to those who continued to support the boycott.[5] Lutuli appears to have appreciated this.

The hazards of such a decision are obvious. The choice before parents is an almost impossible one—they do not want Bantu Education and they do not want their children on the streets. They have to choose between two evils, and no rule of thumb indicates which is the greater. The chances of universal agreement are small, not because of hesitation about whether

[1] Mandela, *No Easy Walk*, p. 26.

[2] *The Personality of the Urban African in South Africa* (London, Routledge & Kegan Paul, 1961), p. 87.

[3] ibid.   [4] Feit, *South Africa*, p. 49.

[5] The Government's response took the form of an ultimatum, which was delivered by Dr. H. F. Verwoerd as Minister of Native Affairs: any child who was absent from school on 25 April 1955, without legitimate reasons would be expelled; where classes or schools were empty on that day, the relevant teaching positions would be abolished. Carter, *The Politics of Inequality*, p. 109.

Bantu Education is evil, but because as Archbishop Clayton of Cape Town told his Synod, 'a rotten education' may be 'better than none'.[1]

The majority of those who initially supported the boycott, and that number was limited, eventually conceded implicitly that Archbishop Clayton was right.[2] African teachers, too, generally chose a job they disliked, rather than no job at all.[3] The A.N.C. campaign again proved a failure. The efforts of Congress leaders to evoke widespread and effective protest on principles obviously central to a liberal philosophy had failed. And they had failed not only because it had proved impossible to organize a national campaign effectively or because the Government held the trump cards,[4] but because Africans themselves partly as a result of these factors, had chosen to compromise. There were factors more important to them than the liberal principle of equality of educational opportunity. Furthermore, in the manner of promoting this principle, Congress leaders had, more than once, lost rather than gained the confidence of Africans. In a desperate and illiberal attempt to enforce the boycott they had embarked on intimidation of their own.[5] And they had promised boycott supporters an alternative education in A.N.C. cultural clubs. These were a stop-gap measure, generally staffed by untrained 'teachers'; such

[1] Luthuli, *Let My People Go*, p. 132.

[2] According to Feit, 6,000 children were affected when the boycott began on 12 April. By the end of April, however, he argues the A.N.C. had had to concede failure. *South Africa*, p. 54.

[3] The dilemma which confronted African teachers is instanced by Leo Kuper's survey conducted in Durban, *An African Bourgeoisie: Race, Class and Politics in South Africa* (New Haven, Yale Univ. Press, 1965), pp. 174–90. Among a sample of ninety-nine, who had apparently 'accepted' Bantu Education, Kuper found evidence of a fundamental antipathy to Government policy. There was, he reports: 'considerable rejection of the basic tenets of apartheid—virtual unanimity in the rejection of separate development, racially restricted franchise, and the revival of the tribal way of life. Solutions to the racial problem elicited from most informants a democratic ideology, or the very antithesis of apartheid—African control. ... And yet the duty of inculcating apartheid falls on these teachers.' ibid., p. 181. The likely outcome of a teacher expressing opposition to Bantu Education is suggested by Ezekiel Mphahlele in his account of his own career as a teacher, his dismissal from his post and his subsequent frustration. *Down Second Avenue*, pp. 165 ff.

[4] The difficulties of organizing the campaign were reflected in the decision of the National Executive Committee to postpone the date of the boycott. But the provincial executives in the Transvaal and the Eastern Cape objected to the delay: they insisted on proceeding with their plans on the grounds that a boycott date had been agreed to earlier at the National Conference in December 1954. Feit, *South Africa*, p. 51.

[5] Feit, *South Africa*, p. 52.

clubs were prohibited from teaching school subjects. Despite their limited success, they proved an inadequate substitute.[1]

The A.N.C. had failed to prevent the Western Areas Removal and the introduction of Bantu Education. In this situation their plans for the Congress of the People to be held on 26 June 1955, took on added significance.[2] At this meeting delegates from local A.N.C. branches throughout South Africa would endorse a Freedom Charter incorporating the aims of the individual branches of Congress. Here, at last, seemed a means of reconciling particular grievances with a restatement of the A.N.C.'s goal of political rights. Sponsored by the A.N.C. and its allies, the Congress of the People was also to be a singular demonstration of interracial solidarity. In the event, it led to a direct confrontation between the A.N.C. and the Government.

---

[1] ibid., pp. 54–55. A report on the Transvaal cultural clubs was made to the Transvaal Provincial Conference, Lady Selborne, 3–4 Oct. 1956, mim., P.A.S. There were, the writer claimed, 1,515 children in A.N.C. cultural clubs in the Transvaal, but the future of the scheme was in doubt, largely because of shortage of money. Despite the writer's obvious enthusiasm for the scheme, he was forced to concede that the boycott had failed: 'The agitation against Bantu Education has dried up. The enthusiasm for the boycott has evaporated: there is a general lull, slackness and negligence in the whole campaign. . . . Just a few people are left to strain every nerve, to persevere whilst suffering persecution . . . to face all forms of tribulation in compliance with Congress objectives, whilst Congress maintains a sickening vigil of silence.'

[2] See below, pp. 163 ff.

CHAPTER VIII

Bridging the gap: co-operation between white liberals and the African National Congress

i

At no time in the fifties—or subsequently—did the Liberal Party make an effective appeal to the white electorate. Initially, they were also unsuccessful in their co-operation with non-whites. In 1954 the A.N.C. sought the Liberals' official support for the proposed Congress of the People, a multiracial demonstration planned in defiance of racial discrimination. The Liberal Party refused to become involved in the project, chiefly because of what they regarded as undue communist influence on the planning and staging of the Congress of the People. Their refusal estranged them from the A.N.C. leadership, whose attitude towards communists was quite different from that of the Liberal Party. The Freedom Charter, which was endorsed by the Congress of the People on 26 June 1955, further alienated the Liberals from the A.N.C. since they saw its 'socialist' elements as further proof of communist influence.

Yet understanding was meanwhile growing slowly and sporadically at the grass-roots level. There were a number of occasions in the mid fifties when Liberals and A.N.C. leaders staged joint protests against *apartheid* laws. Moreover, as Liberals became increasingly involved with non-whites, they were gradually driven to the realization that their original policies and methods were inadequate.

In December 1956 those who had been involved in the Congress of the People were arrested on charges of treason. This large-scale attack on extra-parliamentary opposition aroused the Liberals, and, during the Treason Trial which followed, drew the Liberals much closer to the A.N.C. Here were unique opportunities for interracial co-operation. Furthermore, the course of the Trial fostered the view that the Government could still be defeated. Such hopes were proved illusory only by the events of the early sixties.

ii

Alan Paton, Vice-President of the Liberal Party, gave an early warning that it would not 'be easy to persuade a majority of the white electorate to consent to the idea of a common society.'[1] In the event it proved impossible. Party campaigners soon learned they had under-estimated the difficulty of converting the white electors. Their failure was reflected in the size of party membership. In September 1955, for example, provincial reports revealed a total paid-up membership of just over 1,000.[2] This was already considerably more than the Congress of Democrats could ever gain,[3] but, unlike the C.O.D., the Liberal Party wanted to function as a political party and achieve parliamentary success. In that context, the figure was hardly impressive.

The party was never an electoral success. True, the number of votes which the Liberals gained in the 1959 provincial elections was an advance on their first attempts to win provincial seats in 1954, but this increase did not indicate weighty support for Liberal policies among whites.[4] In the national election of 1958 the party's three representatives were heavily defeated.[5] With these failures in white electorates, the party's only parliamentary spokesmen were those members elected as Native Representatives—Mrs. Margaret Ballinger and Mr. Walter Stanford[6] in the House of Assembly, and in the Senate, Mr. William Ballinger and Dr. Leslie Rubin. However, this kind of representation was abolished under the terms of the Promotion of Bantu Self-Government Act of 1959,[7] and consequently the four Liberal thorns in the Nationalist flesh were removed from the legislature in 1960. Thus the Liberals' original decision to concentrate on gathering white rather than non-white support proved relatively fruitless. At no point in the fifties did they threaten to become a force

[1] Letter of Alan Paton on the Occasion of the Launching of the Party in Cape Town, May 1953, mim., P.A.S.

[2] Minutes of the Meeting of the National Executive of the L.P., Cape Town, 14 Sept. 1955, mim., P.A.S.

[3] Using figures suggested by C.O.D. leaders (author's interview, London, 12 Oct. 1965).

[4] The party contested four seats, two in the Transvaal and one each in Natal and Cape Province; they gained a total of 4,697 votes in the four constituencies. *A Survey of Race Relations in South Africa 1958–1959*, pp. 9–10.

[5] *A Survey of Race Relations in South Africa 1957–1958*, p. 1

[6] Late in 1959 Stanford left the Liberal Party to join the Progressive Party. See below, p. 198.

[7] See below, p. 188.

to be reckoned with in the white political world. Apparently then, they gained little from their initial commitment to parliamentary means. However, their frustration in the parliamentary field was an important factor making for fundamental changes in party policy by the end of the decade.[1]

iii

This lack of any marked success in the white world made it more imperative that the Liberals gain the co-operation and support of non-whites. Initially, they had been sharply rebuffed by the leaders of the A.N.C. and the S.A.I.C.[2] and relations deteriorated further when the Liberal Party refused to support the A.N.C. and its allies in their plans to hold a Congress of the People. The underlying purpose of the proposed Congress was to mobilize mass support for the A.N.C. Confronted with declining membership in the months after the Defiance Campaign, the A.N.C. Executive had sought a new rallying point. Z. K. Matthews, as Cape Provincial President, had made public a proposed solution at the Provincial Conference in August 1953:

I wonder whether the time has not come for the African National Congress to consider the question of convening a national convention, a congress of the people, representing all the people of this country irrespective or [sic] race or colour to draw up a Freedom Charter for the democratic South Africa of the future.[3]

In a subsequent memorandum, Matthews revealed the hopes which the Congress leaders had for such 'a national convention'; it was intended to be the means by which the anti-*apartheid* forces could regain the initiative in the struggle against the Government.

From such a congress [wrote Matthews] ought to come a Declaration which will inspire all the peoples of South Africa with fresh hope for the future, which will turn the minds of the people away from the sterile and negative struggles of the past and the present to a positive programme of freedom for all in our lifetime. Such a Charter properly conceived as a mirror of [the] future of South African society, can galvanize the people of South Africa into action and make them go over [to] the offensive against the reactionary forces that work in this country instead of being perpetually on the defensive, fighting rearguard actions all the time.[4]

[1] See below, pp. 198 ff.   [2] See above, p. 119.
[3] Presidential Address to the Cape Provincial Conference, Cradock, 15 Aug. 1953, mim., P.A.S.
[4] Draft Memorandum of the Congress of the People by Z. K. Matthews, n.d., mim., P.A.S.

The concept of a charter was germane to the planning of the Congress. Here at last appeared a means by which the over-all political aims of the A.N.C. leadership might be closely linked to the day-to-day needs and ambitions of the rank-and-file membership.[1] Local committees were to be established to gather together details of the people's grievances and demands. In this way, all A.N.C. members would be given 'a vested interest in the freedom struggle'.[2] Local demands were to be sifted and co-ordinated into a 'freedom charter' which would be ratified at the mass assembly planned to mark the climax of the campaign.[3]

Matthews's memorandum was submitted to a conference on 21 March 1954, at which the national executives of the A.N.C., the S.A.I.C., the C.O.D., and the South African Coloured People's Organization (S.A.C.P.O.) were all present.[4] They agreed to form a Congress Alliiance and to co-sponsor the proposed national assembly. Thus the Congress of the People would be an unprecedented opportunity for a multiracial demonstration on the part of the Nationalists' opponents.

The Congress was an unprecedented chance, too, for the Liberals to redeem themselves in the eyes of the A.N.C. and its allies, for the Liberal Party was invited to participate in the Congress of the People. Their reputation was to suffer immeasurably from their failure to respond to this invitation. Leaders of the Congress Alliance found it impossible to appreciate the Liberals' initial diffidence and their eventual withdrawal. To them, the whole idea had great emotional appeal apart from the chance to increase the popular support of the A.N.C.[5] Africans were specially angered because a reluctance to accept African leadership appeared to be a central reason for the Liberals' rejection of the proposal.[6]

[1] Supplementary Report of the Secretariat of the A.N.C. on the Congress of the People, submitted to the A.N.C. National Conference, Durban, 16–19 Dec. 1954, mim., P.A.S. The Report said *inter alia* that the 'acceptance of the plan for the Campaign of the Congress of the People, which laid down the basis of obtaining mass support and which charged the organisations concerned to work on the broadest possible front by reaching the people in all walks of life, on the farms and reserves, in the cities, villages, towns, mines, factories and homes, afforded us a unique opportunity of consolidating our organisations.'

[2] Duma Nokwe, in an interview with the author, Dar es Salaam, 15 Nov. 1965.

[3] *A Survey of Race Relations in South Africa 1953–1954*, p. 11.

[4] Supplementary Report of the Secretariat on the Congress of the People, submitted to the A.N.C. National Conference, Durban, 16–19 Dec. 1954.

[5] Author's interview with Joe Matthews, London, 8 Oct. 1965.

[6] Author's interview with Duma Nokwe, Dar es Salaam, 15 Nov. 1965.

For the Liberal Party, however, there was a major stumbling-block. The communist-controlled C.O.D. appeared to have a dominant role in preparations for the Congress. The Liberals were generally much more aware of the dangers inherent in 'co-operation with the communists' than they were appreciative of the way in which they might improve their standing with non-whites by commitment to the Congress of the People. In 1953 the Liberals had officially stated their opposition to communism.[1] When the plans for the Congress of the People were being discussed in 1954, many Liberals—and certainly the leaders—still cherished the belief that they could gain some political power in South Africa. They were reluctant to hazard their chances of this by accepting communists as 'temporary allies', as the A.N.C. had done. Moreover, such a strategic move might oblige them to consider communist claims to share any degree of political power which they won.

The extent to which the communists engineered the preparations for the Congress and prearranged the terms of the Charter itself is difficult to assess. Most Liberals remain convinced that the communists wielded disproportionate influence and prevented the Charter from being genuinely representative.[2] Part of the Liberals' evidence for this lies in the way in which the actual Congress was conducted and in what they considered to be the socialist reforms which the Charter envisaged. But long before the Congress of the People met on 26 June 1955, the Liberals were disillusioned and hostile as a result of their experiences at the provincial level.

In the Cape, for example, the disenchantment was rapid and complete. The Liberal Party sent a delegation of about fifteen people to the first C.O.P. meeting in May 1954.[3] There they found widely diverse groups represented, ranging from the A.N.C. and other political groups to various trade unions and vigilance associations. The delegates seemed to be required solely to express support for the idea of a Congress. They were not required—or allowed—to discuss

[1] See above, p. 113.
[2] This is the author's impression after talking to a number of people who have been active in the Party, e.g. Margaret Ballinger (interviewed, Cape Town, 9 Dec. 1965), Neville Rubin (interviewed, London, 26 Aug. 1965). In Rubin's opinion, the Congress of the People was 'a farce from beginning to end'.
[3] G.M.C. interview with Peter Hjul, Cape Town, 26 Jan. 1964. My account of of the Liberal Party in the Cape and their experiences during the planning of the Congress of the People is based on this source, except where other references are given.

M

policy. Consequently, when Lutuli made a formal request for the Cape Liberals' support, they decided to refuse, chiefly on the grounds that their influence would be minimized by the fact that so much had apparently been preplanned. Meanwhile, two Liberals, Peter Hjul and Jimmy Gibson, had each been elected to a local committee of the C.O.P. They were given the party's permission to act on these in an unofficial capacity. Their experiences verified their original suspicions. They were merely required to rubber-stamp prearranged decisions, rather than formulate policy. In addition, they were subjected to propaganda at a number of meetings by representatives of the World Council of Peace, which appeared to be a communist front organization.[1] They were occasionally asked to endorse resolutions which related to issues unconnected with the proposed C.O.P., one instance being a motion condemning the London Conference of N.A.T.O. powers which had approved the rearming of Germany.[2] This kind of preoccupation irked the Liberals who, in any case, were pro-Western in their sympathies. Hjul's and Gibson's decision to resign from the Cape committees coincided with a Liberal Party National Committee meeting in Johannesburg in January 1955. Here the question of the party's commitment was reopened.[3] In Natal there had been comparatively little dispute over involvement with the Congress Alliance. The C.O.D. was less active there than in the Transvaal and relations between leading Liberals, like Leo Kuper, Provincial Vice-Chairman, and the Natal Indians were excellent.[4] Not so in Johannesburg. The National Committee's discussions with leading C.O.D. people there did nothing to allay their fears and, despite some dissident Transvaal Liberals, they decided to abandon the Congress of the People.[5]

With this decision, reached on 26 January 1955, the Liberals appeared to have dealt an irreparable blow to their relations with the A.N.C. However valid their reasoning, they had rejected another opportunity for identifying themselves with the non-white cause. As Anthony Sampson explains:

[1] See Letter from Jimmy Gibson and Peter Hjul to the Chairman of the Cape Western Region, A.N.C., dated 2 Nov. 1954, mim., P.A.S.

[2] G.M.C. interview with Peter Hjul, Cape Town, 26 Jan. 1964.

[3] Minutes of the Meeting of the National Executive Committee of the L.P., Johannesburg, 26 Jan. 1955, mim., P.A.S.

[4] Author's interview with Neville Rubin, London, 26 Aug. 1965; also Sampson, *Treason Cage*, p. 105.

[5] Minutes of the Meeting of the National Executive Committee of the L.P., Johannesburg, 26 Jan. 1955.

There were reasons enough for the Liberals, who were generally people with ideals and integrity, to shun Congress. Like every workers' movement, it had many and obvious faults. Its demand for a universal franchise was alarming to anyone who had watched a beer-hall mob; its speeches, particularly on foreign affairs, smacked of crude Communist dogma; its sensitivity and lack of confidence inclined it to high-handedness with critics; its members included extreme nationalists, opportunists and Communists—undesirable bed-fellows for respectable European liberals. *But Congress was the representative of the African people: to avoid it was to avoid the problem of the country* [author's italic].[1]

The Liberal Party's suspicions antagonized A.N.C. leaders. Their own attitude towards communists as allies was fundamentally different from that of the Liberals. In the early fifties Congress leaders had already accepted the strategic necessity of their co-operation with the communists.[2] And the events of the mid fifties served to increase this tolerance. Yet, at the same time, there also emerged, within the A.N.C. ranks, fresh opposition to communist influence. There persisted in the fifties the threat of defections from Congress ranks on the grounds that the C.O.D., in particular, was exerting unwarranted influence on the A.N.C. policy and practice. The Congress of Democrats was suspect on two different counts— members of the C.O.D. were white, and numbers of them (especially the leaders) were communists. These two charges, by no means necessarily the same, were made by too distinct kinds of Congress critics in the mid fifties.

Those whose primary concern was the influence of communists *per se* were most powerfully represented by Jordan Ngubane, one of the few original Youth Leaguers whose hostility towards communists grew, rather than declined, in the fifties. There was clearly nothing 'anti-white' about Ngubane's attitude. His crucial clash with Lutuli drove him from the ranks of the A.N.C. in 1956. He then devoted himself more to the Liberal Party, which in the mid fifties was still obviously a party dominated by its white founders. The overriding factor in his 'conversion' was his conviction that white and Indian communists wielded an inordinate influence on what he considered should be more clearly independent-minded decisions on the part of Congress leadership.[3] The Liberal Party provided the

---

[1] Sampson, *Treason Cage*, pp. 102–3.   [2] See above, pp. 69 ff.

[3] Strong evidence of this appears in Jordan Ngubane's own book, *An African Explains Apartheid.* For instance, he condemns what he describes as 'organized bids' by the Communitsts 'to sow suspicion and confusion among Leaguers in

perfect home for someone with Ngubane's misgivings—as well as his temperament and *penchant* for theorizing. For one of the chief distinguishing marks of Liberal Party policy in the fifties—and one which was to persist—was a vocal animosity towards communists. In this sense, Ngubane was never more characteristically 'liberal' than in his anti-communism.[1]

The group which had, in December 1953, formed themselves into an Africanist movement within the A.N.C. were far more vociferous than Ngubane in their allegations of communist control.[2] But their charges against the C.O.D. and the S.A.I.C. were not made primarily because they were anti-communists. The classic liberal objections to communists were of minor importance to the Africanists. They did not attack the white and Indian members of the Congress Alliance because they wanted necessarily to purge the A.N.C. of all communistic principles and rule communist methods out of court. Rather, they were convinced that 'foreign elements' had deliberately diverted the energies of the African nationalists, and had crucially hindered the progress of the liberation movement.[3] They were concerned, for example, that by accepting the Freedom Charter, the A.N.C. was yielding to the influence of other racial groups whose interests were not identical with those of the Africans.[4] This was the chief charge which the Africanists levelled at the C.O.D. and the S.A.I.C.: that as minority groups they had virtually imposed their views on the Africans, whose interests far from coincided with those either of the C.O.D. whites, or the Indian merchant class, who, they claimed, dominated the S.A.I.C.[5]

---

particular and A.N.C. members in general' (p. 99). Further, he claims: 'The League's program of action was shelved in favor of the Freedom Charter; critics of the Communists were elbowed out of the Congress, and the new line increasingly tended to see virtue in the people's republics and vice in the Western democracies' (p. 100).

[1] The chapter of *An African Explains Apartheid* in which Ngubane describes the development and value of the Liberal Party is entitled, presumably with care, 'Communists versus Liberals' (p. 191).

[2] The formation of the Africanist group was described to the author by Z. K. Molete who, at the time of the interview (Dar es Salaam, 13 Nov. 1965), was a leading figure in the P.A.C.

[3] ibid.   [4] ibid.

[5] See 'The Kliptown Charter', in *The Africanist* (June–July 1958). The Charter, the writers claimed 'did not emanate as a finished document from the A.N.C. It emanated as such from the Vodka Cocktail parties of Parktown and Lower Houghton. ... The black masses who met at Kliptown were merely

These misgivings were not shared by the A.N.C. leadership. Nor did Congress leaders sympathize with the objections raised by Ngubane. They were willing to accept that the number of African members on the Co-ordinating Committee for the C.O.P. was, in terms of the numbers which the A.N.C. represented, disproportionately low.[1] This did not, in their view, indicate, as the P.A.C. claimed, that after white domination had been overthrown, minority groups would enjoy an influence out of proportion to their comparatively small numbers. Nor did they consider that temporary acceptance of communist allies prejudiced the kind of state and society which would be established after liberation.

The A.N.C.'s co-operation with communists in the mid fifties was due to their willingness (under pressure of necessity) to accept help from anyone who appeared to offer it on African terms. A.N.C. leaders were 'interested in the arch enemy'; they agreed with Lutuli that they 'must not be side-tracked by witch hunts'.[2] In addition, the white communists of the C.O.D. were notably free of the self-consciousness and partronizing attitude which characterized so many white Liberals in their contacts with non-whites. As Lutuli argued:

All we know is that these men come to help us. I don't deny that some might have ulterior motives, but all I am concerned about is that they came to assist me fight racial oppression, and they have no trace of racialism or being patronizing, just no trace of it at all.[3]

Devoid of the Liberals' persistent paternalism, communists were apparently willing to treat African leaders as equals. In the face of this relatively new experience, which the Africans no doubt relished,

---

pawns in the game of power politics. The Whites who were at Kliptown, apart from the special branch, were mainly members of the Congress of Democrats. They are part of the ruling class in South Africa . . . they are in reality concerned with the maintenance of the *status quo*.'

[1] Mangaliso Sobukwe, the President of the P.A.C., referred in critical terms to both these groups in his address to the Africanist Inaugural Convention, 4–6 Apr. 1959. For example, the Indian merchant class, he said 'identifies itself by and large with the oppressor but, significantly, this is the group which provides the political leadership of the Indian people in South Africa.' By contrast, he continued, the 'down-trodden, poor "stinking coolies" of Natal who, alone, as a result of their material conditions, can identify themselves with the indigenous African majority . . . have not yet produced their leadership.' Reprinted in *The Basic Documents of the Pan-Africanist Congress of South Africa* (Lusaka, Zambia, March 1965), p. 15.

[2] Quoted in Benson, *Chief Albert Lutuli of South Africa*, p. 31.   [3] ibid.

the Liberals' opinion that the Africans were being unconsciously manipulated was particularly irksome.

In the view of the A.N.C. leaders, the Congress Alliance was a strategic necessity. Moreover, additional factors strengthened A.N.C. conviction that the communists were *worthy* allies. The C.O.D. as a group, and particularly its leaders, were extremely energetic, and threw themselves tirelessly into political activity. The degree of their commitment seemed beyond question, especially in view of the increasing risks they ran by virtue of involvement in interracial politics.[1] By the time the Congress of the People was held, a number of C.O.D. leaders, including Piet Beyleveld and Rica and Jack Hodgson, were under bans severely limiting their political activity.

In addition, communist countries were welcoming visits by Africans.[2] Opinion within the A.N.C. varied as to the wisdom and value of such visits.[3] But when travellers returned home, as Duma Nokwe and Walter Sisulu did late in 1953, they helped spread an interest in, and knowledge of, the communist systems. The favourable impressions of Sisulu, for example, particularly as he was not un-critical, must have further encouraged Congress leaders to co-operate with local communists.[4] Also, of course, Russia continued to challenge the system of *apartheid* in the U.N., in a voice apparently much less equivocating than that of the Western powers.[5]

Furthermore, as so often has been true in Asia, communist doctrine on imperialism and capitalism was very attractive to Africans. And not unexpectedly, nationalists throughout Africa borrowed heavily from the communist vocabulary in their struggles for freedom and independence.[6] There were excellent reasons for Africans to sympa-thize with communist anti-imperialism. Agreement on this score was displayed in the A.N.C.'s Executive Committee Report to the National Congress in 1954:

> The expulsion of colonial powers in the great land of Asia is a source of inspiration to the African people. The emergence of the two great powers in this continent, China and India, both enemies of imperialism have

---

[1] At least the leaders of the C.O.D. had earlier been members of the Communist Party; they were obvious targets for Government prosecution under the terms of the Suppression of Communist Act (1950).
[2] Benson, *The African Patriots*, p. 200.   [3] ibid.
[4] ibid., pp. 199–200.   [5] ibid., p. 246.
[6] Benson notes the irony of the right-wing as well as the left-wing of the A.N.C. using 'Marxist' language (*The African Patriots*, p. 200).

shattered the hopes of the imperialist powers and made their rule impossible even under the military might of the United States of America, Great Britain and France.[1]

Clearly, the A.N.C. saw themselves and their fellow Africans in South Africa as a colonial people who were suffering exploitation, and must be liberated. This much was obviously consistent with communist theory. But the use of characteristically communist terms[2] provides no conclusive evidence of the A.N.C.'s being communist-dominated. During the Treason Trial, Lutuli conceded the indisputable fact that the A.N.C. leaders had 'picked up the language'. 'But [he insisted] they learnt the language without becoming communists.'[3] The judgement handed down at the conclusion of the Trial supported his claim.[4]

African leaders found it difficult to appreciate, certainly impossible to share, the hostility which white liberals evinced on the issue of socialism. An increasing number of Africans were an integral part of the labour force in a capitalist system but had not the same role in it as the whites; there was an apparent difference of class interest between black and white. The idea of a more equitable distribution of wealth had a strong appeal to Africans whose lives were constantly circumscribed by the glaring, and apparently permanent, economic inequalities between white and non-white. But the extent to which the A.N.C. delegates to the Congress of the People accepted socialism *per se* varied considerably—if they asked themselves the question in those terms at all. There was divergence among A.N.C. leaders on the issue. During the Treason Trial, Lutuli recalled that he had hoped for a more adequate discussion of the economic clauses of the Freedom Charter. But when the last opportunity for this came at a special conference in March 1956, the Africanists expressed their opposition to the whole concept of the Freedom Charter. In their view, the 1949 Programme of Action remained an adequate statement of A.N.C. objectives and they claimed that the methods which it had proposed were not yet fully explored. In

[1] Annual Report of the National Executive Committee to the 42nd Annual Congress, Durban, 19 Dec. 1954, mim., P.A.S.

[2] e.g. the 1954 National Executive Report, for example, pointed out that 'the dynamics of history say that the imperialists are doomed to ignominious defeat at the hands of the oppressed Africans'. ibid.

[3] Statement taken from Chief Albert J. Luthuli in the case *R. v. Adams and Others*, p. 10.

[4] See below, p. 179.

particular, the Programme had envisaged the Africans striving independently for their freedom. The violence of these Africanist objections to the Freedom Charter forced those who might otherwise have
sought qualifications to the economic clauses to close ranks against
what Lutuli called Africanist 'obstructionism'.[1] And the majority of
conference delegates endorsed the Charter without seeking any
changes. Those from Natal who shared Lutuli's misgivings about
the inclusion of some of the economic clauses were 'certainly not
prepared to split Congress on it.'[2] With such Congressmen, the
necessity to preserve Congress unity and strength was of paramount
importance. They were not 'playing at politics'; they were 'bent on
liberation'.[3]

iv

The Freedom Charter was a unique statement of A.N.C. ideology
in the fifties. For the first time since 1949 Congress produced, with
the help of their allies, a document which stated their major aims.[4]
In view of the ways in which Congress, and the circumstances in
which it worked, had changed since the Programme of Action had
been ratified, it is important to examine the Freedom Charter to see
how far the clearly liberal stamp of the late forties had survived, and
alternatively, what signs there were of a movement away from liberal
principles.

The Charter provides no evidence that the A.N.C., by co-sponsoring
the Congress of the People and ratifying the Charter, had abandoned
the liberal principles outlined in the earlier Bill of Rights and the
Programme of Action.[5] On the contrary, in terms of political theory,
the Freedom Charter included principles fundamental to Western
liberal democracy. For example, under the heading 'THE PEOPLE
SHALL GOVERN!', the Charter declared, 'Every man and woman shall

---

[1] Statement taken from Chief Albert J. Luthuli in the case *R* v. *Adams and
Others*, p. 15.
[2] ibid., p. 16.
[3] Lutuli, quoted in Benson, *Chief Albert Lutuli of South Africa*, p. 31.
[4] c.f. above, p. 68. Congress spokesmen had emphasized the A.N.C. objective
of full political rights in the letters which they had sent to the Government prior
to the Defiance Campaign in 1952. But these letters were primarily intended to
explain why the A.N.C. was resorting to the use of passive resistance. See above,
pp. 81–2.
[5] See above, pp. 31, 68.

have the right to vote for and to stand as a candidate for all bodies which make laws . . .'; and where the Charter elaborated on the general principle 'ALL SHALL BE EQUAL BEFORE THE LAW!' it insisted that no one should be 'imprisoned, deported or restricted without a fair trial' and that laws which discriminated 'on grounds of race, colour or belief' should be repealed.[1]

What was new—and provided grist for the mill of those who wished to characterize Congress as radical and even communistic—was the attention paid to economic change. The sections, for instance, headed 'THE PEOPLE SHALL SHARE IN THE COUNTRY'S WEALTH!' and THE LAND SHALL BE SHARED AMONG THOSE WHO WORK IT!' reflected clearly that Congress had additional interests, besides the winning of political rights which the earlier Bill of Rights and Programme of Action had stressed.[2] This new emphasis was a tacit acknowledgement on the part of the Congress leaders that, if they wanted mass support, they must do more than pursue the abstract principle of political rights; they must champion the immediate interests and preoccupations of the rank and file.

In terms of how liberal a document the Freedom Charter was, these economic prescriptions which it sought were of crucial importance. In this area, the Charter was ambiguous in a way it was not in its references to political and civil liberties. If, as Congress critics argued, the Freedom Charter was a socialist document in its economic aspects, it meant at the very least, that the Africans who accepted it had moved to a position fundamentally different from that of all but a handful of white liberals. To almost all white liberals, and certainly to whites in general, any recognition that the A.N.C. endorsed socialist principles, immediately and automatically deprived Congress of a liberal character.

It is arguable that what in isolation were undoubtedly socialist principles were, in the South African situation, part of what Joe Matthews called an 'essentially bourgeois ideology'.[3] Such a claim rests chiefly on the grounds that the changes in ownership which the Charter envisaged were sought as much to allow Africans with money some outlets to invest their capital and make a profit, as they were to redistribute wealth on a socialist basis. As Mandela pointed out in 1956:

[1] Luthuli, *Let My People Go*, Appendix B, pp. 211–12.
[2] ibid., see above, pp. 31, 68.
[3] Author's interview, London, 8 Oct. 1965.

Under socialism the workers hold state power. They and the peasants own the means of production, the land, the factories, and the mills. All production is for use and not for profit. The Charter [he argued] does not contemplate such profound economic and political changes. Its declaration 'The People Shall Govern!' visualizes the transfer of power not to any single social class but to all the people of this country, be they workers, peasants, professional men, or petty-bourgeoisie.[1]

He explained further:

The non-European traders and businessmen are potential allies, for in hardly any other country in the world has the ruling class made conditions so extremely difficult for the rise of a non-European middle class. . . . The law of the country prohibits non-European from owning or possessing minerals. Their right to own and occupy land is very much restricted and circumscribed and it is virtually impossible for them to own factories and mills.[2]

Yet by far the larger proportion of Africans were wage-earners, rather than businessmen, even on a small scale. And no doubt it was an awareness of the 'proletarian' character of the vast majority of non-whites which encouraged whites to see the Freedom Charter as a socialist, if not a communist, document.

In view of the white minority's monopoly of wealth—and tangibly superior living conditions which depended on that monopoly—the economic changes which the Charter envisaged were radical in the extreme. Talk of the 'mineral wealth beneath the soil, the banks and monopoly industry' being 'transferred to the ownership of the people as a whole', and of all the land being 'redivided among those who work it'[3] was tantamount to revolution. But in the Charter all such changes were set firmly in the context of a multiracial South Africa, and were certainly not deliberately anti-white. Broadly speaking, what the 'socialist' clauses of the Charter implied was that in a multi-racial situation where one race monopolized economic as well as political power, it was not sufficient to seek only specified political changes.[4] Provision must be made also for redistribution of wealth

---

[1] Reprinted in Mandela, *No easy Walk*, p. 57.   [2] ibid., p. 60.
[3] Luthuli, *Let My People Go*, Appendix B, pp. 211–12.
[4] cf. Lutuli's comment: 'The Charter . . . is, line by line, the direct outcome of conditions which obtain—harsh, oppressive, and unjust conditions. It is thus a practical and relevant document. It attempted to give a flesh and blood meaning, *in the South African setting*, to such words as *democracy, freedom, liberty*.' ibid., p. 154.

to underpin the new political structure. In this Congressmen were doing no more than adding socialist planks to their well-worn platforms of political and civil liberties.

The Liberal Party was not to review its economic policy until the late fifties.[1] Meanwhile, they found it impossible to accept the Freedom Charter for reasons quite distinct from its 'socialist' elements. The Charter neglected to make clear—in fact, failed to discuss—the methods by which the Congress Alliance planned to achieve their aims. Such an omission was unthinkable to Liberals; for almost all of them, the liberal end would, under no circumstances, justify the use of illiberal means. And the Charter's failure to discuss methods was readily interpreted as a sign that the communists had, at the very least, lulled the non-whites into ignoring this fundamental question.

Mistrustful of communist influence, the Liberals failed to appreciate the purpose of the Congress of the People and the necessary limitations of the Freedom Charter. Both were intended to provide the 'liberatory movement' with fresh impetus in the face of the increasingly severe Government reprisals which countered Congress Alliance moves in the fifties. The minimum demand of those who endorsed the Charter at Kliptown, as well as the strongest bond between the diverse elements which made up the Congress of the People, was their hatred of racial discrimination.[2] And the specific demands which they made were all, in some way, particular examples of this general principle. Ironically, it was a principle which the Liberals shared, but they failed to see the important way in which it supported what appeared to them as an ideological hotch-potch, with a 'socialist' emphasis that bespoke communist domination of the Congress Alliance.

v

The Congress of the People had been an occasion for grand-scale, spectacular co-operation across the colour line; the Liberal Party had not been involved. Yet they had, at the same time, made progress of another kind. They became involved in multiracial joint enterprises

[1] See below, pp. 197–8.
[2] cf. Thomas Karis's comment: 'In the main, . . . the Charter rang the changes on one theme: all racial discrimination must be abolished and equal rights must be granted for all.' See 'The Trial and its Political Meaning', in *The Treason Trial in South Africa: A Guide to the Microfilm Record of the Trial* (Stanford Univ.: The Hoover Institution, 1965), p. 6.

on specific issues, and also involved in the most basic kind of social work among non-whites. It was slow and sporadic progress, often imperceptible, and the full effects of these experiences could not immediately be seen. But they were eventually to draw the Liberal Party and the A.N.C. much closer together; they also helped transform the party into the more radical body which it became in the late fifties.[1]

The area and extent of successful co-operation varied from province to province. The Natal Liberals were consistently the most successful in interracial enterprises in the mid fifties.[2] They had some difficulty in attracting Indian support—the Natal Indian Congress feared competition for members and, in any event, the party's programme was not sufficiently radical to appeal to Indian intellectuals and professional men.[3] But relations with the Natal A.N.C. were generally very cordial. The bond of respect and friendship between Lutuli and Paton was an influential factor here.[4] Also important was the initially weak position of the C.O.D. in Natal;[5] in the Transvaal, by contrast, Liberals had to compete continually with the white communists for African friendship and co-operation.

The Natal Liberals rapidly identified themselves with the needs of non-whites in the province. At their Provincial Congress in October 1955 (at which they recorded a 60 per cent increase in membership over the preceding year) official protests were made about the impact of *apartheid*. Police raids received special mention, as did the system of racial classification under the Population Registration Act, removal of people under the Group Areas Act and the Government's

[1] See below, pp. 194 ff.

[2] For instance, on the evidence of two Transvaal Liberals, Neville Rubin (interviewed, London, 27 Aug. 1965) and Marion Friedmann (interviewed, London, 23 Sept. 1965). In the Cape, in the fifties the leaders' preference for electoral politics as well as the presence of Parliament in the Cape, meant that the Party's main activities were centred on the parliamentary arena. One of the Cape Division's chief roles was to register protests against laws passed in the face of Liberal Party opposition. Meanwhile, younger Cape members like Peter Hjul, Randolph Vigne, and Patrick Duncan were making contact with Africans; their experiences were to encourage them and others to support radical changes in party policies in the late fifties. (G.M.C. interview with Peter Hjul, Cape Town, 26 Jan. 1964; author's interview with Randolph Vigne, Greenwich, England, 2 Sept. 1965.)

[3] Author's interview with Hans Meidner (ex-President of Natal L.P.), Reading, England, 20 Sept. 1965.

[4] Author's interview with Mhalani Njisane (an African sociologist, who was a member of both the L.P. and the A.N.C.), London, 20 Sept. 1965.

[5] Author's interview with Hans Meidner, Reading, England, 20 Sept. 1965.

proposal to make Crown lands in Zululand available for Europeans.[1] The Congress agreed that the party's main activity during the following year would probably be that of 'investigating and publicising and opposing plans to remove people under various acts in Natal.'[2]

In July 1956 the Natal Indian Congress called a Group Areas Conference, from which grew a Vigilance Committee including Liberal Party members.[3] The Committee's self-appointed task was to study the implications of the proposals of the Group Areas Act, alert those likely to be affected, and awaken white opinion to the hardships which the implementations of Group Areas would cause.[4] An A.N.C. Study Conference was held in Durban in October of the same year, 1956. Four of the eight speakers, who discussed the significance of the Tomlinson Report, were Liberal Party leaders: the Provincial Chairman, Alan Paton; Leo Kuper, the sociologist who was Provincial Vice-Chairman; Violaine Junod, lecturer in Native Law and Administration at the University of Natal; and Leslie Rubin, Native Representative in the Senate.[5]

In November 1956, Violaine Junod and a number of other white women who were members of the Liberal Party were arrested in Pietermaritzburg, Natal. They had been among the 623 women marching in protest against the extension of passes to African women. The mass arrest was at that time the largest in South African history.[6] In Miss Junod's opinion: 'The whites' readiness to identify to the hilt with Africans in their protest and to face the consequences immediately made for a warm atmosphere of solidarity which no amount of talking could previously encourage.'[7]

Meanwhile in several country areas of Natal, the Liberals were making progress at a different level. At the time of the party's inauguration, Jordan Ngubane had stressed the importance of 'taking Liberalism to the man in the Location'.[8] He added: 'When we have got it there it will have to have specific and practical meaning in his daily life.'[9] Christopher Gell had been equally concerned that party members should be more than 'tea and sympathy' liberals. 'Liberalism [he said] has got to leave the drawing rooms and go out among the

---

[1] *Contact* (Oct. 1955).   [2] ibid.
[3] Violaine Junod, 'The White Liberals and the Treason Arrests', in *Africa South* (April–June 1957), pp. 23–4.
[4] ibid.   [5] *Contact* (Oct. 1956).
[6] Junod, 'The White Liberals and the Treason Arrests', p. 24.   [7] ibid.
[8] *Memorandum on the African and The Liberal Party*, c. 1953, p. 4, P.A.S.
[9] ibid.

people, the dirt and the stubborn intractable facts.'[1] The middle and late fifties were active years for the Nationalist legislators. The plethora of restrictive laws provided ample scope for the Liberal Party to become involved with non-whites and their problems at the location level. Those Liberals who took 'Liberalism to the man in the Location' skirted the barriers perpetuated by residential segregation. They came to know Africans on their own terms, as individuals rather than as representatives of a racial group. In involving themselves in the mundane problems of non-whites, whether Africans, Indians, or Coloureds, they short-circuited the whole system of *apartheid*. This fact was eventually to make them dangerous opponents of the Government in the sixties.

The person initially responsible for this 'Ambulance Work'[2] in the Natal countryside was Peter Brown. Brown had led the Natal delegation to the meeting at which the Liberal Party was formed, and subsequently became Natal Provincial Secretary. In the Kokstad area, on the Transkei borders, he worked in conjunction with Mlaheni Njisane, the African sociologist who was a member of both the L.P. and the A.N.C.[3] Brown and Njisane went out to recruit Liberals, and did so as a result of the kind of welfare work into which they were immediately drawn. They went to talk of Liberal Party policies; they stayed to explain municipal regulations to bewildered Africans and help defend their rights over issues like influx control and housing. It was, in Njisane's opinion, the 'unequalled dedication' of Brown which helped immeasurably to blur race distinctions in the area.[4]

Such Liberal efforts had the most direct impact on Elliott Mngadi. Mngadi was a young African whose first contact with the Liberal Party came with his work in the Ladysmith 'blackspot' area, which had been scheduled for removal under the Group Areas Act.[5] Here he was responsible for organizing a Land Owners' Association, set up under the auspices of the A.N.C. and the Liberal Party, the latter paying his salary. So effective was his work that the party was flooded with Africans' applications for membership. Mngadi himself considered that without the appearance of the Liberals he would

---

[1] *Some Immediate Suggestions for Liberals*, May 1953, mim., P.A.S. p.4.
[2] Lutuli's phrase; see above, p. 153.
[3] Author's interview with Mhaleni Njisane, London, 23 Sept. 1965.
[4] ibid.
[5] The author is not free to disclose the source of this information about the work of Elliott Mngadi. To do so could possibly cause embarrassment to the leading Liberal who supplied it.

have become a 'black racialist'. Instead he was elected to the Provincial Committee of the party.

vi

On 5 December 1956, members of the Security Branch arrested 156 men and women, most of them closely associated with the Congress Alliance. The subsequent Treason Trial and the events surrounding it provide a curious paradox. Here was a unique challenge and opportunity for the Liberal Party to identify itself with the A.N.C. And their experiences relating to the Trial forged new bonds between the A.N.C. and the Liberal Party. But this increased understanding was not symptomatic of the general tenor of relations between black and white; before the Trial was concluded in 1961, a marked polarization over the colour question had taken place. In these altered circumstances, the A.N.C. and the Liberal Party could not effectively promote a liberal solution to the colour problem, despite their improved relationship.

The gravamen of the Prosecution's case was that the accused were pledged to overthrow the Government by violence, and furthermore were inspired in this aim by their connections with international communism.[1] True, there were instances of Congress officials, in their individual capacities, stressing the need for non-whites to be *prepared* for violence,[2] but the Government failed spectacularly to prove that official Congress policy had been anything but non-violent. In presenting judgement, Mr. Justice Rumpff emphasized *inter alia* that it had 'not been proved that the form of State pictured in the Freedom Charter' was that of 'a Communist State'.[3] Nor, the judges agreed, had it 'been proved that the African National Congress had become a Communist organisation.'[4] Justice Rumpff granted that the A.N.C.'s demands were 'far-reaching'. But, he added, the Court was 'not convinced that the African National Congress had acquired a policy which caused it to cross the dividing line between non-communism and communism in the spectrum of socialist belief.'[5] In ways such as this, the judgement which concluded the Treason

[1] Karis, 'The Trial and its Political Meaning', p. 17.
[2] The classic instance of this was Robert Resha's speech to the A.N.C. Freedom Volunteers in the Transvaal; the speech is quoted in Karis, op. cit., p. 19.
[3] In the judgement of the Special Criminal Court, Regina v. F. Adams and Others, the full text of which is reproduced in Karis, *The Treason Trial in South Africa: a Guide to the Microfilm Record*, pp. 68–76.   [4] ibid.
[5] Karis, 'The Trial and its Political Meaning', p. 23.

Trial, and resulted in the dismissal of the charges, provided food for thought for those Liberals who had, during the mid fifties, consistently baulked at any closer or more formal co-operation with the A.N.C.

In 1953 the Liberal Party had deliberately chosen to employ constitutional and parliamentary means.[1] In contrast, the A.N.C. had by then endorsed the use of passive resistance, strike, and boycott to pursue their aims.[2] Such strategies had increased at least the possibility of violence, if only because of the way in which they attracted the attention of the police.[3] Yet, the Treason Trial judgement provided conclusive evidence of the A.N.C.'s attachment to non-violence in the mid fifties; this suggested that the common ground between the Liberals and Congress might then have been wider than the Liberals had thought at the time. Furthermore, the Treason Trial judgement implied that the Liberals had been wrong at least about the *extent* of communist influence in the Congress Alliance.

Had such an impartial judgement been available earlier, as proof of Congress' innocence, it is possible that more of the Liberals would have urged the Liberal Party to identify itself with an interracial body like the Congress Alliance. Ironically, by the time the judgement was delivered—29 March 1961—the process of polarization in the relations between white and non-white had accelerated beyond the point where the Liberal Party could make the same kind of alliance with the A.N.C. which would have been possible in the fifties. By that time white Liberals were working under ban or threat of ban, and Congress itself had been declared an illegal organization.[4] Violence had become closer to reality—in fact, almost inevitable—in any confrontations between white and non-white. Plans for sabotage were being made. Coming belatedly as it did, the Treason Trial judgement, which referred to the period from February 1954 to December 1956, appeared tragically irrelevant.[5] It was quite useless,

---

[1] See above, p. 112.   [2] See above, pp. 69, 78 ff.

[3] See above, pp. 150, 156.

[4] The A.N.C. (and the P.A.C.) were banned in March 1960, under the terms of the Unlawful Organizations Act. During the following month a number of Liberals were detained under the State of Emergency regulations. See below, p. 215.

[5] All the accused were involved in the Preparatory Examination which lasted until 30 Jan. 1958. The First Indictment issued in June 1958 listed 92 accused. The Second Indictment (22 Nov. 1958) listed only 30 accused; their trial began on 19 Jan. 1959, and concluded with the verdict of not guilty on 29 Mar. 1961. Karis, *The Treason Trial in South Africa: a Guide to the Microfilm Record*, pp. 32–4.

in the crucially altered circumstances in which political opposition groups worked, or attempted to work, in the sixties, finally to have conclusive evidence that *in the fifties* Congress had been, in fact, a more respectable potential ally for liberal whites than they had at the time been able to see.

Meanwhile, the Trial provoked the Liberals into serious soul-searching. Treason Trial detainees were noticeably diverse in both background and political belief, as well as in colour. Members of the Liberal Party were conspicuously absent from their ranks. The fact that Liberals had *not* been arrested in December 1956 was a tacit sign of their failure; the Government did not consider them opponents worthy of attention. Thus, the Treason Trial prompted a reappraisal not only of the extent to which individuals were prepared to commit themselves, but also of the role of the Liberal Party and the future direction of its policy.

Members of the Liberal Party tackled the multiple practical problems which the Trial produced for the detainees. This was especially useful since the arrest of so many of the Congresses' leaders had caused a hiatus in Congress Alliance activities. Members of the Liberal Party provided transport for Africans to help them sustain the Alexandra Bus Boycott, which coincided with the opening of the Trial in the first months of 1957.[1] Together with other white liberals they payed a prominent role in organizing and administering the Treason Trial Defence Fund.[2] Liberals helped, too, in the exhausting and vital task of preparing the case for the Defence; a number of Liberal lawyers, such as A. P. O'Dowd, were directly involved. Women members of the Liberal Party provided lunches for the detainees while the Trial was in progress.

This shared 'political' activity encouraged social contact between black and white. Detainees (usually the most prominent) gathered in the homes of white Liberals in an unprecedented way. Lutuli recalls:

The colour bar dropped away like the fictitious and beastly thing it is, within the borders of the unexpectedly free world which the Trial had created. These were not chance encounters—part of Johannesburg's generosity was shown in the way in which, recognising the barren quality of our days, a section of its people set themselves to make our lives liveable in the evenings.[3]

[1] *Contact* (Feb. 1957).
[2] ibid. Lutuli paid a tribute to these white liberals and their work in his Foreword to Helen Joseph's *If This Be Treason*, p. 8.
[3] *Let My People Go*, p. 152; also Sampson: 'Among the white liberals it became

N

Moreover, detainees now met and talked with other whites whose political views were clearly at variance with their own. Unique opportunities arose for dialogue with such people as United Party leaders and some of the Afrikaner professors at Potchefstroom.[1] Congressmen found these new experiences exciting. In particular, exchanges with a variety of Nationalist critics fostered a sense of the solidarity of the Government's opponents.[2] In fact, however, the common bond of being anti-Nationalist did not guarantee a common goal. Moreover, the comparative goodwill which was so encouraging to A.N.C. leaders was confined to a small minority of the white population.

Just as ironic was the way in which the Treason Trial promoted the view that the pressure of world opinion would swing the balance in favour of the Government's opponents. 'World attention', said Lutuli, 'is something which we of the resistance need and desire.'[3] Such a hope was rooted in the ways in which the world appeared to have changed since 1945. The emergence of independent Asian nations, as well as sovereign African states, coupled with the avowed aims and status of the United Nations had seemed proof that eventually the Nationalists and their policy of *apartheid* must be defeated. The Government's attack on the rights of 'white institutions' had directed the glare of overseas publicity onto the South African scene in the fifties.[4] The Treason Trial, attracting as it did to South Africa, numbers of foreign observers, especially newspapermen and lawyers, no doubt seemed to the Government's opponents just the kind of strategy which must inevitably provoke the degree and kind of indignant protest which would topple the Nationalists, or cause them to modify their policy.[5] By the time the Trial was concluded, however, it was clear that only a minority of foreign governments were willing to do more than protest; that minority was not likely to be

---

the fashion to invite one or two of the most respectable 'drawing-room' Congress leaders to tea or dinner—an operation which, because of the physical difficulties of communication, had previously been almost impossible. Names like Lutuli, Matthews, Sisulu and Tambo, which had hardly been mentioned before, were now on every liberal's lips.' *Treason Cage*, p. 205.

[1] Lutuli, *Let My People Go*, pp. 152–3; also Sampson, *Treason Cage*, p. 205.
[2] Lutuli, *Let My People Go*, p. 154.
[3] ibid., p. 161.   [4] See above, p. 133.
[5] The presence of observers from the International Commission of Jurists—and their unequivocal comments—seemed of particular significance to Government opponents. Benson, *The African Patriots*, p. 249.

able to muster sufficient support in the United Nations for presenting South Africa with the kind of ultimatum which would bring the Nationalists to their knees.

In October 1958, Chief Lutuli addressed the Liberal Party Provincial Congress in Pietermaritzburg. The A.N.C.'s view of the party which he expressed was noticeably more cordial even allowing for the fact that Lutuli had generally been more kindly disposed towards the Liberals than some of the other A.N.C. leaders. 'I welcome the presence of the Liberal Party,' he said:

It stands for and represents lasting values, values which would make South Africa a country to be honoured. We in the A.N.C. would particularly like to work with the Liberal Party. I must say that we do usually co-operate in those matters where we agree and *as the years have gone by, we have found ourselves more and more in agreement with the Liberal Party* [authors's italic].[1]

Such a reaction was markedly different from that which Lutuli and other Congress leaders had expressed when the Liberal Party had been formed.[2] The change in attitude was due in part to the Liberal Party's activities in relation to the Treason Trial. Ironically, those members of the Liberal Party and Congressmen who saw their experiences during the course of the Trial as chiefly good omens for the future of multiracialism were seriously deluded. Just how crucially they misinterpreted what was happening is suggested by Thomas Karis in his essay, 'The Trial and its Political Meaning'.

The trial, in short, epitomized the alienation of the whites in political power from Africans who demanded a share and eventually majority control of that power. The realist or defeatist saw the trial as symptomatic, epitomizing the conflict of Afrikaner nationalism and African nationalism—or, more ominous, white racialism and black racialism—as forces that cannot be separated or reconciled. ... For the liberal or multiracialist, however, the trial was tragic. It ex-communicated moderate figures with whom it was necessary for whites to consult if they were to bring about the conciliation and eventually the consent that was the only hope for multiracial peace.[3]

[1] *Contact*, (1 Nov. 1958).   [2] See above, p. 119–20.
[3] Karis, 'The Trial and its Political Meaning', p. 26.

CHAPTER IX

The 1958 election and further realignment of liberals

i

The Nationalists' return to power in the general election of 16 April 1958, helped provoke a realignment of Government opponents. The United Party was sharply divided over the issue of future non-white policy; the Progressive Party which emerged as a result in November 1959 was composed of those still left in the U.P. with liberal views on the colour question. The new party advocated policies very like those which the Liberal Party had supported at its inauguration in 1953, most notably the gradual extension of the franchise to all civilized people regardless of race.

The Progressives could succeed to the Liberal Party position because the Liberals had by 1959 moved further to the left. Before the 1958 election the Liberals were already considering drastic policy changes as a result of their experiences on both sides of the colour line. The outcome of the election further encouraged them to rethink their policies. The position which they had adopted by the end of the fifties was considerably more radical than that of 1953. Their endorsement of the use of boycott, their unqualified acceptance of universal adult suffrage, and their consideration of a more radical economic policy were all part of a move away from their original character. Such policy changes earned them the approval of the African National Congress.

Congress, by contrast, did not have the freedom that the Progressives and Liberals had enjoyed to modify their principles and methods in the face of new pressures. Under the shadow of the current Treason Trial (1956–61), the A.N.C. continued to organize campaigns in the quest for mass support, but they were increasingly ineffectual. Even so, optimism remained: for the exodus of the Africanists from the A.N.C. left Congress free from internal division, and the trend towards freedom and independence elsewhere in Africa fostered hope of inevitable success for A.N.C. objectives.

ii

The cohesion of the United Party was subject to increasing strain before the 1958 election. Lack of consensus on the race question was evident despite the fact that party M.P.s had spoken in a common voice against Nationalist legislation infringing the rights of whites and the autonomy of their institutions.[1] In November 1956, Mr. J. G. N. Strauss was replaced as party leader by Sir de Villiers Graaff; the choice of de Villiers Graaff was interpreted by outsiders as a move to secure the loyalty of the widest range of U.P. supporters—it was a selection, said the *Natal Witness*, 'which would give offence to no one.'[2] But the U.P. leaders could not easily disguise the presence of dissident liberals within the party ranks. The Nationalists continually focused attention on this element: in their view, the continued presence of the 'progressives' within the party signified that the U.P. represented a threat to white supremacy. The Minister for Lands, Mr. Paul Sauer, for example, claimed that the Opposition had deviated from the colour policy of Smuts which had been closer to that of the Nationalists; they had, he said, made a 'basic shift towards Liberalism'.[3] Two weeks before the election, the Minister of Native Affairs, Dr. H. F. Verwoerd, spelt out the cost of a United Party victory: 'If the U.P. comes to power we shall experience in our time a Kenya and a mingling together.'[4]

This was first-rate propaganda rather than precise prediction. The United Party was liberal on the race question only in comparison with the Government. The 'progressive' minority had made little headway after the party's racial policy was revised in 1954.[5] In February 1956 the Nationalists had finally secured the removal of the Coloureds from the common roll. The struggle against the Government on this issue had previously provided a focal point for party unity; after the Government's success, the United Party confronted the divisive question of how they would act on the Coloured vote,

[1] See above, pp. 132, 134.
[2] 20 Nov. 1956 (*P.D.* No. 44, 22 Nov. 1956). Strauss had been in ill health for some time and unable to fulfil his duties as Party leader; with the 1958 election in view, active leadership appeared crucial to U.P. success.
[3] *Die Burger*, 22 May 1957 (*P.D.* No. 20, 29 May 1957).
[4] *Die Transvaler*, 1 Apr. 1958 (*P.D.* No. 14, 9 Apr. 1958); also *Die Transvaler*, 17 Jan. 1958: 'The United Party is today in the hands of the Copes, the Suzmans, the Fouries. . . .' (*P.D.* No. 3, 23 Jan. 1958).
[5] See above, pp. 125–6.

if returned to power.[1] Meanwhile, the party caucus refused to relinquish the principle of 'white leadership'. The statement made by de Villiers Graaff at the Union Congress of the U.P. in 1956 continued to be the official party view:

> We believe that the European should, in the interest of Western civilization, retain the leadership, but . . . we must get the confidence, goodwill and co-operation of the non-European population. If we deny them their place they may turn their backs on White civilization. *Our policy is not equality. It never has been, is not and never will be our policy* [author's italic].[2]

The only immediate cause for 'progressive' optimism lay in the United Party Senate plan announced in August 1957. This was a scheme providing for the representation of all racial groups in an expanded Senate, and seemed, especially in contrast with Nationalist policy, to represent a more liberal alternative.[3] It was, however, specifically intended to 'entrench white political leadership'.[4] Such ambiguities in U.P. colour policy left the 'progressives' room for hope and reconciled the party's conservative elements.

In addition, there was nothing to be gained, and much to be lost, by forcing the racial issue prior to the election. If one still believed that the Nationalists could, and would, be voted out of power— and the 'progressive' element within the U.P. did—it was of prime importance not to weaken the Opposition before the election. Here the strategic necessity to beat the Nationalists at the polls became an overriding argument for party unity, just as unity had been imposed on Government opponents for the same reason before 1953.[5]

Moreover, the issues which the party agreed to stress in their election campaigning were those on which widespread agreement could be guaranteed. Both wings of the party were able to deplore the Government's mismanagement of the colour problem, which was a favourite U.P. theme. Generally, U.P. spokesmen stressed the importance of the unity of the white races, deplored Nationalist enthusiasm for a republic and discussed economic prosperity.[6] The 'progressives' no doubt regretted that U.P. campaigning in working-

---

[1] G.M.C. interview with Colin Eglin, Cape Town, 24 Jan. 1964. In the mid fifties, Eglin was a U.P. provincial councillor; he was elected as a United Party M.P. in 1958.

[2] *Star*, 21 Nov. 1956 (*P.D.* No. 44, 22 Nov. 1956).

[3] *P.D.* No. 15, 19 Apr. 1956.

[4] *Rand Daily Mail*, 16 Aug. 1957 (*P.D.* No. 32, 22 Aug. 1957).

[5] See above, p. 95.   [6] *P.D.* No. 24, 27 June 1957.

class areas emphasized 'bread and butter before ideology',[1] but they had to concede that such an emphasis might make possible the party's return to political power. This remained the most urgent concern of all U.P. members.

The national election of 16 April 1958 resulted in a third successive victory for the Nationalists, and a third successive defeat for the United Party. The U.P. representation had fallen from 57 to 53 seats, whereas the Nationalists, who had won 94 seats in 1953, now had 103.[2] The election report in the *Rand Daily Mail* claimed that the U.P. had polled a majority of votes.[3] But the writer was forced to acknowledge that the Nationalists' total of 103 seats was the second biggest ever gained in the Assembly, that the new Parliament would be the first with representatives of only two parties, and that, also for the first time, a political party had been returned to office for a third term.[4] All these facts indicated increasingly strong support for the Nationalists and made the prospect of an early return to power by the U.P. extremely remote. The defeat further divided the U.P.: it drove a sharper wedge between those with different views on the colour question.[5] Rumours that a cleavage threatened were fed by such stands as that of Mr. H. G. Lawrence, a U.P. parliamentarian, who publicly criticized his party for vacillation on the question of race relations:

> Either we are a multi-racial country or we are not. If we are, then the non-European sections must be accorded their rights. I am not thinking necessarily of political rights at the moment. But attempts by this Government to diminish and reject these rights must be resisted now. . . . I do not think the United Party can evade this question. We are not a pale shadow of the Nationalist Party and deserve neither respect nor credit if we do not make our position clear-cut and unambiguous.[6]

Nationalist newspapers hastened to explain the significance of such a statement. *Die Transvaler*, for example, spoke of the race question as the great watershed in Union politics. It continued:

---

[1] *Star*, 20 Feb. 1958 (*P.D.* No. 8, 27 Feb. 1958).
[2] *A Survey of Race Relations in South Africa 1957–1958*, p. 1.
[3] 18 Apr. 1968. There was considerable controversy as to which party gained a majority of votes (*P.D.* No. 16, 24 Apr. 1958).
[4] *Rand Daily Mail*, 18 Apr. 1958.
[5] G.M.C. interview with Colin Eglin, Cape Town, 24 Jan. 1964, and with R. A. F. Swart, Durban, 31 Mar. 1964. Swart was elected as a United Party M.P. in 1953.
[6] *Star*, 3 Nov. 1958 (*P.D.* No. 44, 6 Nov. 1958).

That a choice—whether for the traditional policy of race separation or for the policy of equality which made its entry with the late Jan Hofmeyr—for the U.P. must have perilous consequences, everybody naturally knows and its own leaders certainly best of all. But can the consequences be more critical than those which the U.P. is already suffering as a result of its indecision in the form of three successive election defeats.[1]

Despite the apparent crisis, de Villiers Graaff avoided for as long as possible the thorny issue of the future direction of U.P. racial policy. But polarization within the party continued; de Villiers Graaff was subjected to pressure not only from the 'progressives', but also from the conservatives who considered that the liberal wing of the party had been a liability during the election, and ought to be irrevocably silenced.[2]

Significantly, the issue was forced by Government initiative. In January 1959, the Prime Minister, Dr. H. F. Verwoerd (who had been elected party leader when Strijdom died in August 1958) announced the Government's intention to implement a degree of territorial segregation by developing a series of independent native states or Bantustans.[3] This plan apparently changed the face of Nationalist non-white policy. The new policy, embodied in the Promotion of Bantu Self-Government Bill, was theoretically far removed from the 'white baaskap' approach which had characterized the Government's attitude in the mid fifties.[4] And it consequently provided the U.P. with an unprecedented challenge on the colour question.[5] Sir

[1] 4 Nov. 1958 (*P.D.* No. 44, 6 Nov. 1958).

[2] This point was stressed by R. A. F. Swart (G.M.C. interview, 31 Mar. 1964). There was, he said, 'a great deal of organisation taking place amongst the ordinary members of the party to attend the [1959] congress to see that more conservative delegates were nominated as party delegates and at the congress to put the liberals in their place.'

[3] *Die Burger*, 28 Jan. 1959 (*P.D.* No. 5, 5 Feb. 1959). Dr. Verwoerd was reported as saying: 'We regard the territorial authorities as legislative bodies in the first stage of development. . . . We must see to it that the outside world and the Bantu realise that a new period is arising. . . .'

[4] The first reading of the bill took place in March 1959. *Die Burger* (25 Mar. 1959) commented: 'The constitutional road on which the 1936 legislation was such a large milestone has now reached the point of no return. General Hertzog envisaged a solution to the political clash between white man and Bantu in the political partition of South Africa: a political home for the white man where he would have the authority, and a political home for the Bantu, where he in turn would be enabled to realise his political ideals to the fulness of his capacities.' *P.D.* No. 13, 2 Apr. 1959.

[5] G.M.C. interviews with Colin Eglin and R. A. F. Swart. cf. the comment in *Dagbreek en Sondagnuus* (2 Feb. 1959) that Dr. Verwoerd's 'recent statement

de Villiers Graaff could no longer delay discussion of the issue. The more conservative U.P. leaders were anxious to capitalize on what they saw as the liberal overtones of Verwoerd's announcement; they wished to pursue more openly the concept of white supremacy.[1] At the same time, the 'progressive' spirits saw as freshly urgent the restatement of U.P. racial policy in more liberal terms.[2] The protracted discussions which followed in caucus revealed, as one 'progressive', Colin Eglin, put it, 'not only the difference in emphasis, or difference in minor interpretation, but ... an absolute cleavage on basic principle on the colour question.'[3] In fact, Eglin argued: 'from that period onwards there was no U.P. in the sense it has been one party. It was a number of people with a range of views which made it virtually impossible for them to continue together for any length of time.'[4]

The fracture was clearly evident at the party Congress in August 1959. The controversy between the 'progressives' and the rest of the party arose on two issues: the restoration of the Coloured voters to the common roll if the U.P. were returned to power, and the purchase of more land for the use of Africans.[5] These had both been essential features of Hertzog's native settlement of 1936 to which the U.P. had subsequently adhered. Now, however, in the wake of a third election defeat, the bulk of the U.P. delegates were prepared to abandon what had previously been the basis of United Party colour policy. This suggested to the 'progressives' that the U.P. could no longer be regarded as having even potentially a liberal colour policy.

The U.P. Congress debate on the common roll issue confirmed earlier signs of a growing conservatism on the question. There was

---

on the further development of apartheid has created new disunity between Liberalists and Conservatives in the United Party's caucus.' *P.D.* No. 7, 19 Feb. 1959.

[1] e.g. the report (*Sunday Times*, 22 Feb. 1959) that Mr. Douglas Mitchell had suggested Verwoerd could be regarded as a liberal because he advocated a policy too favourable to the Bantu (*P.D.* No. 8, 26 Feb. 1959). See also *Rand Daily Mail*, 31 July 1959 (*P.D.* No. 31, 6 Aug. 1959).

[2] e.g. Mr. John Cope reported in the *Star*, 9 Apr. 1959 (*P.D.* No. 14, 9 Apr. 1959).

[3] G.M.C. interview, 24 Jan. 1964. cf. the claim in *Die Volksblad* (15 May 1959) that the U.P. was powerlessly crippled 'in the jaws of the monster of inherent division. It could not move to the liberal side for it would not—the provincial elections are too close at hand. And equally it could not move to the conservative side because the liberalists have slammed down the brakes.' (*P.D.* No. 20, 21 May 1959).

[4] G.M.C. interview with Colin Eglin, 24 Jan. 1964.   [5] ibid.

now a minority of influential United Party M.P.s who were prepared to abandon the principle entirely. But it was the Congress' acceptance of Douglas Mitchell's land resolution which forced the 'progressives' into a clear statement of their position. Mitchell had urged that the United Party oppose further land purchases for native settlement until they were returned to power.[1] He made this move on the grounds that any increase in the area of the reserves would be used by the existing Government to develop Bantustans. Mitchell and the conservative wing of the U.P. argued that these would pave the way for sovereign African states within South Africa, a development they were determined to prevent. Once the Congress supported Mitchell's resolution, eleven delegates, including six United Party M.P.s, immediately issued a statement of protest.[2] In their view, such a counter to the Government's scheme was blatantly opportunistic; it constituted a 'clear breach' of Hertzog's settlement of 1936 as well as the party's racial policy adopted in 1954.

Immediately after this confrontation, nine M.P.s resigned from the party; these included the six who had signed the protest, one of whom was Dr. Jan Steytler, former leader of the U.P. in the Cape.[3] They were shortly followed by two other M.P.s, Prof. I. S. Fourie and Mr. C. van Ryneveld, as well as by a number of U.P. provincial councillors.[4] In October, one of the most prominent older members of the party, Mr. H. G. Lawrence, joined this 'progressive' group.[5] In November 1959, they agreed to form a new political party.[6]

The Progressive Party appeared to many liberal-minded whites to offer solid hopes of a solution to the South African racial problem.[7] The policy agreed upon at their Inaugural Congress in November

[1] ibid. cf. Luthuli, *Let My People Go*, p. 164.

[2] A handwritten statement, mim., P.A.S.; also *Cape Times*, 14 Aug. 1959 (*P.D.* No. 33, 20 Aug. 1959).

[3] *Rand Daily Mail*, 18 Aug. 1959 (*P.D.* No. 33, 20 Aug. 1959).

[4] *Star*, 21 Aug. 1959 (*P.D.* No. 34, 27 Aug. 1959). Mr. van Ryneveld subsequently realigned himself with the U.P., but only briefly; he eventually resigned from the U.P. (*P.D.*, No. 34, 27 Aug. 1959). Prof. Fourie did not join the Progressive Party immediately (*Star*, 16 Nov. 1959, quoted in *P.D.* No. 46, 19 Nov. 1959). He remained as an Independent M.P. until June 1961 when he finally became a Progressive (*A Survey of Race Relations in South Africa 1961*, p. 18).

[5] *Rand Daily Mail*, 26 Oct. 1959 (*P.D.* No. 43, 29 Oct. 1959).

[6] *P.D.* No. 46, 19 Nov. 1959.

[7] cf. the sober comment in the *Star* (16 Nov. 1959): '. . . not in their wildest imagination can the Progressives expect to gain power in normal conditions within the foreseeable future. But they can and should act as a leaven to vitalise the thinking and action of this and coming generations in a world of dynamic change.' (*P.D.* No. 46, 19 Nov. 1959.)

1959 was an essentially liberal response to the trend of the events of the fifties. How far had the Progressives moved from the United Party? In what ways was their programme a liberal one?

The traditional U.P. position was clearly reflected in the statement of Principles issued by the Progressives at their party's inauguration. Of the six principles outlined, at least four revealed unmistakably the United Party origin of the Progressives. Typical signs of this heritage were the party's concern with the 'maintenance and extension of the values of Western Civilisation, the protection of fundamental human rights and the safeguard of the dignity and worth of the human person, irrespective of race, colour or creed', and the 'promotion of friendly relations with other nations, more particularly the members of the Commonwealth and those who share the heritage of Western Civilization.'[1] Thus much was not new. In so far as the Progressives' breakaway was an attempt to express more effectively such liberal principles as these, their liberalism was essentially conservative. Yet one of the factors which had driven them to form a separate party was their conviction that they could no longer satisfactorily act out these old U.P. principles within the confines of the United Party.[2]

The area where the Progressives most clearly diverged from traditional United Party principles was on the question of rights for non-whites. Here again they did not disagree on grounds that were in themselves new; what they sought was an extension of the old Cape rights for non-whites. But the United Party had never *as a party* supported the immediate *extension* of the vote to non-whites, even on a qualified basis. It was their awareness of this which encouraged the Progressives after their breakaway to see themselves as revolutionary. Yet it was only *by contrast* with their United Party brethren that their liberalism on the racial issue was striking.

The Progressives' Constitutional and Franchise Proposals included a prospective constitution for a plural society and an entrenched Bill of Rights. The right to vote would be granted to all 'suitably qualified

---

[1] *Principles of the Party*, issued by the Inaugural Congress, Johannesburg, 13–14 Nov. 1959, mim., P.A.S.

[2] cf. Dr. Jan Steytler's explanation: 'We have come to the conclusion that the temper of the ... [U.P.] congress showed a complete unwillingness on the part of most delegates to face up to the challenge of contemporary events here and in Africa. The impression we have is of a Party congress reluctant to move with the times, unwilling even to interpret its own principles in a forward-looking manner.' *Africa South*, iv, 2 (1960), 14.

citizens of a defined degree of civilisation belonging to any population group . . .' Voters would be registered 'on a common electoral roll' and 'special permission' made for the representation of people not qualified to vote.[1] In terms of political rights, the Progressives were clearly concerned to woo the white electorate by extending the Cape liberal practice to South Africa as a whole.[2] Their franchise policy was amost identical to that of the Liberal Party at the time of its formation in 1953.[3] Apparently the Progressives did not think it significant that events had edged the Liberal Party towards an acceptance of universal adult suffrage.

The Progressives' Economic and Labour Policy provides further evidence of the character of the new party's liberalism. Their policy should, they agreed, 'be directed to the conquest of poverty by increasing the National Income, maintaining a high and stable level of employment and hence improving the living standards of all sections of the population.'[4] As means to these ends they envisaged the abolition of job reservation and influx control, the payment of a 'rate for the job' wage, an increase in trade union rights (more gradual for unskilled than for skilled and semi-skilled) and the extension of social security benefits.[5] There seems no doubt that the Progressives were concerned that economic stability should be maintained as a guarantee of continued industrial and commercial expansion. Harry Oppenheimer's support for the Progressives was typical of the interest which businessmen and investors had in a party which could guarantee them a stable economy, and hence consistently good dividends. But the changes envisaged to ensure this were, nevertheless, ones which in terms of traditional white politics in South Africa, were singularly drastic. It is true that the Progressives' specific (and, presumably, deliberate) mention of 'free enterprise' struck an old-fashioned note. But it was clear that, in practice, the

[1] Constitution and Franchise Proposals, endorsed at the Inaugural Congress, 13–14 Nov. 1959, mim., P.A.S.

[2] This impression is borne out by the tenor of Dr. Zach de Beer's argument in 'The Progressive Party', in *Africa South*, iv, 3 (1960), 19. Dr. de Beer was an M.P. and Chairman of the Progressives' National Executive Committee.

[3] cf. Dr. Zach de Beer: 'We believe that constitutional government demands institutions which can be successfully operated only by civilised people. Therefore, we propose a civilisation barrier, which is not a race barrier, since any citizen of any race can cross it.' ibid.

[4] *Economic and Labour Policy*, endorsed at the Inaugural Congress, 13–14 Nov. 1959, min., P.A.S.

[5] ibid. Also *Cape Argus*, 3–4 Dec. 1959 (*P.D.* No. 49, 10 Dec. 1959).

Progressives were prepared to restrict the freedom of free enterprise in ways necessary to build a welfare state for non-whites as well as whites.

Measured by what the U.P. had offered in the past, the Progressives' policies were a marked liberal step forward. But they did not constitute enough of a step forward to bring them to an area from which they could easily bridge the gap dividing white from non-white. Still, the Progressives' chief expectation lay in influencing the white community rather than non-whites. Consequently, to the Progressives, the qualified franchise was the wisest *tactical* move in 1959, as well as a matter of principle. In 1953 the Liberals had gone into the political wilderness in a way the Progressives never envisaged doing. The Liberals had never possessed the financial backing nor the parliamentary weight which the Progressives enjoyed. The situation which confronted the Progressives seemed considerably more hopeful. The factors which had influenced the Liberals in their decision in 1953 were now much more glaring: the bankruptcy of United Party colour policy, the multiracial nature of South African society, the political awareness and maturity of non-white leaders in South Africa, the growth in the number of independent African states, and the climate of world opinion about the racially oppressed—all these factors had, during the fifties combined, it seemed, to generate a temper among the white community which would make it more amenable to a liberal prescription for the colour problem. An African, writing in the Congress Alliance journal *Liberation*, conceded something of this. The Progressive Party marked he said, 'a welcome turn in the direction of political sanity and realism.'[1]

It is true [he said] that the Progressives have nothing to say to White South Africa which the Congress of Democrats and the Liberal Party have not been saying, more forcefully and unambiguously, for the past six years. But the bulk of the European public is timid and conventional; it is fearful of losing its passport or being spied on by the special branch; it has long persuaded itself that Conscience is an impractical luxury. There are thousands who agreed secretly with what the Congress and the Liberals were saying, but feared to show their agreement. They were not prepared to listen to Alan Paton [of the Liberal Party] and Piet Beyleveld [of the C.O.D.] but they are prepared to applaud and support Harry Lawrence and Ernest Oppenheimer when they say the same things because they seem to offer some assurance of respectability and security.[2]

[1] *Liberation*, No. 39 (Dec. 1959), p. 5.   ibid.

It is no doubt true that a good deal of the Progressives' attractiveness was due to their 'respectability'.[1] Even so their new direction was fully acceptable only among a minority of whites. Caught up in the initial rush of enthusiasm for their party, the Progressives missed the fundamental fact that what to them had seemed good reasons for moving in a liberal direction, were to the majority of white South Africans overwhelming arguments in favour of conservatism.[2] They had underestimated the width of the gulf between white and non-white which they planned to bridge. In the sixties, starting with Sharpeville, that gulf was to widen further, as the prejudices and fears that were bred in the bone of South African whites (and non-whites) were to be at last finally and openly revealed as a factor of crucial importance in South African society. The Progressives, even more than the Liberals, could be characterized by the dying words of an earlier great South African, Cecil Rhodes: so little done, so much to do. Or by that very harsh epitaph: too little and too late.

iii

Liberal Party policies underwent serious review in the years 1958–9. The party's parliamentary experience had been sobering.[3] They had failed to gain substantial electoral support. Their M.P.s, all Native Representatives, had sustained a bitter attack on the nature of Government legislation in the middle and late fifties, but without success. Their involvement here had emphasized in their own minds, and to the party as a whole, just how relentlessly non-white rights were being whittled away. Furthermore, U.P. compromises made them realize that most whites were concerned primarily, if not exclusively, with the preservation of white rights. This was a distinction unacceptable to the Liberals. The party's contact with non-

---

[1] cf. Stanley Uys's contention that 'the Progressives represent . . . not a liberal flutter, but an alarmed reaction to a deteriorating situation by persons who, if they had lived in any country other than crazy South Africa, would be the respectable pillars of society.' *Africa South*, iv, 2 (1960), 16.

[2] cf. *Cape Argus*, 17 Aug. 1959: 'Whatever happens to the United Party— and it is the only weapon at the disposal of the anti-Nationalists—let it be remembered that the vast bulk of the electorate is conservative.' (*P.D.* No. 34, 27 Aug. 1959); also *Die Burger* (4 Oct. 1957): 'Everyone who looks deeper than the violently stirred surface of our colour problem, finds a greater degree of agreement than comes to expression in party politics. In reality the great majority of the European population is not basically divided on the colour problem.' (*P.D.* No. 39, 9 Oct. 1957.)

[3] See above, pp. 162–3.

whites had been equally instructive. Here they had eventually been relatively successful at the grass-roots level, and the increasing number of non-whites interested in party membership drove the Liberals to consider modifications to their policies which would encourage this trend.

In addition, Liberals were influenced, as was every politically-minded person in South Africa, by events in the rest of Africa. The pace of these events quickened during and after 1960, but the direction was clear several years earlier. Ghanaian independence in 1957, the first All-African People's Conference in Accra in 1958, and the tensions in the Central African Federation were only some of the straws in the wind. Margaret Ballinger publicly voiced the Liberal Party's concern early in 1959:

The whole face of Africa is changing, not in years but in months. These last few months have shown us that we are facing an entirely new life on this continent. . . . Black Africans are emerging all over the continent in positions of political power, which creates for us problems of accommodation of the most vital importance.[1]

In the face of these incontrovertible facts, the Liberals were doubly dismayed at the spate of discriminatory legislation which had been introduced in their own country during the fifties. Events north of the Limpopo River had helped to polarize white and black opinion in South Africa. And the Government had little difficulty in finding sufficient white support to pass a series of laws which made it abundantly clear that few whites were interested in the kind of 'accommodation' which Margaret Ballinger and the Liberals recommended.

After the election in 1958 the Liberal Party publicly acknowledged their defeat in the parliamentary field; such a step was especially significant in view of the party's initial commitment to constitutional and parliamentary means. Barely five years after Alan Paton's optimistic *Letter on the Occasion of the Launching of the Party in Cape Town*,[2] he argued: '. . . there is one overwhelmingly sound reason for believing that planned gradualism is impossible, and that is that the Nationalist Government will, by all ordinary reckoning, never again be defeated at an election.'[3] Also, in 1958, Peter Brown made unequivocal comment at a public meeting in Durban:

---

[1] Reference dated 28 Jan. 1959, at Chatham House, Press Library, London.
[2] See above, p. 114.
[3] Alan Paton, *Hope for South Africa* (London, Pall Mall, 1958), p. 60.

Parliament is no longer a democratic organ. It is an institution which the
Nationalists find convenient to use. But they hold reasonable argument
and debate in contempt. Parliament is a rubber-stamp which gives the
mark of respectability to their obnoxious laws.[1]

Once the Liberals had relinquished the parliamentary arena, the
party's focus changed. They no longer needed to soft-pedal policies
to attract the hesitant European voter, but could afford to think
more in terms of policies which would put them on better talking
terms with non-whites. Most important, the Liberals' virtual abandonment of parliamentary methods raised the question of alternate
means.

They now endorsed the use of boycott as a legitimate means of
protest. In their *Statement on the Overseas Boycott*, issued in 1958,
Paton and Brown, as the party spokesmen, conceded that white
supremacy would never yield 'to mere verbal persuasion'.[2] They condoned passive resistance and boycott as 'the only two kinds of
[non-violent] weapons left to non-white people who resist Apartheid.'[3]
Subsequently, the Liberals agreed to support the A.N.C.-sponsored
Boycott Movement which was initiated in London late in 1959.[4]
Visiting London at the time was Patrick van Rensburg, the Organizing Secretary of the Transvaal Liberal party; he took an active part
in the Boycott Movement with the approval of the party Chairman,
Peter Brown.[5]

Boycott was 'hardly a traditional liberal instrument of opposition',[6]
a fact which van Rensburg acknowledged. But Brown, and most of
the party, appreciated that 'new pressures' were 'inevitable and
necessary'.[7] In this, they were partly influenced by the African
members of the party who scornfully dismissed the argument that
non-whites would be the first to suffer in any boycott.[8] These
Africans agreed with Ngubane that they would 'be lucky merely to
starve in order to break Apartheid's back.'[9] Paton, too, held no
doubts that the Africans '. . . would choose without exception to risk
economic and personal suffering, rather than consent to the pro-
longation of a system which denies them and their children status

---

[1] *Contact*, 4 Oct. 1958.
[2] *Statement on the Overseas Boycott* (*1958*), issued by the L.P., mim., P.A.S.
[3] ibid.   [4] Van Rensburg, *Guilty Land*, p. 39.
[5] ibid., p. 40.   [6] ibid., p. 49.
[7] Peter Brown, 'Not to Boycott is to Surrender', in *Contact*, 8 Aug. 1959.
[8] See *Statement on the Overseas Boycott* (1958).   [9] ibid.

and recognition . . .'[1] Here, as the A.N.C. had done,[2] the Liberals underestimated the degree of conservatism which poverty and fear could breed among non-whites.

The vexed question of the franchise was re-opened in 1959.[3] It could no longer be side-stepped. White Liberals had come to know Africans and Coloureds much better through the interracial contact which the party had provided.[4] They could not offer these people the second-class citizenship which the qualified franchise implied, any more than they could expect non-whites outside the party to be attracted by a programme which offered them anything less than one-man, one-vote. A Franchise Commission finally reported to the Liberal Party National Congress in May 1960, and, as a result, the party resolved 'to extend the right of franchise on the common roll to all adult persons.'[5]

The party's economic policy also came under fresh scrutiny. Initially, the Liberals had been concerned to alleviate economic hardship, but generally they failed to comprehend how deep-rooted the causes of these inequities were.[6] In 1953, to talk in terms of a planned economy or equitable redistribution of and would have been to split the party irrevocably. However, the Liberals' experiences in the mid fifties were edging them in the direction of fundamental change. In their efforts to abolish the colour bar, the Liberals came out clearly against job reservation, the exclusion of non-whites from official trade unions, and the inadequacy of the education and training offered to non-white apprentices.[7] By 1958 the Liberal Member for the Cape Provincial Council, B. P. H. Curran, fought successfully in the African constituency of the Eastern Cape on the issue of a 'minimum living wage'.[8] A year later, in April 1959, this was accepted by the Liberal Party National Congress as a cardinal element of party policy.[9] At the same time, the Congress made their land policy

[1] Speaking on 'Racial Problems in the Modern World', in St. Paul's, London, 1959, mim., P.A.S.

[2] See above, pp. 155 ff.

[3] Minutes of the National Congress of the L.P., Johannesburg, 4–6 Apr. 1959, mim., P.A.S.

[4] Van Rensburg, *Guilty Land*, p. 36.

[5] Minutes of the National Congress of the L.P., Cape Town, 28–30 May 1960, mim., P.A.S.

[6] Peter Brown, 'The Liberal Party of South Africa', in *Contemporary Review* (1961), p. 589.

[7] Minutes of the National Congress of the L.P., Durban, 13–16 Dec. 1957, mim., P.A.S.

[8] *Contact*, 22 Mar. 1958.   [9] *Contact*, 18 Apr. 1959.

o

considerably more explicit, acknowledging as it did, that some 'redistribution of land will clearly be necessary so that the wants of hitherto landless people can be met.'[1] It was not until 1964 that the party's economic policy appeared markedly socialist.[2] No longer hoping to make any great impact on white electors, it became less necessary to keep a conservative economic line. On the other hand, if they wanted to attract non-white support, they had no counter to the promises of the Freedom Charter. The A.N.C. had, meanwhile, staged their spectacular £1-a-day wage campaign, and in Natal, for instance, there were a large number of African factory workers who were members of the party, and whose loyalty the Liberals were anxious to keep.[3] These Africans already within the party provided a crucial additional pressure. Furthermore, after the Liberals had endorsed universal adult suffrage, they came to realize that, to Africans, this was a political gain only, a gain which left the whites with a monopoly of economic privilege. At the same time, the secession of older members made it easier to introduce the moot point of a more radical economic policy.

It would be misleading to suggest that there was no serious opposition within the party to these changes in policy. Casualties in the Cape were by far the heaviest. There, fifty people resigned within two years.[4] The majority of these were older members, wedded to the original tenets of the party, and concerned that this new militancy would alienate prospective white supporters.[5] Most of them shared the feelings of Gerald Gordon and Oscar Wollheim, who stated explicitly that they considered '. . . the franchise should be exercised only by those whose education and civilized standards gave them the necessary sense of responsibility.'[6] The Progressive Party provided a new political home for those to whom the Liberals' unequivocal stand for universal adult suffrage was unpalatable. In their franchise policy in particular, the Progressives had inherited the Liberals' original position of 1953.[7]

Among those who resigned on the franchise issue and subsequently joined the Progressives was Dr. Wollheim,[8] the man responsible for the Liberal Association out of which the Liberal Party had developed.

---

[1] *Contact*, 5 Sept. 1959.   [2] See below, pp. 223.
[3] The author is not free to disclose the identity of the leading Liberal who claimed that these were straws in the wind.
[4] *Cape Argus*, 14 Sept. 1960.   [5] ibid.
[6] *Cape Times*, 14 Sept. 1960.   [7] See above, pp. 112, 116–7.
[8] *Cape Argus*, 14 Sept. 1960.

In a sense, his resignation and others like it signified the failure of the Liberals on their stand of 1953. They had hoped to gain—and keep—support from as wide a political spectrum as possible. Yet Wollheim himself saw what had happened to the Liberal Party:

> The Progressives have to some extent stepped in where moderate Liberals operated among the White voters until a year ago [i.e. until 1959]. This has to a certain extent pushed the Liberal Party out of the electoral field and among the South Africans who are voteless. In this sphere the Liberal Party is at present the only bridge between White and non-white.[1]

iv

Late in 1959, the Liberal Party earned the commendation of Oliver Tambo, an A.N.C. leader who had earlier been a Treason Trial detainee. Addressing a non-white audience at an Africa Day Meeting in Alexandra township, he said: 'Europeans in South Africa should, as soon as possible, follow the policy of the Liberal Party before the Africans reach a point of no return.'[2] The note of urgency which Tambo struck bespoke the frustration which the A.N.C. leadership felt. The Treason Trial had brought members of the Congress Alliance into closer contact with each other,[3] but in every other way it aggravated the organizational difficulties which had hobbled the A.N.C. in the mid fifties. Even so, while the Congress policy of non-violence was subjected to close scrutiny in the court-room, A.N.C. leaders encouraged Congress officials to explore more fully the possibilities of non-violent protest.[4] However, it appeared increasingly clear that such a strategy would be ineffective in achieving the A.N.C.'s major aim of full political rights. The Potato Boycott (1959) helped force limited concessions from the Government with regard to the working conditions of farm labour.[5] But such success never threatened the white power structure. Furthermore, where protests for particular objectives failed they did harm to the A.N.C.'s reputation among non-whites. This was so with the 1958 stay-at-home

---

[1] ibid.   [2] *Contact*, 2 June 1959.
[3] Lutuli pointed out: 'What distance, other occupations, lack of funds, and police interference had made difficult—frequent meetings—the Government had now insisted on. We could at last confer *sine die*, at any level we liked.' *Let My People Go*, p. 148. Duma Nokwe also mentioned this particular 'bonus' of the Treason Trial (author's interview, Dar es Salaam, 15 Nov. 1965).
[4] Benson, *The African Patriots*, p. 111.   [5] ibid., p. 263.

strike, planned to coincide with the election of 16 April.[1] Many Africans resented the A.N.C. appeal to strike for £1-a-day. They were being asked to hazard their jobs and their wages with very little chance of success.[2] Also, in this instance, the A.N.C. resorted to intimidation, and police moved in to protect African workers.[3] Moreover, with non-white campaigns there was always the possibility of violence developing from even a studiously non-violent protest. On such occasions there were frequent clashes with the police and mass arrests. Congress leaders knew that any outbreak of violence involving Africans, whatever the complexity of its cause, would be easy pickings for the Nationalists to add to their existing wealth of propaganda against the non-whites.[4]

Still the Congress leaders had no alternatives, and they continued to recommend the use of non-violent protest. There were, in any case, some apparent causes for optimism. One was the final departure of the Africanists from the ranks of the A.N.C. in March 1959. There were a number of ways in which the Pan-Africanist Congress differed from the A.N.C.: these were differences which must have encouraged A.N.C. leaders to see the A.N.C. *by contrast* as moderate. True, Robert Sobukwe, the President-General of the P.A.C., claimed that his followers accepted 'political democracy as understood in the west', and opposed 'totalitarianism in any form'.[5] But such an endorsement of apparently liberal principles had a hollow ring, for the P.A.C. frankly accepted the inevitability of violence; as well they displayed a general temper which appeared to welcome the possibility of an open conflict.[6]

---

[1] The success of the 1957 strike and the comparative failure of the 1958 'stay-at-home' are discussed by Feit, *South Africa*, pp. 55–8; also Luthuli, *Let My People Go*, p. 163.

[2] Feit, *South Africa*, p. 56.

[3] ibid., p. 57.

[4] See above, pp. 80, 87, 156.

[5] In his Opening Address at the Africanist Inaugural Convention, 6 Apr. 1959, reprinted in *The Basic Documents of the Pan-Africanist Congress of South Africa* (Lusaka, Zambia, March 1965), p. 12.

[6] This was implied by Peter Molotsi in a discussion with the author, Evanston, Illinois, 31 May 1965. The Pan-Africanists' acceptance of violence is discussed—and underlined—by Bloke Modisane in his autobiography, *Blame me on History* (London, Thames & Hudson, 1963), pp. 251 ff. Modisane was reluctantly and, it appears, never totally converted to the Pan-Africanist viewpoint, but his interpretation of their principles was recommended as just by Z. B. Molete while Molete was still a P.A.C. leader (author's interview, Dar es Salaam, 13 Nov. 1965).

Moreover, they were distinctly exclusivist.[1] Whites had in their view beguiled African nationalists from what must in future be a single-minded pursuit of their freedom. For this reason, those who were essentially more closely akin to the white world and its privileges must prove, as individuals, their total identification with the Africans' cause.[2] Until they did so, whites must be assumed to be at least potential traitors to the movement for African liberation. In addition, to endorse multiracialism, as the A.N.C. persisted in doing, was to accept the fact that the 'old separate [i.e. racial] identities and divisive forces'[3] breaking up the community would be perpetuated in any new state established after the whites' monopoly of power was broken. Thus the P.A.C. rejected multiracialism and endorsed instead the comparatively difficult and frequently nebulous concept of non-racialism.[4] In their mistrust of whites, they denied any credit to white communists or white Liberals for their increasingly costly attempts to confront the colour question. In fact, the P.A.C. tarred ardent Nationalists and passionate Liberals with the same brush. This may be an understandable oversimplification. But it was a serious distortion of some of the facts of interracial co-operation in the fifties.

The A.N.C. leaders were angered by this distortion as well as by much else about the P.A.C. But the Africanists had been a thorn in

[1] Sampson comments on the P.A.C.'s preoccupation with black nationalism. Of the clash between the Africanists and the main body of A.N.C., he says: 'It was an acrimonious quarrel, and fundamentally the oldest argument in Congress—the argument between nationalism and liberalism.' *Treason Cage*, p. 112.

[2] cf. Sobukwe's explanation in an outline of the Africanists' case which appeared in *Contact*, 30 May 1959: 'We have admitted that there are Europeans who are intellectual converts to the African's cause, but, because they benefit materially from the present set-up, they cannot completely identify themselves with that cause.'

[3] Author's interview with Z. B. Molete, Dar es Salaam, 13 Nov. 1965.

[4] Sobukwe explained the grounds of the Pan-Africanists' objections to multi-racialism in his Opening Address to the Africanist Inaugural Convention. See *The Basic Documents of the Pan-Africanist Congress of South Africa* (Lusaka, Zambia, 1965), pp. 16–17. cf. the article, 'They were Right and So are We', in *The Africanist* (June–July 1958): 'By far the most serious charge that has been levelled against African Nationalism is that it is racialistic. Our line of attack, or presentation of the subject-matter and our chain of reasoning all refute this allegation. We have depicted African nationalism as a social force whose inner-springs are the assessment of the interplay, the determination of the interrelation and the evaluation of the correlation between economic elements and socio-historical factors and forces. For us there is no "race" problem but only a social problem.'

their flesh, particularly in the Transvaal, since 1953 and Congress leadership was relieved to be rid of such a persistent and dangerous irritation. Congress leaders thought their own image would be enhanced by the now clear dividing line between the A.N.C. and the Pan-Africanists. But the formation of the P.A.C. proved of only very temporary and limited advantage to Congress. P.A.C. spokesmen addressed their audiences in a much more rabble-rousing manner than the A.N.C. had ever attempted, or thought desirable. This search for mass support encouraged just the kind of over-simplification and catch-cries which, through Press reports and Government responses, generated fresh fear among the vast majority of South African whites. And most of them, when confronted with the possibility of a black take-over of power, found little reason, if they looked for any, to distinguish between the P.A.C. and the A.N.C.

Meanwhile, the A.N.C. found another good omen, besides the exodus of the Africanists, to reconcile them to their frustration in the late fifties. When Congress leaders had sought recognition from the whites in the early fifties, they had lacked a powerful weapon which the late fifties appeared to have given them. The emergence of independent African states, Ghana, for instance, in 1957, and Guinea in 1958, seemed to A.N.C. officials as an irrefutable argument in support of their faith in a change in South Africa. With the prospect of a number of other African states gaining independence in 1960, the tide of hope among Congress leaders ran high. This optimism was expressed by Lutuli in an address to a white audience in Johannesburg in April 1959.

> The yearning for freedom [he said] is not peculiar to South Africa. The whole of Africa is emerging into Freedom. We live in the midst of what has rightly been described as 'Emergent Africa'. Why should it be thought [he asked] that Africans in this part of Southern Africa are different from Africans in Ghana? Africans in Ghana have received full democracy. In Nigeria they are about to receive full democracy. How can it be suggested that the Africans in the Union of South Africa will not yearn, like their brothers in the North, for freedom. The very fact that Africa is emerging to freedom should be a sign to all of us that our vision of democracy, is coming and *will* be realised.[1]

Yet the emergence of independent African states was not the sign of hope which Lutuli considered it to be. His argument could, and did,

---

[1] The address was entitled 'Freedom is the Apex', mim., P.A.S.

exert a *conservative* influence on a different kind of white audience. No doubt the whites who heard Lutuli speak on that occasion were newly impressed with the logic of the argument that the Government could not permanently subject non-whites to second-class citizenship. But the meeting had been sponsored by the Congress of Democrats, and most of the audience would probably have been earlier converted to at least sympathy with the A.N.C.'s purposes. The occasion was, in this way, typical. Congress' most fruitful interracial activity during the fifties had been strictly limited to a *minority* of whites.[1] These opportunities were new and exciting, an incredible advance on the possibilities ten years before; they were also seriously misleading. For they fostered the conviction that interracial co-operation on a limited scale was the precursor of a fundamental change of heart on the part of a majority of South African whites. And this was to prove a mythical hope.

In the late fifties, it was by no means clear that the sixties would provide the setting for a stark confrontation between white and black nationalism. It was not until the hammer-blows of Sharpeville and Langa shattered the political balance in March 1960, and drove a deeper wedge between those who wanted a genuinely integrated society and those who were at bottom white supremacists, that the degree of polarization along racial lines became amply evident.

[1] Benson claims that Lutuli impressed an increasing number of South African whites in the late fifties. *Chief Albert Lutuli of South Africa*, pp. 36–8.

CHAPTER X

White unity and the dismantling of the liberal state (1960—1963)

i

Sharpeville, Langa and the subsequent state of emergency declared in March 1960 appeared at first to vindicate the reasoning of the Nationalists' opponents. Now, at last, it seemed inevitable that the tide must turn. Foreign governments expressed outrage, foreign confidence in the South African economy plummeted, support for U.N. censure widened. At home dissident Nationalists expressed misgivings, and a cleavage threatened in those seemingly indestructible pillars of Afrikaner nationalism, the Dutch Reformed Churches. The direction of the winds of change seemed unmistakable. The Nationalists would have to concede ground to the combined—and irresistible—force of their opponents at home and abroad.

Sharpeville *was* important. White liberals and others were right to predict that it was a crisis which would bring change. But they were wrong about the nature of that change. Sharpeville did not precipitate the Nationalists' defeat. Instead, it galvanized the Government into even stronger measures against their opponents, particularly against those who advocated an integrated society and the extension of non-white rights. In this way, Sharpeville far from being a turning-point served to accelerate a process already well advanced. Between 1960 and 1963 it became palpably clear that the majority of white South Africans would never accept a liberal solution to the colour problem. As a consequence of this choice, the period is marked by the diminution of the rights of whites as well as non-whites. For it was only in this way that white minority rule could be preserved.

ii

During the first weeks of 1960 a wide range of Government critics expressed their opposition to the pass laws, one of the oldest forms of racial discrimination in South Africa.[1] The Pan-Africanist Congress, formed in March 1959,[2] announced their first major campaign aimed at the abolition of the pass laws. Their members were asked to deliberately leave their passes at home and surrender themselves at their local police stations to be arrested for not being in possession of their passes. Robert Sobukwe, the President of the P.A.C., had stressed that the campaign to be launched on 21 March was to be non-violent.[3] However, the anti-pass demonstrations in the Sharpeville location near Vereeniging in the Transvaal culminated in the police opening fire on a crowd estimated between 15,000 and 20,000; sixty-seven Africans were killed and a hundred and eighty-six wounded.[4] On the same day there was also violence in the location of Langa near Cape Town. There were fewer casualties than at Sharpeville, but the same pattern involving a large African demonstration, misunderstanding with the police, police reaction, and death and injury most commonly to Africans.[5]

In the days that followed 21 March the Government adopted unprecedentedly drastic measures to restore order. On 24 March they banned public meetings of all races in specified districts. On 26 March the Commissioner of Police announced the temporary relaxation of the pass laws; these were reinforced on 10 April, after there had been widespread incidence of passbook burning, either voluntarily or under threat from intimidators. On 28 March the Government introduced the Unlawful Organizations Bill, designed to ban the A.N.C. and the P.A.C.; it also increased tenfold the penalties for intimidation.[6] On 30 March a state of emergency was declared;[7] before this was publicly known, 1,200 people of all races were detained in pre-dawn arrests.[8] During April and May, police made large-scale raids on Africans townships; by 6 May 18,011 arrests had been made as a result.[9] The emergency regulations which gave extensive and arbitrary power to the Government were finally lifted on 31 August five months after the crisis had begun.[10] In retrospect,

[1] *Days of Crisis in South Africa* (*Events up to 15th May 1960*), compiled by Muriel Horrell (Johannesburg, S.A.I.R.R., 1960), pp. 1–3.
[2] See above, p. 200.   [3] *Days of Crisis in South Africa*, pp. 7–8.
[4] ibid., pp. 9–10.   [5] ibid., pp. 11–12.
[6] These details are taken from *A Survey of Race Relations in South Africa 1959–1960*, pp. 68–70.
[7] ibid., pp. 73–8.   [8] *Contact*, 16 July 1960.
[9] *A Survey of Race Relations in South Africa 1959–1960*, p. 84.
[10] ibid., p. 78.

it appears that the Nationalists were never seriously in danger of losing control of the situation.

The Government's opponents deplored not only Sharpeville itself, but the Government's strong-arm measures. Yet, in fact, support for the Nationalists' racial policy increased in the early sixties. The overwhelming majority of white South Africans were now clearly conservative on the colour question. Those who pursued the idea of a multiracial society and the extension of rights to non-whites after 1960 did so with a new conviction, but their numbers were few.[1] Between this minority and the bulk of the white electorate, there was no common basis for political intercourse.

In particular, the United Party proved themselves loyal to the practice, if not the theory, of white supremacy. This is most clearly demonstrated by the United Party's attitude towards the punitive measures which the Nationalists introduced in the early sixties. The Unlawful Organizations Bill (1960) provided for the banning of the A.N.C. and the P.A.C. The General Law Amendment Bill (1961) which enabled the Government to detain people for twelve days without trial was followed, in 1962, by a General Law Amendment Bill which made sabotage an act of treason, and hence a capital crime, and, in 1963, by a further General Law Amendment Bill which legalized detention without trial for ninety days.[2] The general grounds on which the Government supported such measures did not vary. The political ambitions of the A.N.C. and the P.A.C. represented a clear threat to the future of white civilization in South Africa. To counter this threat, the most drastic action was necessary and defensible: there was, the Nationalists stressed, no greater priority than 'the security of the State'.[3]

The Government's proposals all allowed for extensive infringement of civil liberty, and their opponents attacked them on this score. Nevertheless, it was only the Native Representatives and the Progressive M.P.s who consistently and unambiguously opposed such

[1] See below, pp. 309–10.
[2] Act No. 34 (1960), Act No. 39 (1961), Act No. 76 (1962), Act No. 37 (1963). The provisions of these laws are outlined in some detail in Muriel Horrell, *Legislation and Race Relations*, pp. 55–60.
[3] J. B. Vorster, the Minister of Justice, in *Ass. Debates*, IV, 21 May 1962, col. 6078. cf. the Nationalist M.P., Dr. Coertze, speaking on the General Law Amendment Bill (1961): 'The rights of the organized community are much more important than the incidental rights of the individual.' *Ass. Debates*, vol. 108, 10 May 1961, col. 6255.

measures.[1] The United Party supported the Unlawful Organizations Bill (1960); they restated their disagreement with the Government over the permanence of economic integration and stressed the need for consultation with non-whites,[2] but de Villiers Graaff conceded that, in the circumstances, the overriding consideration was the maintenance of law and order.[3] In 1961 and 1962 the U.P. opposed the General Law Amendment Bills;[4] this opposition was grounded in the kind of liberal principles which they had defended in the fifties.[5] Sir de Villiers Graaff's objections to the 1961 Bill, which provided for detention without trial, were characteristic:

> This is legislation of a kind which gives inordinate power to the Executive, interferes with the freedom of the subject, prevents the ordinary individual getting the protection of the courts, and in no way deals with the problems with which we are faced.[6]

Yet, in 1963, the United Party supported the introduction of ninety-day detention without trial. The only parliamentarian to oppose this measure was the solitary Progressive M.P., Mrs. Helen Suzman.[7] In her view, the U.P. had now given 'the green light to the Government'; they had 'meekly acquiesced in South Africa's abdication from the ranks of democratic countries.'[8] Clearly, the view which Mrs. Suzman represented was a minority one. Moreover, the United Party, in supporting such extensive interference with the rights of the individual, had entirely abandoned the liberal principles to which they had clung so fervently in the fifties.[9]

[1] e.g. both Margaret Ballinger, the Native Representative, and Dr. Jan Stetyler, the Progressive Party leader, moved amendments at the Second Reading of the Unlawful Organizations Bill (1960). When a division was called at the Third Reading, only Margaret Ballinger and the Progressives opposed the bill. *Ass. Debates*, vol. 104, 4 Apr. 1960, col. 4735. The Native Representatives did not sit in the Assembly after 1960, and after the election in October 1961, there was only one Progressive M.P., Mrs. Helen Suzman.

[2] e.g. *Ass. Debates*, vol. 104, 29 Mar. 1960, col. 4318; ibid., 30–1 Mar. 1960, col. 4558.

[3] ibid. vol. 104, 29 Mar. 1960, col. 4318.

[4] ibid., vol. 108, 15 May 1961, col. 6355; ibid., IV, 12 June 1962, col. 7649. For Sir de Villiers Graaff's amendment, see ibid., col. 7631.

[5] See above, pp. 44–51.

[6] *Ass. Debates*, vol. 108, 8 May 1961, cols. 6068–9.

[7] *Ass. Debates*, VI, 29 Apr. 1963, col. 4927.   [8] ibid., col. 4929.

[9] cf. Scott Haigh in the *Sunday Tribune*, 12 May 1963: 'The Nemesis of death hovers over the United Party on its chronic sick-bed. One dawn the South African electorate may awake to be confronted with a reactionary, cumbersome and mostly abhorrent Common-Front White Laager Government.' (*P.D.* No. 18, 16 May 1963.)

There were still a number of issues over which the United Party and the Nationalists disputed, publicly and bitterly. Some of these contentious questions, such as the future 'place' of the Coloureds, the respective rights of Boer and Briton, and the value of the Commonwealth connection, were old debates. And there were additional areas of new dispute. In 1961, for instance, Sir de Villiers Graaff introduced a race federation plan as the United Party alternative to separate development. This scheme provided for a central federal parliament, with each racial group represented; the Coloureds were to be regarded as part of the white community, and 'white leadership' was to be retained.[1] To the active supporters of the U.P. such a plan constituted a clear option to the Government's policy. Yet in practice the misgivings which the United Party expressed all failed to materialize into basic disagreement. There was always, on crucial issues, a vital measure of consensus.

The course of the Republican crisis, as well as the 1961 election, provide further evidence of increasingly large numbers of whites moving, for all practical purposes, into the Nationalist-designed laager. Non-Nationalists, including the United Party, held high hopes that the referendum on the Republic would indicate a rejection of the Government and its policies.[2] In fact, the vote revealed that in all provinces but Natal a majority of whites favoured the change to Republican status.[3] In the first months of 1961 South Africa became a Republic and withdrew from the British Commonwealth.[4] At the same time, the Nationalists, attuned to white fears of the 'black peril', made an unprecedented appeal for English-speaking support. Verwoerd decided to hold an early election; although he

[1] *Ass. Debates*, vol. 107, 28 Mar. 1961, cols. 3860–1. The U.P. leader planned *inter alia* that the rights of the urban Africans would be extended by measures such as a system of pass exemptions and the grant of freehold title, and that job reservation would be replaced by the principle of 'the rate for the job'.

[2] e.g. the comment in the *Sunday Express* (18 Sept. 1960): '. . . [the referendum] gives the Opposition voter a unique opportunity to register his opinion, not merely about the republic but about the whole record of this Government over the past 12 years.' (*P.D.* No. 36, Sept. 22, 1960); also Dr. Jan Steytler, leader of the Progressive Party's campaign against the Republic (*Rand Daily Mail*, 3 Feb. 1960).

[3] The results of the Republican referendum are detailed, in a provincial breakdown of votes, by W. H. Vatcher, *White Laager: The Rise of Afrikaner Nationalism* (New York, Praeger, 1965), p. 192.

[4] The Republic of South Africa Constitution Act (No. 32 of 1961) provided that South Africa would become a Republic on 31 May 1961. Meanwhile, in March 1961, South Africa withdrew from the Commonwealth (*P.D.* Nos. 10–11, 16 Mar., 23 Mar. 1961).

need not have gone to the country before 1963, he chose to hold a general election in October 1961. There were several likely advantages for the Government. They hoped to capitalize on the current violence in the Congo, recapture the loyalty of dissident Nationalists, exclude the Progressives from Parliament, and confirm their electoral hold before there were any serious economic repercussions from leaving the Commonwealth.[1]

The election of 20 October 1961, vindicated Verwoerd's timing; it again increased the Nationalists' power. For the first time since the National Party had gained office in 1948, they had clearly won more votes than the Opposition.[2] Moreover, they now had 105 seats compared with 102 in the 1958 election; United Party strength had dropped from 53 to 49 since 1958.[3] The Nationalists now held two-thirds of the 156 seats in the House of Assembly. Clearly the United Party was losing its popularity, even with English-speakers;[4] more and more whites wanted to take an unequivocal stand against the 'black peril' and the Government had an impressive record for coping with non-white disturbances and political protest.

The Progressives retained only one seat. But they were only narrowly defeated in a number of other constituencies and their 69,042 votes surprised all but the most sanguine liberals.[5] Commenting on the emergence of the Progressives as a 'new star', Verwoerd added:

[1] *A Survey of Race Relations in South Africa 1961*, p. 14.
[2] The 800,590 who went to the polls cast their votes as follows:

National Party	370,431
United Party	302,875
National Union	35,905
Progressive Party	69,042
Conservative Workers' Party	6,229
Liberal Party	2,461
Independents	10,404

(*Africa Digest*, ix, 3 (1961); cf. *A Survey of Race Relations in South Africa 1961*, p. 21.)
[3] *A Survey of Race Relations in South Africa 1961*, p. 19.
[4] This was in spite of the U.P.'s marked move to the right prior to the election. They rejected the offer of an election pact with the Progressives; instead they made a pact with the National Union which had been launched in 1960 by Mr. Japie du P. Basson to capture support from dissident Nationalists and to promote co-operation between Afrikaners and English-speakers. *A Survey of Race Relations in South Africa 1961*, pp. 17–18.
[5] Mr. J. Cope lost the Johannesburg seat of Parktown by only 85 votes, and Mr. G. Forder lost in Pietermaritzburg District by 175. In four other constituencies, the U.P. majority over the Progressive candidate was less than 900.

But is this really a star, or is it a meteor? I would not wish to spoil the pleasure of its members in their minor successes, but to me the figures in which they exult tell the story of personal popularity of a lively group of middle-aged idealists and of another Natalian stand.[1]

Certainly the Progressives had won substantially larger electoral support than the Liberal Party ever enjoyed. However, in the face of the general trend of voting, the Progressive (and Liberal) votes did not represent a sign of hope. Instead, they indicated just how deeply divided the liberal minority was from the rest of the white community on the issue of non-white rights.

Yet the Progressive Party refused to abandon their hopes of the gradual extension of non-white rights within an integrated society. Their opposition to the punitive laws introduced between 1960 and 1963 was unambiguous and fearless, albeit ineffective.[2] Progressives had firmly believed that the Government would eventually have to concede to the non-whites' demands for political rights in order to maintain the rate of industrial growth and economic stability.[3] Such a hope was seriously shaken by the way in which the threat of econo-mic disaster following the 1960 emergency was averted without major modification to the existing pattern of race relations.[4] Even so, the Progressives had pushed ahead with the development of their political ideals. In December 1960 they had endorsed the Molteno Report, the product of their own commission appointed to discuss franchise qualifications and constitutional safeguards.[5] By August 1962, the Progressives had planned a federal constitution for a multiracial society.[6] By then, too, they had recruited as party members a number of non-whites who fulfilled the Progressive franchise qualifications.[7] Yet it was increasingly apparent that they had no chance of winning any degree of effective political power in South Africa.

The significance of the 1961 election result had been further borne out by the Government's increasing success in wooing the English-speakers to the Nationalist viewpoint. The post-election move of promoting two English-speakers, Mr. A. E. Trollip and Mr. Frank

[1] *Africa Digest*, ix, 3 (1961).
[2] e.g. Mr. Harry Lawrence, *Ass. Debates*, vol. 108, 8 May 1961, col. 6099; Dr. Zach de Beer, ibid., cols. 6120–8.
[3] See above, p. 126.   [4] See below, pp. 212–3.
[5] Molteno Report, vol. I (Nov. 1960).
[6] *A Survey of Race Relations in South Africa 1962*, p. 2.   [7] ibid.

Waring, to the Cabinet may have been rather an unsubtle tactic, but it paid the Nationalists considerable dividends by allaying fears that political power in South Africa was irrevocably an Afrikaner preserve.[1] Electorally secure, and anxious to promote white unity and strength, in contrast to their earlier preoccupation with Afrikaner identity, the Nationalists also relented on the question of white immigration.[2] They now conceded that it was of prime importance that the numbers of the white community be increased as rapidly as possible. Their sole stipulation was that newcomers to South Africa would have to subscribe to the practice of *apartheid*.[3] Their immigration policy had achieved marked success by 1963.[4]

The Nationalists' steady increase in electoral support was underpinned by other sources of power. One of these was their monopoly of armed strength. The importance of such a monopoly had been seen during the 1960 emergency. Armoured cars, helicopters, and planes had been used to intimidate non-whites and, when violence erupted, to crush the disturbances.[5] Between 1960–1 and 1963–4 defence spending nearly quadrupled.[6] The largest increase in expenditure was for the purchase of arms and ammunition. The strength of the police force was not greatly increased in the early sixties. The staff of the Special Branch, however, was more than trebled between January and July 1963, a white police reserve was established, and, under the terms of the Defence Amendment Act of 1963, members of the Citizen Force or Commando could carry out police duties.[7] The

[1] *Africa Digest*, ix, 3 (1961).
[2] Publicity was given to National Party plans for increased immigration in the early months of 1960—plans made despite, or perhaps because of, the existing state of emergency (e.g. *P.D.* No. 15 21 Apr. 1960; No. 20 24 May 1960; cf. *P.D.* No. 26 12 July, 1962).
[3] The Minister of the Interior, Mr. J. F. Naudé, for instance, spoke of the need to 'educate' new arrivals because of the 'country's particular demographic circumstances'. Immigrants who had previously settled elsewhere in Africa would, he conceded, adapt more easily (*Star*, 13 Apr. 1960 in *P.D.* No. 15 21 Apr. 1960).
[4] In January 1963 the Minister of Labour and Immigration, Senator A. E. Trollip, reported a net gain of 11,000 immigrants over emigrants in the preceding year; these were, he said, the best immigration results in the past ten years. *Africa Digest*, x, 5 (1963).
[5] *A Précis of the Reports of the Commissions appointed to enquire into the Events occurring on March 21 1960 at Sharpeville and Langa* (Johannesburg, S.A.I.R.R., 1961), pp. 10, 18–20; also *Days of Crisis in South Africa*, p. 9.
[6] *Apartheid in South Africa* (New York, United Nations, n.d.), p. 33.
[7] ibid., p. 34. Early in 1963, it was announced that within three years there would be a countrywide two-way radio system linking the 1,000 police stations in South Africa and South-West Africa to their divisional headquarters and, through these, to the police headquarters in Pretoria (*Africa Digest*, x, 5 (1963)).

number of independent African states increased in the sixties, and voices critical of South African racial policy gathered volume in international forums such as the United Nations.[1] As a consequence, the Government openly admitted that its military priorities were internal security and defence against a direct attack from the North.[2]

Furthermore, the South African economy proved able to recover from the slump which had followed Sharpeville. Government opponents had previously hoped that a serious economic crisis would force political concessions from the Nationalists, but such hopes were illusory. The 1960 emergency did have a serious effect on the South African economy;[3] the withdrawal of foreign investment produced a unique economic crisis; the consequent difficulties were not easily overcome. But the Government acted swiftly, readily gained the co-operation of South African businessmen, and in view of the gravity of the crisis stabilized the situation with remarkable speed.[4] Outside attempts to undermine South Africa's economy through the imposition of sanctions, for example, were resented by all but a minority of the whites and contributed to their growing solidarity on the colour question. Increasingly, they felt themselves to be, in Douglas Brown's phrase, 'against the world'.[5] In addition, the Government acted astutely in offering useful and profitable concessions to industrialists, which mollified them considerably but in no way threatened the continuance of *apartheid*. The extent of the rapport which had developed between the Nationalists and big business in the economic and political crisis of the sixties is indicated by

[1] In November 1962, for the first time in the history of the United Nations, the necessary two-thirds majority in favour of sanctions was forthcoming (*Africa Digest*, x, 3 (1962)).

[2] e.g. In April 1961 Mr. J. J. Fouché, Minister of Defence announced a scheme to strengthen the Citizen Force as well as other defence developments, such as a plan for the local manufacture of a greater range of weapons: 'At present the tendency is for unrest to spread southward, and it has already affected Angola. We are watching the situation extremely closely in case it spreads further south so that we can take timely action to meet whatever dangers confront us.' (*Africa Digest*, viii, 6 (1961)). cf. the publicity given to South Africa's military strength on the occasion of the 50th anniversary of the establishment of the Defence Force in June 1962 (e.g. *P.D.* No. 23 21 June 1962).

[3] How seriously the Government—and its opponents—regarded the economic crisis is suggested by the space devoted to the issue in both Afrikaans and English papers. e.g. *P.D.* Nos. 21–4 incl., June 1961.

[4] e.g. the analysis of the current economic situation in *Africa Digest*, viii, 6 (1961); also *Africa Digest*, ix, 5 (1962); xi, 2 (1963).

[5] Douglas Brown, *Against the World: A Study of White South African Attitudes* (London, Collins, 1966).

the work of a body like the South African Foundation. Created late in 1959, the Foundation was composed of businessmen of different shades of political opinion, and included Afrikaners and English-speakers.[1] The Foundation's self-appointed task was to reconcile the world to South Africa by the skilful use of diplomacy, hospitality, and friendship among the international network of their business contacts.[2]

The Nationalist Government was well served by Afrikaans news-papers, directed at those who comprised the base of the Nationalists' electoral support. Generally, *Die Burger* in Cape Town was less aggressive in tone than the Transvaal papers, *Die Transvaler* and *Die Vaderland*; its editors and readers cherished the belief that their Cape Nationalism was less crude and emotional than that of the Transvaal Nationalists.[3] Yet, *Die Burger* was four-square behind the Government and *apartheid*. Whenever a crisis loomed, *Die Burger* as a good Nationalist paper helped to close the ranks. For example, when, in May 1961, the Government took special powers to combat a threatened non-white national stay-away from work to mark Republic Day, *Die Burger* told its readers that the safety of the state outweighed considerations of individual justice.[4]

Enthusiastic support was not the only connection between the Afrikaans dailies and the Government. Cabinet Ministers and other party leaders sat on the boards controlling the newspapers. Malan, Swart, Strijdom, Dönges, and Verwoerd, to name the most obvious instances, were all, at some time, on such boards.[5] In addition, many Nationalist politicians were once journalists, and maintained close contact with the newspapers. The editors of *Die Burger* and *Die Transvaler* enjoyed the right to attend and speak—though not vote—at the caucus meetings of the National Party, a right unknown in Western democracies.[6]

Facts such as these encouraged liberals to regard the English-speaking newspapers, by comparison, as the defenders of liberty.

[1] South African *Sunday Times*, 13 Dec. 1959, (*Africa Digest*, vii, 4 (1960)).

[2] e.g. the favourable response of Lord Birdwood, chairman of the Foreign Affairs Committee of the British Conservative Party Association, who visited South Africa in August 1961. *Africa Digest*, ix, 2 (1961).

[3] This was borne out by the author's interview with Mr. Piet Cillié, editor of *Die Burger*, Cape Town, 15 Dec. 1965.

[4] *Die Burger*, 31 May 1961 (*P.D.* No. 20, 1 June 1961).

[5] Dr. Verwoerd's direct connections with the Afrikaans press are discussed in *Africa Digest*, x, 1 (1962).

[6] Carter, *The Politics of Inequality*, p. 39.

P

This was, of course, partly a carry-over from their view of the United Party, whose policy the English-speaking Press supported in the fifties. As it became clearer to more and more liberals that the United Party was moving right rather than left, the *Rand Daily Mail*, in particular, switched its support to the 'progressive' point of view; and then to the Progressive Party.

But there was still no genuinely 'open forum'.[1] Only rarely did an editor make an unequivocal plea for a radical redirection of racial policy. More frequently, the virulent attacks and detailed prescriptions of 'liberal' papers were aimed at the particulars of the policies of the Government or the United Party. Discussion of such issues as manhood suffrage for non-whites, redistribution of wealth, residential and social integration were virtually taboo.

Despite this, however, the English-speaking papers were sufficiently liberal to irritate and apparently alarm the Nationalists. In 1960 the Government proposed a censorship Bill, ostensibly aimed at obscene publications but carrying a deadly political sting in its tail. After protests, and in the shadow of Sharpeville, the Bill was withdrawn.[2] But, in 1961, the Government made a new move for censorship, by introducing the Undesirable Publications Bill.[3] This provided for censorship of newspapers, books, periodicals, and every other conceivable kind of publication. In many ways it was similar to the Bill withdrawn earlier; but it differed importantly in that under the terms of the new Bill, the courts, and not the Government, were to decide what was 'undesirable'. The courts' powers, however, were wide; besides the usual tests for obscenity and blasphemy, a publication could be declared 'undesirable' if it brought any section of the inhabitants of the Republic into ridicule or contempt; was harmful to the relations between sections of the community; or was prejudicial— a very wide word—to the safety of the State, the general welfare, or peace and good order.

At the same time as the Bill received its First Reading and was sent to a Select Committee, there was a marked intensification of the onslaught on the English-speaking Press. The timing and number of legal attacks made on journalistic critics of the Government appear

[1] cf. Douglas Brown's comment on the relative ineffectiveness of the 'journalistic ways of undermining, or appearing to undermine, apartheid'. *Against the World*, p. 145.

[2] *Africa Digest*, viii, 5 (1961).

[3] The terms of the bill are detailed in *A Survey of Race Relations in South Africa 1961*, pp. 87–8.

to be more than a mere coincidence. Among these were the prosecution and conviction of the editor of the *Evening Post* (an Eastern
Province newspaper) for printing a subversive statement within the
terms of the emergency regulations,[1] and the commitment to gaol of
a reporter on the staff of the *Rand Daily Mail* for refusing to disclose
to the authorities the identity of a person who had given him the
information used in an article he wrote.[2] Attacks such as these
proved sound strategy; the individuals immediately involved might—
and often did—remain defiant, but newspaper owners generally
conceded to Government pressure. The Opposition Press agreed to
consult with the Government in an attempt to work out a code of
behaviour which would satisfy both Press and Government. A
muzzle was preferable to a gag; but in neither case could the English
Press act effectively as the 'watchdog' of liberty.

iii

There is common agreement among leading Liberals that the
years 1960 and 1961 saw their party at the height of its achievement.[3]
For a short time, the Liberal Party made a striking impact as a group
dedicated to the extension of non-white rights. The part which
Liberals played during the Emergency in 1960 enhanced their reputation with non-whites. When the Government ordered the mass
arrests of 30 March, party members, black and white, were included
among those detained.[4] Such action against Liberals was entirely
without precedent. Some members, for example, Peter Brown,
Elliot Mngadi, and Hans Meidner, were to remain imprisoned for
ninety-eight days, until early July, and others for even longer.[5]
Non-whites were impressed by this evidence of commitment to the
cause of their rights. In Brown's words, 'Nationalist persecution'
had become the party's 'badge of honour'.[6]

The mass arrests precipitated further demonstrations, including
sporadic rioting, notably in Durban and the Western Province of
the Cape.[7] Here it seems that the Liberals played a valuable role,

---

[1] *The Times*, 18 Oct. 1960 (*Africa Digest*, viii, 3 (1960)).
[2] *The Times*, 14 Oct. 1960 (*Africa Digest*, viii, 3 (1960)).
[3] A conclusion reached from the evidence of a number of different Liberals,
e.g. Randolph Vigne, Neville Rubin, John Shingler, Hans Meidner.
[4] See above, p. 205.   [5] *Contact*, 16 July 1960.
[6] 'Year of Crisis', in *Contact*, 31 Dec. 1960.
[7] Horrell, *Action, Reaction and Counteraction*, p. 30.

despite their knowledge that the Government now considered them sufficiently dangerous to detain. This was seen on 30 March when a column of 30,000 Africans made their way into Cape Town rallying near the Houses of Parliament. Philip Kgosana, the young member of the P.A.C. who had assumed leadership of the march, persuaded the marchers to disperse, after he had been assured by the police that he would be granted the interview he had requested with the Minister of Justice.[1] Earlier that day, Kgosana had gone to the Liberal Party office in Cape Town. There he had a number of friends, partly through his working as a sales agent for *Contact*.[2] The Liberals had also advised him to disband the demonstration.[3] They had done so without duplicity, solely because they feared a repetition of the 'misunderstanding' at Sharpeville. Anthony Delius, the top-ranking South African journalist, who could be a pitiless critic of the weaknesses inherent in the liberal position, was, on this occasion, prepared to say that the Liberal Party had been chiefly responsible for averting a blood-bath.[4]

The Government responded to the magically sudden appearance of 30,000 Africans in the heart of Cape Town by sealing off most of the African townships. In particular, Langa was virtually under siege.[5] The P.A.C. had established order there when the police had failed, and its leaders now sought an ally in the Liberal Party. Their leader, Nana Mahomo, had recommended that the Liberals and the Black Sash women be sought out, if the P.A.C. should need assistance in the aftermath of its campaign against the passes.[6] The Liberals contacted businessmen and wholesalers, and within one week raised £1,500 to feed the people of Langa, Nyanga East and Nyanga, as well as families outside these townships.[7] They helped the P.A.C. in the transportation and distribution of the food until the Government prevented further supplies from entering on 3 April. After that they helped feed families of those Africans arrested in the large-scale pick-ups by the police.[8]

The state of emergency had also involved the Liberal Party in Johannesburg and Durban. After it ended, in August 1960, member-

---

[1] ibid. [2] G.M.C. interview with Peter Hjul, Cape Town, 26 Jan. 1964.
[3] Author's interview with Randolph Vigne, Greenwich, England, 2 Sept. 1965.
[4] ibid. [5] Horrell, *Action, Reaction and Counteraction*, p. 30.
[6] Author's interview with Randolph Vigne, 2 Sept. 1965. Such a recommendation was in striking contrast to the P.A.C.'s initial rejection of the Liberal Party. See above, p. 201.
[7] *Contact*, 16 Apr. 1960. [8] ibid.

ship of the party increased steadily partly because of the Liberals' witness during the preceding months. In addition, the party filled a vacuum caused by the banning of the A.N.C. and P.A.C. in March 1960. There were few avenues of expression left open to Africans who wished to remain politically active;[1] the Liberal Party still remained legal, despite the fact that individual Liberals had undergone severe penalties. In December 1960, Brown wrote of his conviction

... that the existence of the Liberal Party, the message which it had been putting out for years and the part which it played in the Emergency was a decisive factor in preventing a large-scale drift towards intransigent racialism on both sides of the colour line. ...[2]

The Liberals' role had changed markedly from that of 1953 when they had formed a political party seeking support from a wide spectrum of the white electorate; now they were a pressure group working to maintain contact with those non-whites not hopelessly alienated by white intransigence.[3] By the time of their 1961 National Congress, their membership had increased to somewhere between 4,000 and 5,000, and a majority of the delegates at the Congress were Africans.[4]

Meanwhile, the party had become engaged in two new enterprises: closer co-operation with African leaders in the A.N.C. and the P.A.C., and political campaigning in the Transkei, a large African reserve in the Eastern Cape. A Consultative Conference of African leaders met in Orlando, Johannesburg, on 16–17 December 1960. Among the thirty-six delegates were former members of the A.N.C. and P.A.C., and a number of African liberals. These included W. B. Ngakane, one of the sponsors of the Conference, Julius Malie, Transvaal Organizer for the party, Jordan Ngubane, National Vice-President, Joe Nkatlo, National Vice-Chairman, and Bill Bhengu, the Natal lawyer who later became National Vice-President (1963).[5] The delegates were concerned to fill the void which had been left in African political life by the banning of the A.N.C. and the P.A.C. Their final resolutions emphasized 'the urgent need for African unity',

---

[1] This was commented on by Leo Kuper, Chairman of the Natal Provincial Division, at the National Congress of the L.P., Cape Town, 28–30 May 1960.
[2] 'Year of Crisis', in *Contact*, 31 Dec. 1960.
[3] cf. Jordan Ngubane, speaking in Pietermaritzburg, Natal, referred to the Liberals' belief that they could 'act as a sort of buffer third party to mitigate the eventual outcome'. *Contact* 2 July 1960.
[4] Minutes of the L.P. National Congress, Durban, 7–10 July 1961.
[5] *Contact*, 31 Dec. 1960.

P 2

an aim for which they pledged to work on the basis of the following principles:

(a) the removal of the scourge of *apartheid* . . .;
(b) the immediate establishment of a non-racial democracy;
(c) the effective use of non-violent pressures against apartheid.[1]

These were all criteria with which the Liberal Party was in the fullest accord. Before dispersing, the Conference elected a Continuation Committee. Ngubane was made Chairman, and Bhengu and Malie were also appointed to the executive.[2] The Committee's brief was to make plans for a non-racial conference which would in turn ask the Government to call a national convention to draft a new constitution.[3]

But, as in the past, divisive forces within the movement for liberation proved too strong. Old sources of dispute reasserted themselves. In particular, a number of delegates, including the members of the Liberal Party, were soon convinced that the communists were manipulating the Committee just as they had largely pre-planned the Conference. Their fears were strengthened by the ready availability of large sums of money, the source of which was never disclosed.[4] Co-operation between the different elements rapidly broke down. A walk-out by the P.A.C. members was followed by the resignation of two independent moderates, Paul Mosaka, President of the African Chamber of Commerce, and Congress Mbata, who had been active earlier in the A.N.C. Youth League. With them went the Liberals, who considered there had been ample evidence of what Ngubane called 'the invisible hand'.[5] Because of their participation, Ngubane, Bhengu, and Malie were promptly arrested and, ironically, were subsequently charged and convicted under the Suppression of Communism Act.[6] It was clear that although Liberals saw themselves

---

[1] Resolutions adopted at the Consultative Conference of African Leaders held at the Donaldson Community Centre, Orlando, on 16–17 December 1960, P.A.S. The Conference apparently agreed to use the P.A.C. term 'non-racial', in preference to 'multiracial'. See above, p. 201.

[2] See Letter from Continuation Committee of African Leaders to All African Political, Cultural, Social and Religious Bodies, dated 12 Jan. 1961, P.A.S.

[3] Ngubane, *An African Explains Apartheid*, p. 169.

[4] ibid., p. 170.

[5] ibid., p. 171. Pamphlets advertising the proposed 'All-In' conferences were issued as official publicity but, in fact, without the Committee's approval (author's interview with Duma Nokwe, Dar es Salaam, 15 Nov. 1965).

[6] Peter Brown, 'The Liberal Party of South Africa', in *Contemporary Review* (1961), p. 591.

as distinct from communists, the Government was not interested in such distinctions.

The Liberals were considerably more successful in the Transkei and their activity here brought even stronger reaction than had their direct involvement with A.N.C. and P.A.C. leaders. The party's work in the Transkei coincided in time with the Government's decision to grant self-government to that territory and with the subsequent setting up of the first Bantustan.[1] The Liberals were to prove an unwelcome influence as the Transkeians moved towards 'political independence'. Liberal Party activity was initiated there in the months following Sharpeville by Patrick Duncan, Randolph Vigne, and Hammington Majija.[2] With the aid of helpful contacts which they had built up, the Liberals were able to disseminate information about Liberal policies among the Tembu especially. The Paramount Chief of the Tembu, Sabata Dalindyebo, was one of the Transkei chiefs willing to hazard his future by open criticism of the Government. The Liberals offered the Tembu more than policies; they supplied practical assistance, including financial aid.[3] Through the medium of *Contact*, they reported a number of instances of suspension of the rule of law in the Transkei.[4] As a result, three leading Liberals faced prosecution in September 1962: the editor of *Contact*, Patrick Duncan; the National Deputy Chairman, Randolph Vigne; and the Cape Provincial Chairman, Peter Hjul.[5] The charges were laid under the terms of Proclamation 400 of the Emergency Regulations, which had been introduced to cope with the uprising of the Pondoland tribesmen early in 1960. Duncan was first banned in March 1961, and on a second occasion, in April 1962. He defied the second ban and moved to Basutoland before he could be seized by the police.[6] Hjul and then Vigne were banned in February 1963, the nature of their bans confining them to a magisterial district for five years, and forbidding them to attend any political or social gathering in that time.[7]

Early in March 1963 four Liberals were arrested and questioned in Umtata, capital of the Transkei. They were Terence Beard, the Deputy Chairman of the party in the Cape, Dr. C. F. Goodfellow, and two leading Africans, Cromwell Nododile and Hammington

---

[1] *A Survey of Race Relations in South Africa 1963*, pp. 80–105.
[2] Author's interview with Randolph Vigne, 2 Sept. 1965.   [3] ibid.
[4] *Liberal Opinion* (Oct. 1962).   [5] ibid.
[6] *Contact*, 7 Mar. 1963.   [7] ibid.

Majija.[1] These men were subsequently warned by the Cape Town magistrate to 'refrain from activities which would further the aims of Communism'.[2] In September, Beard was served with a five-year banning order.[3] It was also early in 1963 that two applications to hold public meetings of the party in Umtata were refused.[4] In the second instance, the magistrate replied that 'he was not prepared to authorise the holding of such a meeting on the said date or on any other prior or subsequent date by the Liberal Party of South Africa . . .'[5]

The first Transkei general election was held on 20 November 1963. Campaigning had been conducted in the most difficult circumstances.[6] Transkeians had no experience in the kind of choices which the election provided. In any case, a large number of their leaders were banned or imprisoned. In the period from February to June 1963, 176 people had been detained under Proclamation 400.[7] No white or non-racial political parties were allowed to take part. Only the frankly pro-Government Chief Mantanzima was allowed to broadcast on Radio Bantu.[8] Despite factors such as these, the election revealed overwhelming support for Chief Victor Poto of Western Pondoland and his lieutenant, Sabata Dalindyebo.[9] They had both come out clearly in favour of 'a state in which the colour of a man's skin plays no part in his civic rights'.[10] This was indisputably a moral victory for those members of the Liberal Party who had worked in the area, as well as for other outsiders and liberally-minded Transkeians themselves. Hammington Majija who had planned to stand for election, as he was entitled to do, was served with a banning order on nomination day.[11] Similar to earlier bans, it also banned him from his newspaper work which was his livelihood. It was the severest order yet dealt to a Liberal.

It would be difficult to deny that the Liberals were effective in the Transkei. The Government's response was evidence of their effectiveness. The party no longer provided only the mere pin-pricks that it had done in the 1950s; it had become a deep thorn in the Nationalists'

[1] 'Liberal Party News', in Liberal Opinion (Mar. 1963).
[2] Contact, 27 July 1963.   [3] Contact, 20 Sept. 1963.
[4] Liberal Opinion (June 1963).   [5] ibid.
[6] Govan Mbeki, South Africa: The Peasant's Revolt (London, Penguin Books, 1964), p. 141.
[7] Horrell, Action, Reaction and Counteraction, p. 85.
[8] Mbeki, South Africa: The Peasants' Revolt, p. 142.   [9] ibid., p. 138.
[10] Quoted by Selby Msimang in a letter to the editor of Contact, 7 Mar. 1963.
[11] Contact, 4 Oct. 1963.

side. The bannings and smear campaign with which the Government responded to the party's activities in the Transkei were only the beginning of a superbly clever and, for the Liberals, disastrously effective crusade which the Nationalist Government was to direct against the Liberal Party on a nationwide scale.

Their campaign had gathered force during the Paarl Riot Inquiry which had been opened in the Transkei following extensive rioting in Paarl in November 1962. At the Umtata hearings Chief Mantanzima had indicted the Liberals on the grounds that they had engineered the killings, and assisted Poqo—the alleged P.A.C. underground—in making petrol bombs.[1] In his interim report Judge Snyman mentioned that Poqo had been influenced by communist agitators 'as well as white people who according to the evidence present appear to be liberals and even members of the Liberal Party'.[2] The demands of the Liberals for evidence to support this kind of accusation were generally ignored. The Government, on the other hand, responded to Judge Snyman's interim report by successfully introducing the General Law Amendment Bill (1963).[3]

One of the Nationalists' least subtle spokesmen on the Liberals was Mr. J. C. Greyling, who used the occasion of the Second Reading of the Transkei Constitution Bill to attack the party:

> The Liberal Party is cleverer than the United Party and much cleverer than the Progressive Party . . . it has fetched its weapons from the camp of the Communist . . . the Liberal Party wants to do battle with us in the Transkei . . . it uses all the weapons with which Communism fights: treachery, murder, conflicts, lies, false reports and the creation of incidents . . . it is a deadly sting . . . we shall have to restrict the Liberal Party.[4]

But the Government did not make a direct move against the Liberals *as a party* until 1968 when interracial political activity was made illegal under the terms of the Prohibition of Improper Interference Act.[5] Rather, they relied on unfavourable publicity such as Snyman's and Greyling's to alienate the white community from the Liberal Party. Furthermore, if the Government could emasculate the Liberal leadership by warnings and bannings, and intimidate rank-and-file support by widespread and relentless Special Branch activity,

---

[1] *Contact*, 7 Mar. 1963.
[2] Quoted in an interview with Alan Paton, as reported in the *Evening Post*, 28 Sept. 1963.
[3] See above, p. 206.   [4] Quoted in *Liberal Opinion* (June 1963).
See below, p. 230.

there would be no need to proscribe the party. Indeed the Government could then cite its continued existence as an example of the freedom of political parties in South Africa.[1]

Many Liberals ceased to be active in the face of Government persecution. This was not immediately reflected in a numerical weakness because, ironically, large numbers of non-whites were joining at the same time. But the 'purging' of the party had begun with the imprisonment of Liberals during the emergency. A number of members were not prepared to be involved in a political party subject to such treatment. And the banning of individuals served to accelerate this process. As early as 1957, Miss Junod had warned her fellow Liberals of the unique hardships which faced any white man (or woman) who deliberately chose to belong to an ostracized political group:

... The fact that his action may be acclaimed by many non-whites and the greater section of the outside world cannot fully compensate for his sense of loss, his immediate unhappiness, his loneliness. Non-whites who become so politically involved stand to lose as much in the material sense—jobs, income, and so on. But rather than becoming outcasts in their own community, they become the acclaimed leaders, the heroes, and the martyrs.[2]

It was not so with white Liberals.

There were those too, who had been active in the party and now chose to leave South Africa. For most of those involved this was an agonizing choice. Voluntary exiles had additional problems. They could never be absolutely certain that they could have achieved nothing by staying, or were achieving anything of real value by their work from outside. There was always the silent, if not voiced, reproach of those who chose differently, and remained behind. And there was the loss of contact—a painful alienation—which exile brought.[3]

Even so, a number of original members stayed, and remained active. One might have expected them to be among the first to leave.

[1] For example, the reply by the South African Embassy in London to criticism by the British Liberal Party included the claim that 'the South African Liberal Party, as any other party, has every opportunity to work out its own destiny'. *African Digest*, xii, 2 (1964).

[2] 'The White Liberals and the Treason Arrests', in *Africa South* (April–June 1957), p. 25.

[3] cf. Helen Joseph's explanation of why she refused to go into exile, *Tomorrow's Sun: a smuggled journal from South Africa* (London, Hutchinson, 1965), p. 281.

Some of them had serious doubts about the new policies of the party, and were uneasy in the extra-parliamentary field of activity. But such people as Margaret Ballinger, Leo Marquard, Alan Paton, and Jack Unterhalter remained a stabilizing element within the party. They were even joined by Dr. Edgar Brookes, the author and teacher, who for many years had been a 'non-party' liberal, but now identified himself with the clearly radical Liberals. He was made National Chairman of the party in 1964.

Despite the increasing difficulty of functioning as a legal group the Liberals continued to consider further radical modifications of their policies. Crucial changes took place in the party's economic policy in the early sixties. In 1961 Brown spoke openly of the party's belief in a 'shared economy'.[1] He spoke too, of the Liberals' commitment 'to an equitable retransfer of land holdings to non-whites, redistributive capital taxation and a planned mixed economy'.[2] By 1962 pressures existed for the acceptance of a future 'welfare state' economy. In 1963 the National Congress agreed to the appointment of a Commission which *inter alia* would 'reconsider the policy of the Party with a view to its restatement' in a form which would 'indicate clearly the Party's social-democratic character . . .'[3] Significantly, this Commission's work was never completed. By the time the 1964 Congress met, over half of the Commission's twenty-two members were banned, detained, or had left the country.

A new pattern of raids and arrests involving white Liberals began in July 1964.[4] Additional cause for a direct attack on the party had been provided by the Security Branch's exposure of Liberals' involvement in sabotage. As the party had moved nearer to the A.N.C. and the P.A.C. in their political and economic outlook, they had found, as the non-whites had done earlier, that their means of effective political expression were increasingly restricted. This frustration eventually led a minority of the Liberals to resort to violence as

[1] In *An Analysis of the South African Political Situation and the Role of the Liberal Party* (Stockholm, 1961), p. 2.

[2] ibid.

[3] Minutes of the National Congress of the L.P., Cape Town, 6–7 July 1963. In an interview with G.M.C., (Durban, 29 Jan. 1964) Peter Brown, Party Chairman, spoke of the 'majority support' for 'a social welfare tone' and 'the importance of having a broader base, and being concerned with the general problems of the under-privileged'.

[4] *Observer*, 2 Aug. 1964. The article claimed that these arrests were 'formal notification to Whites that if they meddle in race politics they do so at their own peril'.

a last alternative. White Liberals initiated the African Resistance Movement (A.R.M.) in December 1961, without the knowledge of party leaders; their declared aim was to 'inconvenience and confuse, disrupt and destroy'.[1] Their acts of sabotage were to be conducted against Government installations and essential services. They specifically rejected the idea of violence against persons.[2] In this, they tragically disregarded the palpable fact that in the political climate of South Africa virtually *any* extra-parliamentary pressure could readily, almost inevitably, lead to violence, and consequently endanger human life. Although a distinction may be drawn, in theory, between violence against property and violence against persons, in practice, such a distinction proves almost impossible to maintain.

Members of A.R.M. had worked undetected for over two years, during which time they remained members of the Liberal Party. One of their explanations for not resigning lay in the fact that were they to publicly dissociate themselves from the Liberals they would attract unwelcome attention from the Special Branch.[3] The collapse of A.R.M., and the widespread arrests of July 1964, provided the Government with ammunition of potent calibre.[4] The saboteurs were indisputably connected with the Liberal Party. Moreover, one of them, John Harris, had been responsible for a bomb explosion in the Johannesburg station, as a result of which a white woman had died and a number of people had been injured. While the sabotage trials were in progress, the editor of the *Die Burger* wrote:

> What has appeared during this time is that, while a wide gulf separates the Communist and the true Liberal, a Liberal Party has grown in our country which offers a home to people whose activities in practice cannot be distinguished from those of Communists.[5]

For the Liberals it was an exigency without precedent. Aware of the level of frustration which had prompted the members of the A.R.M., they stressed that the 'primary cause of sabotage in South Africa was the policy of apartheid'.[6] Yet, whatever their private reservations as to the justification for sabotage, as a party, they were forced to judge the saboteurs harshly. Paton expressed the official view at the National Congress in Johannesburg in October 1964:

---

[1] *Contact*, 3 July 1964.
[2] Interview with Randolph Vigne, London, 15 Sep. 1965.   [3] ibid.
[4] The trials were held in November 1964; details are available in *Africa Digest*, xii, 3–4 (1964–5).
[5] *Die Burger*, 27 Nov. 1964.   [6] *Contact*, 23 Oct. 1964.

Any person who while a member of the Liberal Party plans to use violence against things or persons is not only guilty of an offence against the law, he is also guilty of grave disloyalty to the Party.

Above all, any person who calls himself a Liberal, and who plans violence against persons is not really a Liberal at all. He may burn against injustices to others, and burn to set them right. He may be a zealot. He may be dedicated to his cause. But he is not a Liberal—And what is more, if he persists in his plans, he is likely to do grave damage to the whole cause of Liberalism; how great such damage might be is at the moment impossible to predict.[1]

But the party could not disown them so completely. For it was not what they had achieved or failed to achieve, but rather the fact that they were white Liberals, which was most significant.[2] In an important sense, this involvement of active Liberals in acts of sabotage signalled the failure of the party. It was not a failure for which the Liberals themselves were entirely, or even chiefly, to blame. But it underlined how far Liberals had been forced by circumstances to move from their prime attachment to parliamentary methods in 1953. The general response of the white community signalled their final rejection of Liberal Party policy. Almost to a man, they moved submissively into the white laager. By contrast, many non-whites were tremendously impressed by the fact that whites were willing to hazard their lives for the ideal of equality of rights, regardless of race.[3] Herein lay the bitterest irony: at the moment when the Liberals had at last won the sympathy and trust of large numbers of non-whites, they had almost totally alienated themselves from the white community.

iv

The fact that the A.N.C. was an illegal organization after March 1960 presents peculiar difficulties for the historian. Underground movements do not have—cannot afford to have—extensive written records. So the lines of their development are not easily traced. Significantly, the most thorough documentation of Congress available in the period is that provided by the trials of those who persisted

[1] ibid.
[2] cf. Revd. Nicolas Stacey, 'White Against Whites', in *The Observer Weekend Review*, 28 Nov. 1965, p. 21.
[3] The impression of Laurence Gandar, editor of the *Rand Daily Mail*, whom the author interviewed in Johannesburg, 2 Dec. 1965.

in their active involvement after Congress was banned. Here the testimony of Nelson Mandela, the most prominent Congress leader active in the early sixties, is of crucial importance. But this again, for obvious reasons, may be admissible as evidence for the historian only if he, or she, exercises great caution. Therefore, although it is relatively easy to talk with certainty about A.N.C. political objectives in the forties and fifties, the different kind of evidence available in the sixties means that one's conclusions are necessarily more tentative.

Several things, however, do seem clear. It was with the greatest reluctance that Congress leadership acknowledged the legitimacy of violence; they did so only on conditions which were intended to severely circumscribe its use; and, despite their adoption of unconstitutional means, their aims remained consistently liberal.

The banning of the A.N.C. did not lead immediately to the Congress leaders' endorsement of violence. That decision was not reached until June 1961.[1] Until then the majority of A.N.C. leaders had insisted on the necessity of fully exploiting the non-violent tactics endorsed in the Programme of Action—passive resistance, boycott, and strike action. But the Government's reaction—in fact, white reaction in general—to the stay-at-home strike sponsored by the A.N.C. in May 1961 destroyed the Congress faith that strike action could be a non-violent means of effecting change. The stay-at-home was unsuccessful in its main purpose of bringing the Government to the conference table, despite a spectacular response in some areas. Furthermore, this failure was obviously due to the whites' monopoly of power. The Government had used multiple strong-arm measures. The General Law Amendment Act (1961) enabled them to detain without trial the organizers of the strike; 10,000 Africans were arrested and gaoled under pass offences; political meetings were banned throughout the country; extra police were deployed in the townships to 'encourage' Africans to ignore the call to strike.[2] 'During the night [says Benson] helicopters flew low over townships flashing searchlights down on the match-box houses and rough roads'.[3] At the time, Mandela refused to admit publicly the true

[1] Mandela's statement to the Court during the Rivonia Trial, the text of which is included in the collection of his articles and speeches, *No Easy Walk to Freedom*, p. 169.
[2] Mandela's speech in the trial of October 1962, *No Easy Walk*, pp. 153–4; cf. *P.D.* No. 19, 24 May 1961.
[3] Mary Benson, *South Africa: The Struggle for a Birthright* (London, Penguin Books, 1966), p. 236.

significance of the Government's successful introduction of 'martial law'. He argued:

The steps taken by the Government to suppress the campaign were a measure of our strength and influence in the political life of the country and of its weakness. . . . Only by mobilizing the entire resources of the State could the Government hope to stem the tide that was running so strongly against it.[1]

But the stark fact of the matter was that the Government—and not the A.N.C.—*could* mobilize the 'entire resources of the State', and that these were easily sufficient 'to stem the tide'. Later, in November 1962, Mandela (on trial for his leading role in the strike, and for subsequently leaving the country illegally) soberly acknowledged the superior strength of the white Government:

In the end if a strike did not materialize on the scale on which it had been hoped it would, it was not because the people were not willing, but because the overwhelming strength, violence, and force of the Government's attack . . . had for the time being achieved its aim of forcing us into submission. . . .[2]

It was their recognition of this which drove the A.N.C. leaders to review their policy of non-violence in the days of fresh disillusionment following the May 1961 strike. There were still those—though now a minority—who considered that non-violent techniques of resistance had not been sufficiently explored. But there were those, and Mandela was among them, for whom the outcome of the strike was conclusive proof of the inadequacy of the existing A.N.C strategy. There had been, of course, earlier instances of South African Governments using force to crush non-white demonstrations which had been deliberately non-violent. And it was the cumulative effect of years of frustration which induced the change in 1961. Mandela later explained:

We have been conditioned to our attitude by the history which is not of our making. We have been conditioned by the history of White Governments in this country to accept the fact that Africans, when they make their demands strongly and powerfully enough to have some chance of success, will be met by force and terror on the part of the Government.[3]

---

[1] From Mandela's analysis of the general strike, dated June 1961 (*No Easy Walk*, p. 95).
[2] ibid., pp. 154–5.   [3] ibid., p. 155.

But the crisis among the policy-makers had another, not unrelated, cause. Congress leaders clearly felt that if they refused to show a willingness to modify A.N.C. policy in the changed circumstances, the status of their organization *among Africans* was in danger.[1] Furthermore, they appear to have felt an obligation to attempt to channel popular opinion which they judged had swung decisively, if not in favour of violence, at least to a point sufficiently anti-white to make violence 'inevitable'. The prospect of spontaneous outbreaks of non-white terrorism was at least in some ways as much of a nightmare to Congress leaders as it was to whites. They envisaged civil war as the likely result,[2] and no doubt judged that such an eventuality would be political suicide for the A.N.C.; it was scarcely possible that a multiracial democracy could be salvaged from such a situation.

The crucial factor, however, was that in view of these other considerations, Congress now appeared to have no alternative but to acquiesce in the use of violence. Mandela explained subsequently:

... [We] felt that without violence there would be no way open to the African people to succeed in their struggle against the principle of White supremacy. All lawful modes of expressing opposition to this principle had been closed by legislation, and we were placed in a position in which we had either to accept a permanent state of inferiority, or to defy the Government. We chose to defy the law. We first broke the law in a way which avoided any recourse to violence; when this form was legislated against, and then the Government resorted to a show of force to crush opposition to its policies, *only then did we decide to answer violence with violence* [author's italic].[3]

Thus the A.N.C.'s decision to endorse the use of violence was a last resort—a tragic Hobson's choice: their reluctance is borne out by the manner in which they implemented their design. The A.N.C. was not, as a body, to be involved in violence. It had a useful role to fulfil of political education which must continue, besides which it was a mass movement and a large proportion of its members had 'joined on the express policy of non-violence'.[4] Hence a separate body was created: Umkonto we Sizwe (Spear of the Nation) was to operate as a subsidiary to the A.N.C. and was to have a small, carefully selected membership, only some of whom were Congressmen.[5] In addition,

[1] Mandela's speech at the Addis Ababa Conference in January 1962 (*No Easy Walk*, p. 120).
[2] Rivonia Trial Statement, ibid., p. 170.
[3] ibid., p. 164.   [4] ibid., p. 170
[5] Author's interview with Joe Matthews, London, 8 Oct. 1965.

Congress leaders determined that the use of violence must be subject at all times to the 'political guidance of the A.N.C.'; it must be 'properly controlled violence'.[1] Moreover, of the four forms of violence which seemed possible—sabotage, guerrilla warfare, terrorism, and open revolution—the A.N.C. initially consented only to the first.

'Sabotage did not involve loss of life [argued Mandela], and it offered the best hope for future race relations. Bitterness would be kept to a minimum and, if the policy bore fruit, democratic government could become a reality.'[2] Consistent with this reasoning the acts of sabotage were to be directed against 'the economic lifelines of the country', and against Government buildings and other 'symbols of apartheid'.[3] Such acts, it was hoped, would without alienating white sympathy sober the Government sufficiently to bring them to the conference table, where they would offer not threats or even palliatives but equal rights to non-whites.

Qualifications such as these may seem distinctions without a difference. And certainly the A.N.C. leaders showed some degree of political naïvety when, like the white communists who supported Umkonto, and the white Liberals who joined the African Resistance Movement, they thought that their use of violence could be 'properly controlled'. Yet, it is comparatively easy, in restrospect, to find fault with the reasoning of those who formed Umkonto we Sizwe. It was only the course of events after their decision in November 1961 which provided irrefutable proof of their miscalculations. As the liberal whites who formed the African Resistance Movement had done, Mandela and his associates failed to appreciate either the size or the strength of the white monolith. In fact, few whites were interested in the kind of distinctions with which Congress leaders had hedged around their decision to embark on sabotage. When explosions occurred in empty public buildings or power houses it was not in white minds 'properly controlled violence', but rather an integral part of a revolutionary pattern. The activities of Umkonto were not contrasted with other outbreaks of violence such as Poqo terrorism, the Paarl riots, or outside South Africa, white deaths in the Congo. Rather, they were interpreted by the Government as part of the same pattern, and accepted by the vast majority of South African whites as justification for further punitive measures.

[1] Rivonia Trial statement, *No Easy Walk*, p. 170.
[2] ibid., p. 171.   [3] ibid.

The leaders of Umkonto we Sizwe were brought to trial in July 1963.[1] As well as any other, this date signifies the virtual paralysis of A.N.C. leadership within South Africa. There were, of course, Congress leaders outside South Africa; Tambo, Resha, Nokwe, and Joe Matthews were among those who had evaded the Government net. But they were in no position to give the kind of direct and relatively effective leadership they and their colleagues had provided in the fifties. Moreover, under these new conditions, Congress was to be forced more and more towards the use of violence and hope of revolution. In such circumstances, Congress leaders could no longer hope for the emergence of a multiracial democracy.[2]

It was not until 1968 that the liberal ideal of equal political rights in a common legislature received its death-blow. In that year, the Prohibition of Improper Interference Act made interracial political activity illegal. Subsequently, it was a criminal offence for any South African to belong to any political organization with a membership of different races. It was, in addition, illegal for any person to address a political meeting if the majority of the audience belonged to a race other than his own.[3] The Liberal Party decided to disband. The new conditions made it clearly impossible for them to function as a multiracial party. The Progressives refused to dissolve their party, but the changed circumstances made a mockery of their purpose.[4]

This Act was a logical extension of earlier *apartheid* measures,[5] and its successful implementation indicated the degree of consensus among whites on the colour question. Even by the early sixties, however, the practice of *apartheid* obviously already had the approval of the vast majority of South African whites. In particular, by then, the final approval of the English-speaking community for *apartheid* had materialized, as the Nationalists had predicted it would at the time of the Liberal Party's inauguration in 1953.[6] In just the way Milner had suggested was possible in 1897,[7] the white races in South

[1] *P.D.* No. 27, 18 July 1963.
[2] See above, p. 228.
[3] *Africa Digest*, xv, 3 (1968).
[4] ibid.; also *P.D.* No. 14, 11 Apr. 1968.
[5] cf. *Die Oosterlig*, 29 Mar. 1968 (*P.D.* No. 14, 11 Apr. 1968).
[6] See Strijdom's speech at the time, quoted in *Information Digest*, No. 8 [1953], issued by the Africa Bureau.
[7] See above, p. 11.

Africa had been united by their common acceptance of a repressive policy towards non-whites. But loss of liberty for non-whites had inevitably meant loss of liberty for whites as well. As South African liberals had forewarned, the determination to maintain white supremacy had proved incompatible with the maintenance of liberal principles.

Bibliography

1. DOCUMENTS

(i) This book is heavily dependent on a rich collection of documents at the Program of African Studies, Northwestern University, Evanston, Ill., U.S.A. These documents are not listed individually in this bibliography. Instead, where such a document has been used in the book, specific reference has been made to its location in the collection.

Several *sets* of documents, however, have been of central importance. They are:

African National Congress Provincial Conference Reports, 1949–59.
African National Congress National Congress Reports, 1949–59.
Letters written by Joe Matthews to his father, Z. K. Matthews, 1952–3.
Liberal Society Minutes, 1952.
Liberal Association Minutes, 1953.
Liberal Party Provincial Congress Reports, 1953–63.
Liberal Party National Congress Reports, 1953–63.

(ii) Treason Trial Record held (on microfilm) at the School of Oriental and African Studies, London University, and (in mimeographed form) in the Library of the South African Institute of Race Relations, Johannesburg.

2. NEWSPAPERS AND PERIODICALS

Africa Digest, 1953–66
The Africanist, 1953–59
Africa South, 1956–61
Africa X-ray Report, 1957–9
The Black Sash: Die Swart Serp, 1956–65
The Cape Times, 1948–53
Contact, 1954–63
Drum, 1955–60
Fighting Talk, 1952–61

The Forum, 1951–60
Information Digest, 1953
Press Digest (Jewish Board of Deputies), 1956–66
Liberal Opinion, 1962–4
Liberation, 1953–9
New Age, 1952–6
Race Relations Journal, 1956–61
Race Relations News, 1948–66
Rand Daily Mail, 1957–63
The Round Table, 1948–61

3. PARLIAMENTARY DEBATES AND PAPERS
Native Laws Commission U.G., No. 28, 1948
South African House of Assembly Debates, 1946–63

4. INTERVIEWS

In the course of preparing this book, the author talked with a number of people who, in different ways, had been involved in the events of the period. Gwendolen Carter and Thomas Karis had previously conducted similar interviews on a larger scale. Frequently their interviews were recorded and copies are held in the documents collection at the Program of African Studies, Northwestern University, Evanston, Ill., U.S.A.

Where evidence from these discussions has been used in the book, the place and date of the interview have been cited in the relevant footnote. There too, where it is not obvious, the identity of the 'witness' has been explained.

A. *Author's interviews*

Margaret Ballinger	Abdul Minty
Piet Cillié	Peter Molotsi
Yusuf Dadoo	Donald Molteno
René de Villiers	Z. B.Molete
Jonty Driver	Nat Nakasa
Colin Eglin	Beyers Naudé
Ruth First	Mhaleni Njisane
Bernard Friedman	William Nkomo
Marion Friedmann	Duma Nokwe
Laurence Gandar	A. P. O'Dowd
Gerald Gordon	Alan Paton
Michael Harmel	W. A. P. Phillips
Emil Jammine	Peter Randall
Marius Jooste	Ambrose Reeves
A. C. Jordan	Robert Resha
Louis Kane-Berman	Leslie Rubin
Wilhelm Kleynhans	Neville Rubin

Raymond Kunene
John Lang
Colin Legum
Julius Lewin
Leo Marquard
Joe Matthews
Congress Mbata
Hans Meidner

John Shingler
Joan Sinclair
Bob Steyn
Helen Suzman
Fred van Wyk
Randolph Vigne
Quintin Whyte
Oscar Wollheim

B. *Interviews held at the Program of African Studies, Northwestern*

Margaret Ballinger
Peter Brown
Patrick Duncan
Colin Eglin
Peter Hjul
Sydney Kentridge
Adrian Leftwich
Albert Luthuli

Joe Matthews
Z. K. Matthews
S. Molema
Z. B. Molete *et al.*
Michael Parkington
Marais Steyn
R. A. F. Swart

5. BOOKS, ARTICLES, PAMPHLETS, AND REPORTS

Books which are autobiographical, or largely so, and can consequently be regarded as 'primary material' are marked with an asterisk.

The articles listed here are those which did not appear in the periodicals listed under Section 2.

*ABRAHAMS, PETER, *Tell Freedom* (London, Faber & Faber, 1954).

African Farm Labour: A Survey (Johannesburg, S.A.I.R.R., 1959).

AINSLIE, ROSALYNDE, and ROBINSON, DOROTHY, *The Collaborators* (London, Anti-Apartheid Movement, n.d.).

ANDREWS, H. T., *The South African Foundation: South Africa in the Sixties* (Cape Town, South African Foundation, 1962).

Apartheid in South Africa (New York, United Nations, n.d.).

*BALLINGER, MARGARET, *From Union to Apartheid: A Trek to Isolation* (New York, Praeger, 1969).

The Basic Documents of the Pan Africanist Congress of South Africa (Lusaka, Zambia, 1965).

BENNETT, GEORGE (ed.), *The Concept of Empire: Burke to Attlee 1774–1947* (London, Adam and Charles Black, 1953).

BENSON, MARY, *The African Patriots* (London, Faber & Faber, 1963)
—— *Chief Albert Lutuli of South Africa* (Cape Town, O.U.P., 1963).
—— *South Africa: The Struggle for a Birthright* (London, Penguin Books, 1966).

Blackout (A Commentary on the Education Policy of the Instituut vir Christelik-Nasionale Onderwys), issued by the Education League, Johannesburg (1959).

*BLUMBERG, MYRNA, *White Madam* (London, Victor Gollancz, 1962).

BRETT, E. A., *African Attitudes: A study of the social, racial and political attitudes of some middle class Africans* (Johannesburg, S.A.I.R.R., 1963).

BROKENSHA, MILES, and KNOWLES, ROBERT, *The Fourth of July Raids* (Cape Town, Simondium, 1965).

BROOKES, EDGAR H., *South Africa in a Changing World* (Cape Town, O.U.P., 1953).

BROOKES, EDGAR H., and MACAULEY, J. B., *Civil Liberty in South Africa* (Cape Town, O.U.P., 1958).

BROUGHTON, M., *Press and Politics of South Africa* (Cape Town, Juta 1961)

BROWN, DOUGLAS, *Against the World: A Study of White South African Attitudes* (London, Collins, 1966).

BROWN, PETER, 'The Liberal Party in South Africa', in *Contemporary Review* (1961).

BULLOCK, ALAN, and SHOCK, MAURICE (eds.), *The Liberal Tradition from Fox to Keynes* (Oxford, Clarendon Press, 1967).

BUNTING, BRIAN, *The Rise of the South African Reich* (London, Penguin Books, 1964).

BURGER, JAN, *The Gulf Between* (Cape Town, Howard Timmins, 1960).

BUTLER, JEFFREY, *The Liberal Party and the Jameson Raid* (Oxford, Clarendon Press, 1968).

CALLAN, EDWARD, *Albert John Luthuli and the South African Race Conflict* (Kalamazoo, Michigan, Western Michigan Univ. Press, 1962).

CALPIN, G. H. (ed.), *The South African Way of Life: Values and Ideals of a Multi-racial Society* (London, Heinemann, 1953).

CALVOCORESSI, PETER, *South Africa and World Opinion* (London, O.U.P., 1961).

CARTER, GWENDOLEN M., *African Concepts of Nationalism in South Africa* (Edinburgh, 1965).

—— *The Politics of Inequality: South Africa Since 1948*, 3rd edn. (London, Thames & Hudson, 1962).

CAWOOD, LESLEY, *The Churches and Race Relations in South Africa* (Johannesburg, S.A.I.R.R., 1964).

COLE, MONICA, *South Africa* (London, Methuen, 1961).

COPE, JOHN, *South Africa* (London, Ernest Benn, 1965).

COWEN, DENIS V., *The Foundations of Freedom* (Cape Town, O.U.P., 1961).

CRONJE, SUZANNE, *Witness in the Dark: Police torture and brutality in South Africa* (London, Christian Action, n.d.).

DAVENPORT, T. H. R., *The Afrikaner Bond: The History of a South African Political Party, 1880–1911* (Cape Town, O.U.P., 1966).

DAVIDSON, BASIL, *Report on Southern Africa* (London, Jonathan Cape, 1952).

DAVIES, IOAN, *African Trade Unions* (London, Penguin Books, 1966).

DE BEER, Z. J., *Multi-Racial South Africa* (London, O.U.P., 1961).

DE GRUCHY, JOY, *The Cost of Living for Urban Africans* (S.A.I.R.R., 1960).

DE KIEWIET, C. W., *The Anatomy of South African Misery* (London, O.U.P., 1956).

—— *A History of South Africa: Social and Economic* (Oxford, Clarendon Press, 1941).

DE PREEZE, A. B., *Inside the South African Crucible* (Cape Town, H.A.U.M., 1959).

DE RIDDER, J. C., *The Personality of the Urban African in South Africa* (London, Routledge & Kegan Paul, 1961).

DE VILLIERS, H. H. W., *Rivonia, Operation Mayibuye* (Johannesburg, Afrikaanse Pers, 1964).

DOXEY, G. V., *The Industrial Colour Bar in South Africa* (Cape Town, O.U.P., 1961).

DRAPER, MARY, *Sport and Race in South Africa* (Johannesburg, S.A.I.R.R., 1963).

DUNCAN, PATRICK, *South Africa's Rule of Violence* (London, Methuen, 1964).

DVORIN, EUGENE P., *Racial Separation in South Africa, An Analysis of Apartheid Theory* (Chicago, Chicago Univ. Press, 1952).

ENGELBRECHT, S. P., *Thomas François Burgers* (Pretoria, J. H. de H. Bussy, 1946).

FAGAN, H. A., *Our Responsibility* (Cape Town, Juta, 1960).

FEIT, EDWARD, *African Opposition in South Africa: The Failure of Passive Resistance* (Stanford Univ., The Hoover Institution, 1967).

—— *South Africa: The Dynamics of the African National Congress* (London, O.U.P., 1962).

*FIRST, RUTH, *117 Days* (An Account of Confinement and Interrogation under the South African Ninety-Day Detention Law) (London, Penguin Books, 1965).

*FIRST, RUTH (ed.), *No Easy Walk to Freedom* (Articles, Speeches, and Trial Addresses of Nelson Mandela) (London, Heinemann, 1965).

FORMAN, LIONEL, and (SOLLY) SACHS, E. S., *The South African Treason Trial* (London, John Calder, 1957).

Franchise Proposals and Constitutional Safeguards (Molteno Report, vol. 1) (Johannesburg, Progressive Party of South Africa, 1960).

FRIEDMAN, DR. BERNARD et al., *Looking Outwards: Three South African Viewpoints* (Johannesburg, S.A.I.R.R., 1961).

*FRIEDMANN, MARION (ed.), *I will still be moved: Reports from South Africa* (London, Arthur Barker, 1963).

The Future of South Africa, issued by the British Council of Churches (London, S.C.M. Press, 1965).

GEYSER, PROF. A. S. et al., *Delayed Action!* (Pretoria, 1960).

GIBBS, HENRY, *Twilight in South Africa* (London, Jarrolds, 1950).

GIBSON, OLIVE, *The Cost of Living for Africans* (Johannesburg, S.A.I.R.R., 1954).

GINIEWSKI, PAUL, *Bantustans: A Trek Towards the Future* (Cape Town, Herman & Rousseau, 1961).

Q

GORDIMER, NADINE, 'Chief Luthuli' in *Atlantic Monthly* (April 1959).
GROBLER, SEN. J. H., *Africa's Destiny* (Johannesburg, Book of the Month Club, 1958).
HAHLO, H. R., and KAHN, ELLISON, *The Union of South Africa: The Development of its Laws and Constitution* (London, Stevens, 1960).
HAILEY, LORD, *An African Survey* (London, O.U.P., 1957).
HANCOCK, W. K., and VAN DER POEL, JEAN, *Selections from the Smuts Papers*, Vols. I–IV (C.U.P., 1966).
HANCOCK, W. K., *Smuts, Vol. I: The Sanguine Years 1870–1919* (C.U.P., 1962).
—— *Smuts, Vol. II: The Fields of Force 1919–1950* (C.U.P., 1968).
HANCOCK, W. K. (ed.), *Survey of British Commonwealth Affairs:*
  Vol. I, *Problems of Nationality 1918–1936*;
  Vol. II, Part 1, *Problems of Economic Policy 1918–1939*;
  Vol. II, Part 2, *Problems of Economic Policy 1918–1939* (London, O.U.P., 1942).
Handbook for Better Race Relations, issued by the United Party (August 1963).
HATCH, JOHN, *The Dilemma of South Africa* (London, Dennis Dobson, 1952).
HEADLAM, CECIL (ed.), *The Milner Papers:*
  Vol. I, *South Africa 1897–1899* (London, Cassell, 1931).
  Vol. II, *South Africa 1899–1905* (London, Cassell, 1933).
HEARD, KENNETH, A., *Political Systems in Multi-Racial Societies* (Johannesburg, S.A.I.R.R., 1961).
HELLMANN, ELLEN (ed.), *Handbook of Race Relations in South Africa* (Cape Town, O.U.P., 1949).
HEPPLE, ALEXANDER, *South Africa: A political and economic history* (London, Pall Mall, 1966).
—— *Trade Unions in Travail* (Johannesburg, Unity Publications, 1954).
—— *Verwoerd* (London, Pelican Books, 1967).
HILL, CHRISTOPHER, *Bantustans* (London, O.U.P., 1964).
HINCHCLIFF, PETER, *The Anglican Church in South Africa* (London, Darton, 1963).
HOERNLÉ, R. F. ALFRED, *South African Native Policy and the Liberal Spirit: Being the Phelps-Stokes Lectures, delivered before the University of Cape Town, May 1939* (Johannesburg, Witwatersrand Univ. Press, 1945).
HOFMEYR, J. H., *South Africa* (1st edn., 1932), ed. John Cope (London, Ernest Benn, 1952).
HOLMES, CHRISTOPHER, *South Africa: a time to choose* (London, S.C.M., n.d.).
*HOOPER, CHARLES, *Brief Authority* (London, Collins, 1960).
*HOPKINSON, TOM, *In the Fiery Continent* (London, Victor Gollancz, 1962).

HORRELL, MURIEL, *African Education: Some Origins, and Development until 1953* (Johannesburg, S.A.I.R.R., 1963).

—— *Action, Reaction and Counteraction* (Johannesburg, S.A.I.R.R., 1963).

—— *Days of Crisis in South Africa* (*Events up to 15th May 1960*) (Johannesburg, S.A.I.R.R., 1960).

—— *A Decade of Bantu Education* (Johannesburg, S.A.I.R.R., 1964).

—— *Legislation and Race Relations* (Johannesburg, S.A.I.R.R., 1963).

—— *The 'Pass Laws'* (Johannesburg, S.A.I.R.R., 1960).

—— *A Précis of the Reports of the Commissions appointed to enquire into the Events occurring on March 21 1960 at Sharpeville and Langa* (Johannesburg, S.A.I.R.R., 1961).

—— *South African Trade Unionism* (Johannesburg, S.A.I.R.R., 1961).

—— *A Survey of Race Relations in South Africa* (annual editions 1951–66).

HOUGHTON, D. HOBART (ed.), *Economic Development in a Plural Society* (Cape Town, O.U.P., 1960).

HOUGHTON, D. HOBART, *The South African Economy* (Cape Town, O.U.P., 1964).

—— *The Tomlinson Report: A Summary of the Findings and Recommendations in the Tomlinson Commission Report* (Johannesburg, S.A.I.R.R., 1956).

*HUDDLESTON, TREVOR, *Naught for Your Comfort* (1st edn., 1956) (London, Fontana, 1960).

HUNTER, GUY (ed.), *Industrialization and Race Relations: A Symposium* (London, O.U.P., 1965).

*HUTCHINSON, ALFRED, *Road to Ghana* (London, Victor Gollancz, 1960).

*JABAVU, NONI, *Drawn in Colour* (London, John Murray, 1960).

*—— *The Ochre People: Scenes from a South African Life* (London, John Murray, 1963).

*JOSEPH, HELEN, *If This Be Treason* (London, André Deutsch, 1963).

*—— *Tomorrow's Sun: a smuggled journal from South Africa* (London, Hutchinson, 1965).

KARIS, THOMAS, 'South Africa', in Gwendolen M. Carter (ed.), *Five African States* (Ithaca, Cornell Univ. Press, 1963).

—— *The Treason Trial in South Africa: a Guide to the Microfilm Record of the Trial* (Stanford Univ., The Hoover Institution, 1965).

KEPPEL-JONES, A., *South Africa: A Short History* (London, Hutchinson's Univ. Library, 1949).

—— *When Smuts Goes* (1st edn., 1947) (Pietermaritzburg, Shuter & Shooter, 1955).

KEYTER, CARL, *Industrial Feeding of African Workers* (Johannesburg, S.A.I.R.R., 1962).

KRÜGER, D. W., *The Age of the Generals* (Johannesburg, Dagbreek, 1961).

KRÜGER, D. W. (ed.), *South African Parties and Policies 1910–1960: A Select Source Book* (London, Bowes & Bowes, 1960).

KUPER, LEO, *An African Bourgeoisie: Race, Class and Politics in South Africa* (New Haven, Yale Univ. Press, 1965).
—— 'The background to Passive Resistance' (South Africa, 1952), in *British Journal of Sociology*, 4 (1953).
—— *Passive Resistance in South Africa* (New Haven, Yale Univ. Press, 1957).
LEGUM, COLIN and MARGARET, *South Africa: Crisis for the West* (London, Pall Mall, 1964).
LE MAY, G. H. L., *British Supremacy in South Africa 1899–1907* (Oxford, Clarendon Press, 1965).
LEWIN, JULIUS, *Politics and Law in South Africa* (London, Merlin Press, 1963).
—— 'The Rise of Congress in South Africa', in *Political Quarterly* (July 1953).
LEWIN, JULIUS (ed.), *The Struggle for Racial Equality* (London, Longmans, 1967).
LEWSEN, PHYLLIS, *Selections from the Correspondence of J. X. Merriman* (Cape Town, Van Riebeeck Society):
Vol. I, *1870–1890* (1960);
Vol. II, *1890–1898* (1963);
Vol. III, *1899–1905* (1966).
LONGMORE, LAURA, *The Dispossessed: A Study of the Sex-Life of Bantu Women in and around Johannesburg* (London, Jonathan Cape, 1959).
LOUW, ERIC H., *The Case for South Africa* (New York, MacFadden, 1963).
*LUTHULI, ALBERT, *Let My People Go* (London, Fontana, 1963).
MCCALLUM, R. B., *The Liberal Party from Earl Grey to Asquith* (London, Victor Gollancz, 1963).
MCCRACKEN, J. L., *The Cape Parliament 1854–1900* (Oxford, Clarendon Press, 1967).
MACCRONE, I. D., *Race Attitudes in South Africa* (Johannesburg, Witwatersrand Univ. Press, 1957).
MACMILLAN, W. M., *Bantu, Boer and Briton: The Making of the South African Native Problem* (Oxford, Clarendon Press, 1963).
*MANDELA, NELSON, *No Easy Walk to Freedom* (articles, speeches, and trial addresses, ed. Ruth First) (London, Heinemann, 1965).
MANSERGH, NICHOLAS, *South Africa 1906–1961: The Price of Magnanimity* (New York, Praeger, 1962).
MARAIS, J. S., *The Cape Coloured People 1652–1937* (1st edn., 1939) (Johannesburg, Witwatersrand Univ. Press, 1957).
—— *The Fall of Kruger's Republic* (Oxford, Clarendon Press, 1961).
MARQUARD, LEO, *Liberalism in South Africa* (Johannesburg, S.A.I.R.R., 1965).
—— *The Peoples and Policies of South Africa*, 3rd edn. (Cape Town, O.U.P., 1962).

*MATSHIKIZA, TODD, *Chocolates for My Wife* (London, Hodder, 1961).

MAYER, PHILIP, *Townsmen or Tribesmen: Conservatism and the Process of Urbanization in a South African City* (Cape Town, O.U.P., 1963).

MBEKI, GOVAN, *South Africa: The Peasants' Revolt* (London, Penguin Books, 1964).

MILLIN, SARAH GERTRUDE, *Rhodes* (London, Chatto & Windus, 1933).

*MODISANE, BLOKE, *Blame me on History* (London, Thames & Hudson, 1963).

MOLTENO, DONALD B., *The Betrayal of 'Natives Representation'* (Johannesburg, S.A.I.R.R., 1959).

*MOLTENO, SIR JAMES TENNANT, *The Dominion of Afrikanerdom: Recollections Pleasant and Otherwise* (London, Methuen, 1923).

*—— *Further South African Recollections* (London, Methuen, 1926).

MOLTENO, P. A., *The Life and Times of Sir John Charles Molteno*, 2 vols. (London, Smith, Elder & Co., 1900).

MOLTENO REPORT, Vol. I., *Franchise Proposals and Constitutional Safeguards* (issued by The Progressive Party, Nov. 1960).

*MPHAHLELE, EZEKIEL, *The African Image* (London, Faber & Faber, 1962).

*—— *Down Second Avenue* (Berlin, Seven Seas, 1962).

NATHAN, H. L., and HEATHCOTE WILLIAMS, H., *Liberal Points of View* (London, Ernest Benn, 1927).

NEAME, L. E., *The History of Apartheid* (London, Pall Mall, 1962).

*NGUBANE, JORDAN K., *An African Explains Apartheid* (New York, Praeger, 1963).

*NICHOLLS, G. HEATON, *South Africa in My Time* (London, Allen & Unwin, 1961).

*NKOSI, LEWIS, *Home and Exile* (London, Longmans, 1966).

Open Minds in Open Universities (Johannesburg, The Education League, 1956).

The Open Universities in South Africa (Johannesburg, Witwatersrand Univ. Press, 1957).

*PATON, ALAN, *Kontakion for you departed* (London, Jonathan Cape, 1969).

—— *Hofmeyr* (Cape Town, O.U.P., 1964).

—— *Hope for South Africa* (London, Pall Mall, 1958).

PATON, DAVID M. (ed.), *Church and Race in South Africa* (Papers from South Africa 1952–7) (London, S.C.M. Press, 1958).

PATTERSON, SHEILA, *Colour and Culture in South Africa* (A Study of the Status of the Cape Coloured People within the Social Structure of the Union of South Africa) (London, Routledge & Kegan Paul, 1953).

—— *The Last Trek: A Study of the Boer People and the Afrikaner Nation* (London, Routledge & Kegan Paul, 1957).

PAUW, B. A., *The Second Generation: a study of the family among urbanized Bantu in East London* (Cape Town O.U.P., 1963).

PIENAAR, S., and SAMPSON, ANTHONY, *South Africa: Two Views of Separate Development* (London, O.U.P., 1960).

PIROW, OSWALD, *James Barry Munnik Hertzog* (Cape Town, Howard Timmins, n.d.).

PISTORIUS, P. V., *No Further Trek* (Johannesburg, Central News Agency, 1957).

PLOMER, WILLIAM, *Cecil Rhodes* (London, Nelson, 1933).

Prison Conditions in South Africa (A factual report compiled by Amnesty International) (London, 1965).

Prisoners of Apartheid (London, Christian Action, n.d.).

PYRAH, G. B., *Imperial Policy and South Africa 1902–10* (Oxford, Clarendon Press, 1955).

REEVES, AMBROSE, *Shooting at Sharpeville* (London, Victor Gollancz, 1960).

—— *South Africa—Yesterday and Tomorrow: The Challenge to Christians* (London, Victor Gollancz, 1962).

RHOODIE, N. J., and VENTER, N. J., *Apartheid: A Socio-Historical Exposition of the Origin and Development of the Apartheid Idea* (Cape Town, H.A.U.M., 1960).

RICHMOND, ANTHONY, *The Colour Problem: A Study of Race Relations* (London, Penguin Books, 1961).

ROBERTS, MARGARET, *Labour in the Farm Economy* (Johannesburg, S.A.I.R.R., 1959).

ROBERTS, M., and TROLLIP, A. E. G., *The South African Opposition 1939–1945* (London, Longmans, 1947).

ROBERTSON, H. M., *South Africa: Economic and Political Aspects* (Durham, N. C., Duke Univ. Press, 1957).

ROGERS, MIRABEL, *The Black Sash* (Johannesburg, Rotonews, 1956).

*ROSE INNES, JAMES, *Autobiography*, ed. B. A. Tindall (Cape Town, O.U.P., 1949).

ROUX, EDWARD, *Time Longer than Rope: A History of the Black Man's Struggle for Freedom in South Africa*, 2nd edn. (Madison, Univ. of Wisconsin Press, 1964).

RUBIN, LESLIE and NEVILLE, *This is Apartheid* (London, Christian Action, 1965).

SACHS, BERNARD, *The Road from Sharpeville* (London, Dennis Dobson, 1961).

*SACHS, E. S. (SOLLY), *Rebels Daughters* (London, MacGibbon & Kee, 1957).

Safeguard Your Future (The Principles and Policies of the Progressive Party of South Africa) (reprinted Sept. 1962).

*SAMPSON, ANTHONY, *Drum* (London, Collins, 1956).

—— *The Treason Cage* (London, Heinemann, 1958).

*SAMPSON, VICTOR, *My Reminiscences* (London, Longmans, 1926).

SAMUELS, HOBART HOUGHTON, and FOURIE, *South Africa's Changing Economy* (Johannesburg, S.A.I.R.R., 1955).
SARON, GUSTAV, and HOTZ, LOUIS (eds.), *The Jews in South Africa: A History* (Cape Town, O.U.P., 1955).
SCHREINER, OLIVE, *Closer Union* (Cape Town, reprinted by the Constitutional Reform Association, n.d.).
SCHREINER, O. D., *The Nettle: Political Power and Race Relations in South Africa* (Johannesburg, S.A.I.R.R., 1964).
*SCOTT, MICHAEL, *A Time to Speak* (London, Faber & Faber, 1958).
*SEGAL, RONALD, *Into Exile* (London, Jonathan Cape, 1962).
—— *Political Africa* (A *Who's Who* of Personalities and Parties) (London, Stevens, 1961).
SEGAL, RONALD (ed.), *Sanctions against South Africa* (London, Penguin Books, 1964).
SOLOMON, W. E. GLADSTONE, *Saul Solomon* (Cape Town, O.U.P., 1948).
SOREF, HAROLD, and GRIEG, IAN, *The Puppeteers* (London, Tandem Books, 1965).
South Africa and the Rule of Law (Geneva, International Commission of Jurists, 1960).
SPENCE, J. E., *Republic under Pressure* (A Study of South African Foreign Policy) (London, Chatham House, 1965).
SPOONER, F. P., *South African Predicament* (London, Jonathan Cape, 1960).
SPOTTISWOODE, HILDEGARDE (ed.), *South Africa: The Road Ahead?* (Cape Town, Howard Timmins, 1960).
*STANTON, HANNAH, *Go Well Stay Well* (South Africa, August 1956 to May 1960) (London, Hodder, 1961).
STULTZ, N. M., 'The Electoral Revival of the National Party in South Africa, 1934 to 1948, unpublished Ph.D. thesis, Boston Grad. School, 1965.
SUZMAN, HELEN (ed.), *A Digest of the Fagan Report* (Johannesburg, S.A.I.R.R., 1952).
TABATA, J. B., *Education for Barbarism in South Africa* (London, Pall Mall, 1960).
TATZ, C. M., *Shadow and Substance in South Africa: A Study in Land and Franchise Policies Affecting Africans, 1910–1960* (Pietermaritzburg, Univ. of Natal Press, 1960).
THOMPSON, L. M., *The Unification of South Africa, 1902–1910* (Oxford, Clarendon Press, 1960).
The Threatened People, issued by the Congress of Democrats (Johannesburg, 1954).
UNESCO, *Social Implications of Industrialization and Urbanization in Africa South of the Sahara* (1956).
*UNGAR, ANDRÉ, 'South Africa', in *Resistance to Tyranny*, ed. Eugene Heimler (London, Routledge & Kegan Paul, 1966).

VAN DEN BERGHE, PIERRE L., *South Africa: A Study in Conflict* (Middletown, Wesleyan Univ. Press, 1965).

VANDENBOSCH, AMRY, 'Nationalism in South Africa', in *Mid-Twentieth Century Nationalism*, ed. William J. Bossenbrook (Detroit, Wayne State Univ. Press, 1965).

VAN JAARSVELD, F. A., *The Awakening of Afrikaner Nationalism 1868–1881* (Cape Town, Human & Rousseau, 1961).

*VAN RENSBURG, PATRICK, *Guilty Land* (London, Penguin Books, 1962).

VATCHER, WILLIAM HENRY, JR., *White Laager: The Rise of Afrikaner Nationalism* (London, Pall Mall, 1965); New York, Praeger, 1965).

WALKER, ERIC A., *The Cape Native Franchise* (a series of articles published in the *Cape Argus*), published by the Continuation Committee of the National Conference on the Native Bills (Cape Town, 1936).

—— *A History of Southern Africa*, 3rd edn. (London, Longmans, 1962).

—— *Lord de Villiers and his Times: South Africa 1842–1914* (London, Constable, 1925).

——*W. P. Schreiner: A South African* (Oxford, Clarendon Press, 1937).

WALKER, IVAN L., and WEINBREN, BEN, *2,000 Casualties* (A History of the Trade Unions and the Labour Movement in the Union of South Africa) (Johannesburg, The South African Trade Union Council, 1961).

WALKER, O., *Kaffirs are Lively* (London, Victor Gollancz, 1948).

WEBB, MAURICE, *In Quest of South Africa* (Johannesburg, S.A.I.R.R., 1945); reprinted as *New Africa Pamphlet*, No. 8 (Johannesburg S.A.I.R.R., 1945).

WEBB, MAURICE, and KIRKWOOD, KENNETH, *The Durban Riots and After* (Johannesburg, S.A.I.R.R., 1949).

The Western Areas Removal Scheme: Facts and Viewpoints (Johannesburg, S.A.I.R.R., 1953).

WOOD, C. T. (ed.), *Where We Stand: Archbishop Clayton's Charges 1948–1957* (chiefly relating to the Church and State in South Africa (Cape Town, O.U.P., 1960).

Index